THE

DEVIL

AND

DR. BARNES

PORTRAIT OF AN
AMERICAN ART COLLECTOR

HOWARD GREENFELD

PENGUIN BOOKS

PENGUIN BOOKS
Published by the Penguin Group
Penguin Books USA Inc.,
375 Hudson Street, New York, New York 10014, U.S.A.
Penguin Books Ltd, 27 Wrights Lane,
London W8 5TZ, England
Penguin Books Australia Ltd, Ringwood,
Victoria, Australia
Penguin Books Canada Ltd, 10 Alcorn Avenue
Toronto, Ontario, Canada M4V 3B2
Penguin Books (N.Z.) Ltd, 182–190 Wairau Road,
Auckland 10, New Zealand

Penguin Books Ltd, Registered Offices:
Harmondsworth, Middlesex, England

First published in the United States of America by Viking Penguin Inc. 1987
Published in Penguin Books 1989

5   7   9   10   8   6   4

LIBRARY OF CONGRESS CATALOGING IN PUBLICATION DATA
Greenfeld, Howard.
The devil and Dr. Barnes: portrait of an American art collector /
Howard Greenfeld.
p.   cm.
Bibliography: p.
Includes index.
ISBN 0 14 01.1735 0 (pbk.)
1. Barnes, Albert C. (Albert Coombs), 1872–1951.   2. Art patrons—
United States—Biography.   I. Title.
[N5220.B28G74   1989]
709′.2′4—dc19
[B]   ·   88-21846

Printed in the United States of America
Set in Sabon

PENGUIN BOOKS

THE DEVIL AND DR. BARNES

Howard Greenfeld is the author of many books, including introductions to the works of Chagall and Picasso and biographies of Puccini and Caruso. He returned to the United States eight years ago, after fifteen years in Italy—where he founded The Orion Press to publish English-language translations of European writers such as Calvino, Primo Levi, and Fellini—and five years in Paris. He lives in Princeton, New Jersey, with his wife, Paola, and his son, Daniel.

FOR CAROL ROSENSTIEL
WITH LOVE

New York; Mary Jo Crawley of the Philadelphia *Inquirer*; Cathy
Henderson of the Harry Ransom Humanities Research Center of
the University of Texas; Leslie A. Morris of the Rosenbach Museum
and Library; Ferris Olin of the Rutgers University Art Library; M.
Jessica Rowe of the Blanden Memorial Art Museum; Louise F.
Rossmassler of the Philadelphia Museum of Art; David Schoonover
of the Beinecke Rare Book and Manuscript Library at Yale University; Dr. Robert Sanders of Central High School in Philadelphia;
and Karen Berch Weiss of the Archives of American Art.

Among the individuals who assisted me were: Carol Ackerman,
Deirdre Bair, Robert Brady, Jack Bookbinder, Marcelle Berr de
Turique, John Crawford, Dr. George Cannon, John Condax, Robert Carlen, Dr. Roderick M. Chisholm, Margit W. Chanin, Barrows
Dunham, Michael Ellis, Helen Fogg, Judge Lois G. Forer, Corinna
F. Fales, Harry Fuiman, Fred Geasland, Kenneth Goodman, Tamara Gold, Harry Harris, Mona Hille, Leslie Jones, Antoinette
Kraushaar, Lim M. Lai, Mary D. Laing, Jon D. Longaker, David
Levine, Eleanor Levieux, Patricia Levieux, Nancy Little, Pierre Matisse, Adele P. Margolis, Henry D. Mirick, Dr. Donald L. Mullett,
Barbara Morgan, Dorothy Norman, Klaus Perls, Peter Paone, Gar
Reed, Joanna Reed, Irma Rudin, Margaret Sharkey, William Schack,
Mrs. John Sloan, Lawrence M. Seiver, Donna Stein, Dr. Harold
Taylor, Dora Vallier, Marvin Wachman, Matthew B. Weinstein,
and C. Clark Zantzinger.

Ira Glackens has been most generous in sharing with me his
memories of Dr. Barnes as well as his perceptive insights into the
collector's behavior, and I am especially grateful to him for giving
this book a title. In addition, I owe special thanks to Amanda Vaill
and Lisa Kaufman of Viking Penguin for their valuable advice and
to my wife, Paola, for her unfailing support at every stage in the
preparation of this book.

ACKNOWLEDGMENTS

This is not an authorized biography. The Barnes Foundation did not, in any way, cooperate with me in my attempts to draw an honest portrait of its founder. Paranoia still reigns at Merion. Most people officially connected with the Foundation, past and present, refused to speak to me; many of them, in rejecting my requests for information, angrily accused me of prying. Some spoke to me or answered my letters once, but on second thought, or, more likely, after consultation with the Foundation's staff, the keepers of its secrets, they changed their minds and refused to continue what might have been an enlightening dialogue. Others did furnish me with valuable insights and information; but, for fear of reprisal, they asked that their names be withheld from this list of acknowledgments, and I have honored their requests.

Many others, however, did cooperate with me, and they gave generously of their time and knowledge. The staffs of a number of libraries and museums were especially helpful, and among them I would like to single out for thanks the following people: Jo Ann Boydston of the Center for Dewey Studies in Carbondale, Illinois; Louisa Bowen and David V. Koch of the University of Southern Illinois; Marietta Bushnell of the Pennsylvania Academy of the Fine Arts; George D. Brightbill of the Temple University Libraries; Judith Cousins and Rona Roob of the Museum of Modern Art in

THE DEVIL
AND
DR. BARNES

"The American art world lost its most bizarre and colorful personality," wrote Emily Genauer, art critic for the *New York Herald Tribune,* following the death of Dr. Albert C. Barnes in 1951. "Behind him he left what is regarded by connoisseurs as the finest privately owned art collection in America . . . and more ill will than any other single figure in American art." The *New York Times,* in its front-page obituary, noted that Barnes was "as acid with his tongue and pen as he was astute in the acquisition of art treasures. Impatient and unpredictable, he had a talent for invective. He alienated many, but no one challenged his right to esteem as a patron of artists, as a connoisseur of paintings and a collector of outstanding moderns." Henry McBride, writing in *Art News,* predicted that "the paralyzing terror which the amazing Doctor managed to put upon the entire American art world of this generation is something that will not fade quickly from memory."

Today, thirty-six years after his death, neither that terror nor Barnes's enormous achievements have been forgotten. The Barnes Foundation, its incomparable collection housed in a cream-colored limestone mansion in the midst of a splendid twelve-acre park in the fashionable Philadelphia suburb of Merion, remains as a monument to the iron-willed, self-made millionaire who created and then dominated it during his lifetime. Classes in the understanding and appreciation of art are held there much as they were when the doctor was alive. They are taught by Barnes's faithful disciples, using the same rigid, "scientific" methods of judging paintings formulated by their master and set forth in massive textbooks he wrote many years earlier. The gallery's twenty-three rooms, their walls literally covered with works of art—often several tiers high and sometimes far above eye level—are exactly as Barnes left them. The seemingly haphazard arrangements whereby paintings, grouped neither by period nor by country, are interspersed with scores of early handwrought iron keys, locks, hinges, bolts, and other pieces of hardware, were meticulously planned by the doctor himself to fortify his aesthetic judgments. Time has, for the most part, stood still at the Barnes Foundation since the death of its creator.

Yet there has been one significant change. During Barnes's lifetime, the contents of his collection was a carefully guarded secret, hidden behind the Foundation's ten-foot-high wall. Permission to view and study it was granted only to the very few, all of them personally chosen by Barnes himself. On March 16, 1961, however, after a lengthy battle with the state of Pennsylvania concerning the Foundation's status as a tax-exempt institution, a new policy was initiated: the Foundation was forced to open its doors to the public, a limited number of whom have been permitted to enter the gallery two-and-a-half days a week—on Fridays, Saturdays, and on Sunday afternoons—on a first-come, first-served basis.

Since that time art lovers have been dazzled and often overwhelmed by the treasures of the Barnes collection. Included in it are some two hundred works by Renoir, affording visitors a unique opportunity to study each period of the artist's development. There are almost one hundred Cézannes, including *The Card Players* and what most critics consider his finest version of *The Bathers,* which are essential to a complete understanding of the artist's work; and some sixty-odd Matisses, among them his huge mural commissioned by Barnes, *The Dance,* its installation supervised by the painter.

There are more than thirty rare, early Picassos as well as countless masterpieces by Seurat, Daumier, Manet, Monet, the Douanier

Rousseau, Utrillo, Modigliani, and Soutine (whom Barnes discovered). American art is represented by a large number of works by Glackens, Prendergast, and Demuth, and old masters by paintings of Tintoretto, El Greco, Titian, and Rubens. Included, too, are examples of ancient Egyptian, African, Persian, and Chinese art, as well as an important sampling of African sculpture.

It is a remarkable collection, all the more so because it is the result of one man's taste, passions, and eccentricities. Nonetheless, though the contents of the Barnes collection have been revealed to the public—curiously, so great was the secrecy that surrounded the Foundation for so many years that even today many are unaware that admission to its gallery can be easily obtained—little has been known about the controversial and mysterious man who created it.

If Barnes had peacefully assembled his paintings, written his books, and directed the educational work of his Foundation, he would have been unqualifiedly respected and universally mourned at his death. Yet such was not the case, and he left behind him far more enemies than he did friends. The former despised and feared him; the latter worshipped him and remain, even today, stubbornly loyal to his memory.

He was unique; his life and character were a maze of confusing contradictions. Though usually blunt and honest to a fault, he repeatedly claimed that he made his millions through the discovery of Argyrol when, in truth, another chemist discovered the medication and Barnes made his fortune by promoting it. His Foundation was meant to be an example of democracy at work, yet he ruled over it like a monarch and banished all those who defied his wishes. He collected paintings in order to educate the masses, but he rarely allowed anyone the privilege of entering his gallery. He shunned publicity, yet he engaged in well-publicized quarrels; supposedly a private man, he aired his disputes in public, bombarding the press with pamphlets, releases, and copies of his frequently vituperous correspondence. A man of intelligence and sensitivity who displayed impeccable taste in building his collection, he engaged in senseless, childish battles and wrote obscene letters to his enemies who, according to *Time* magazine, believed he got his temper from the devil himself.

Though a sincere early champion of the cause of black Americans, he was often patronizing in his treatment of them, and none played a role in his foundation—until after his death. According to Bertrand Russell, with whom Barnes waged his most famous battle, "he could only get on with dogs and coloured people because he did not regard them as equals."

For Jean Renoir, Barnes was "simply the High Priest of Art, to which his whole life was devoted"; yet he refused to cooperate with art historians and critics who were equally impassioned in their devotion to the world of art and artists. For Thomas Hart Benton, Barnes was "both friendly, kindly, hospitable, and at the same time a ruthless, underhanded son of a bitch . . . a magnificent son of a bitch."

Barnes was not "nice." He was an outsider fighting to get inside, an unpleasant man in a society that valued good manners, a self-made millionaire of little breeding in a city ruled by men of superior upbringing. Yet his personality and his outrageous behavior should not be allowed to overshadow his very real achievement: his collection. And his story deserves to be told.

There are few clues to Barnes's future in his background or his early years and no indication that he would one day become a wealthy and powerful figure in the world of twentieth-century art. He had no inheritance to speak of, financial or cultural. His father, John J. Barnes, whose Irish ancestors were said to have been among the original settlers of Pennsylvania, was born in Philadelphia in January 1843 and drifted from job to job throughout his lifetime. When in 1864 he enrolled as a private in the 82nd Regiment Infantry, he gave his occupation as butcher. Among his fellow workers at the slaughterhouse was one man who made a name for himself: Peter Widener, who became the supplier of mutton to the Union Army during the Civil War and soon afterward made millions by cornering the market in streetcar lines. Widener later developed a taste for expensive masterpieces of art, which he passed on to his son Joseph.

Though his own son was many years later to amass a collection of paintings that would rival Widener's, John Barnes did not fare so well as the elder Widener, nor was he responsible for his son's interest in art. After less than four months in the army, he was wounded at the bloody Battle of Cold Harbor, Virginia, and his right arm was amputated. After another year, he was discharged and granted a pension of eight dollars a month.

His disability, however, did not deter him from seeking work wherever he could, and when, on April 4, 1867, he married the twenty-one-year-old Lydia Schafer, he was earning his living as a letter carrier. The couple had three sons in five years: Charles, the first, was born in 1868; the second, John J., was born in 1870 and lived less than a year; their third son, Albert Coombs, was born on January 2, 1872.

At the time of the birth of this third son, the Barnes family lived in a small two-story row house at 1466 Cork (now Wilt) Street in the Kensington section of northwestern Philadelphia. Albert Barnes later resented tales of his impoverished beginnings, and he was to some extent justified. Kensington, between the Delaware River and the ghetto of North Philadelphia, was not a slum. The residents of what was predominantly a factory district were not rich, but neither were they poverty-stricken. Instead, they were tough and proud, flag-waving working men, for the most part of English, Scotch-Irish, or Irish origin. It was the neighborhood that later gave birth to Sylvester Stallone's Rocky, a neighborhood of fighters.

Most childhood memories are unreliable—we remember what we want to and what best fits into the picture we have of ourselves—and Barnes's were especially so. Because he enjoyed making fun of those who questioned his past, it is hard to take his comments on his early years too seriously. Nonetheless, he never forgot that his early years were difficult ones and that his family knew poverty and, occasionally, hunger. He remembered, too, that during his childhood he developed interests that would turn into passions as he matured. By the time he was six years old, he showed more than the ordinary child's enthusiasm for drawing, for expressing himself through the visual representation of objects and scenes that excited him. His greatest source of inspiration was from the neighborhood firehouse. He made chalk drawings of it and of the shiny red metal wagon and the gracefully moving horses that pulled it, and he proudly showed them to his parents. As time passed, he enjoyed not only drawing but being surrounded by pictures as well.

Barnes later remembered, too, that at the age of eight he had what he would later characterize as his first religious experience. The occasion was a Methodist camp meeting to which his mother took him in Merchantville, New Jersey, the small town across the Delaware River where she had been born. The young boy was held enthralled by the spontaneous singing and rhythmic movement of the black participants, was transported from his own everyday world to the realm of mysticism. From this experience, he believed, came his lifelong desire to increase his knowledge and understanding of the black people of America.

If Barnes's interest in art, black culture, and, to a lesser extent, his fascination with fire fighting can be traced to his earliest years, so can the trait that would best characterize his behavior as a man. He learned to be tough and to fight back.

When he was ten years old, his family moved from the relative well-being of Kensington to one of the oldest and poorest sections of the city, known as The Neck, in South Philadelphia. Survival in The Neck was difficult. When the neighborhood kids stole his toys—which he had bought with his own money, earned by working at odd jobs—he protested; when he did so, he was beaten up. Unable and unwilling to accept their domination, Albert and his older brother bought a set of boxing gloves and practiced in their basement. They increased their skill by attending local boxing matches and observing how real fighters used their fists. Before long the Barnes brothers were able to defend themselves successfully against their enemies. Albert Barnes recalled the experience many years later as his first contact with science: using knowledge gained by experience and observation to attain practical, beneficial goals.

Young Barnes's life changed radically in 1885, when he enrolled in Philadelphia's Central High School. It was no ordinary school. In the years following its founding in 1838, its arts curriculum compared favorably to that of the University of Pennsylvania—it was known to some as the poor man's college, and Central High gave its graduates B.A. or B.S. degrees, though they had no real meaning. The second oldest high school in the country, Central was dedicated to the education of carefully chosen boys, who had demonstrated signs of superior intellectual potential. When Barnes enrolled at Central it was said, generally, that Philadelphia's Catholics went to parochial school, its wealthy to private school, and its promising poor to Central High.

It was Barnes's mother who first recognized her son's promise. Her older son, Charles, showed no such potential—uninterested in higher education, he eventually earned his living as a lead worker—but Albert was different, and Lydia Barnes's belief in him was vindicated when he met Central High's high standards and was admitted to the school. The Barnes family left The Neck three years later—for a small house at 1331 Tasker Street, in a better, middle-class area of South Philadelphia—but Albert had already distanced himself from both The Neck and its inhabitants by that time. Central High became more than just a school for him; it represented a huge step forward and a definitive break with a past he chose to forget. The atmosphere there challenged a boy of his bright curiosity and keen intelligence, and he found in his gifted and eager-to-learn companions a source of stimulation. During his years there, he was introduced to the world of science, and in the laboratory he learned to apply the methods of science, which he would never forget. He learned how to fight battles in defense of his ideas rather than his possessions, and often recalled incurring the wrath of one teacher by protesting the latter's statement that "work is always irksome, put forward only for the sake of the object to be gained." Even as an adolescent such an idea was abhorrent to him, and it had to be vehemently challenged, as did all ideas incompatible with his own.

Barnes's interest in art, too, was nurtured at Central High through his friendship with a classmate and teammate—both played baseball at school—William J. Glackens. For Barnes painting was a pastime, an increasingly satisfying one since the days he painted scenes of the firehouse; but for Glackens, who already showed a remarkable talent as a draftsman, it was a passion. When Barnes showed his own paintings to his gifted friend and the latter laughed, he was more intrigued than angered or discouraged. "I wanted to find out what he was laughing at," Barnes remembered years later, "and I learned a lot from him."

Barnes's academic record during his four years at Central High was mixed. At the end of his first term, he was fourth in a class of thirty-three—remarkable for a boy who was forced to get up at four in the morning to deliver copies of the *Public Ledger* (his father worked in the newspaper's circulation department at the time). When he graduated in June 1889, he was twenty-fourth in a class of twenty-six, but he still had reason for pride: graduation from Central High was in itself a considerable achievement.

Again at the urging of his mother, though it would involve considerable financial sacrifice, Barnes entered the medical school of the University of Pennsylvania in the fall of 1889. Practical considerations had compelled him to set aside his interest in the arts and develop instead his aptitude for science. He could never hope to make a living as a painter, but after three years of study he would be granted a degree that would permit him to practice medicine.

His first year at Penn was difficult. To pay for his education and to support himself, he was forced to earn money by working as a tutor and playing semiprofessional baseball. In spite of this rigorous schedule, his academic record during his first year was good enough to earn him a scholarship for the second year. During his next two years, he again excelled, and upon graduation in 1892 his three-year average was a more than respectable 84.5.

Information concerning Barnes's activities during the years immediately following his graduation from Penn is scarce and frequently contradictory. Nonetheless a pattern emerges from it: that of a young man—he was twenty years old when he earned his M.D.—stubbornly determined to obliterate his past and expand his horizons. Emotionally and intellectually he was already far removed from the environment in which he had been raised. He was now eager to reap the practical benefits of his education and distance himself economically from his origins. In other words he wanted to get rich, and he would be as obstinate in his efforts to make money as he had been in pursuit of his education.

His first decision was made immediately following graduation. He abandoned the idea of a career in physical medicine—building a practice as a doctor required time and money, and he had little of either—and accepted an internship at the State Hospital for the Insane at Warren, in northwestern Pennsylvania. The internship would fulfill his postgraduate academic requirements and would also enable him to gain greater insight into human behavior, knowledge he felt certain would be of value no matter what career he eventually chose.

Exactly what Barnes did immediately following his year at Warren remains a mystery. Though his friend Henry Hart and others have written that he set up practice as a doctor at the family home on Tasker Street for a few years, Barnes himself stated categorically that he never practiced medicine. Instead, according to Barnes—and his version seems reliable—he returned to Penn for graduate courses in chemistry and philosophy, earning his living playing baseball, tutoring in chemistry, and translating scientific articles from the German (which he must have learned on his own, since there is no record of his having formally studied the language).

In any case, within a few years he had decided to become a chemist. He had excelled in chemistry at Penn, and it had continued to fascinate him since graduation. This was an intelligent decision, for he was a born chemist. Quick and methodical, he was unrelenting in his search for answers and truths, temperamentally far more suited to laboratory study than to the care and comfort of the sick. Most important, as a chemist he would be in a position to make money, and quickly. The late nineteenth century was a period of unprecedented activity in the development of therapeutic pharmaceutical products. The world eagerly awaited new preparations to cure its ills, and many of these preparations could be produced with only a minimum of capital expenditure. Newspapers as well as scientific journals were filled with stories of pioneering chemists who had made fortunes from their inventions, and Barnes confidently believed that he could be one of them.

In 1896, his decision made, Barnes set out for Berlin. Germany was in those years the center for chemical research, and German-inspired products were already firmly established on the American market. As a result, German-born, German-trained chemists were in great demand in America.

During this extended visit, Barnes took courses in both chemistry and philosophy—he liked to call himself a "philosophical chemist"—and he perfected his knowledge of the German language, then an essential requirement for a student of science. He had little money—only the small savings he had been able to accumulate since his graduation from Penn—but he managed to live on his earnings as an English teacher and as a sales representative for an American stove manufacturer. After eighteen months, however, he ran out of money and was forced to return home. He paid for his passage by working as a deck hand on an oil steamer destined for Bayonne, New Jersey. (During the voyage, he also entertained the captain and the crew by singing German college songs and Negro spirituals.)

Once back in Philadelphia, Barnes lost little time in finding a job with H. K. Mulford and Company, one of Philadelphia's leading pharmaceutical manufacturers. His training in chemistry and his knowledge of psychology served him well, and before long he was appointed the firm's advertising and sales manager. Apparently, he was so successful that by 1900 the firm agreed to his request to return for a brief period to Germany—this time, to Heidelberg—to hire a young, German-trained scientist who might help in the development of new products for the firm. At the same time, Barnes reasoned, he would be able to take refresher courses in physiological chemistry, which would make him an even more valuable Mulford employee.

Barnes was enrolled at the University of Heidelberg from May 9 to August 6, 1900. During that period he took a course in therapeutics as well as a laboratory course at the university's Pharmacological Institute. In addition, he attended a seminar given by Professor Kuno Fischer, a prominent philosopher, who led his students in analyses of the works of Leibnitz, Fichte, Kant, and Hegel.

While pursuing his own studies, Barnes also carried out his assignment for Mulford: he found a research chemist, Hermann Hille, who was willing to come to Philadelphia. Hille, who had just received his Ph.D. from the university, was uniquely qualified. Before coming to Heidelberg, he had received his degree in pharmacy from the University of Würzburg and had worked with the physicist Wilhelm Roentgen during the latter's researches which led to the discovery of x-rays. Hille enjoyed traveling—he had worked in pharmacies in London and in Nice—and was eager to leave Germany once again. Though he felt the pay being offered was low for a man of his education and experience, he was assured by Barnes that he would be given substantial raises and would receive royalties on the sales of the products he developed, so he accepted the offer.

His mission successfully completed—he had no idea then of just how successful he had been from his own point of view—Barnes returned to Philadelphia. A few months later, in September 1900, he was joined by Hille.

The German chemist's arrival in America, which would prove to be of great significance to both men, coincided with an event of at least equal importance in Barnes's life: his meeting in the late summer of 1900 with a small, blue-eyed blonde, Laura Leighton Leggett of Brooklyn. The couple became acquainted shortly after Barnes's return to Philadelphia, in the quiet town of Milford, Pennsylvania. Barnes was visiting a cousin, and Miss Leggett was spending her summer vacation with her mother and sister at the small Poconos resort. It didn't take Barnes, a man of quick and confident decision, long to realize that the young woman would make an ideal partner.

She was twenty-five years old—three years younger than Barnes—and her background sharply contrasted to his own. While John J. Barnes, a private during the Civil War, drifted from job to job, Richard Lee Leggett, a captain during the war, had achieved considerable financial success as a partner in his family's wholesale grocery business. While it was impossible to trace the lineage of Barnes's parents, Laura's pedigree was clear and impressive: her father's family had emigrated from England in the early seventeenth century and had settled in New York's Westchester County, and her mother's ancestors were early settlers of French and English origin. Unlike the Barneses, the Leggetts had never known poverty; their daughter had been raised in a five-story brownstone, staffed by at least four servants, in a comfortable Brooklyn neighborhood where the family still lived.

During their short time together at Milford, the couple found that despite their different backgrounds, they shared many interests, especially music—Laura's education had prepared her for life as a concert artist. In addition, their personalities were both compatible and complementary. Laura Leggett was a lady, with none of her suitor's rough edges; she could bring dignity to his home and to his life. She deeply admired Barnes's keen mind and wealth of brilliant ideas and, most important, was willing to listen to him expound them relentlessly. While Barnes was frequently short-tempered and bombastic, the young woman was soft-spoken and gentle. Nonetheless, behind her mild, courteous demeanor, she was as strong-willed and as disciplined as Barnes. It was not without reason that she had been called "The Boss" by the five brothers and sisters among whom she was raised.

In October, Albert Coombs Barnes and Laura Leighton Leggett officially announced their engagement. They were married on June 4, 1901—only nine months after they had first met—at Saint James Protestant Episcopal Church in Brooklyn, and immediately embarked on an extended honeymoon trip to Europe. Their first stop was the northwest German port of Bremerhaven, after which they traveled to Heidelberg, where Barnes had a chance to present his bride to his associates at the University and where he was able to conduct a few experiments to test ideas which had been germinating in his mind since he had left there. After Heidelberg, they toured through Switzerland, traveled to Rome, and then left for home from Genoa.

Shortly after their arrival in Philadelphia, the couple rented a house on Drexel Road in the exclusive Main Line suburb west of the city. This area was, according to John Gunther, the home of "an oligarchy more compact, more tightly and more complacently entrenched than any in the United States." Barnes's first home there was a modest one, not entitling him to a role in the oligarchy, but it represented an auspicious beginning. The Main Line, though only a few miles distant, was light-years away from the world in which he had been raised.

2

Hermann Hille was among the guests at the Leggett-Barnes wedding. Since his arrival in America, he and Barnes had been on friendly, if not intimate, terms, and Barnes had been helpful during Hille's first months at the new job in a foreign country. When the German chemist complained that his research was being hampered by insufficient work space and a lack of equipment, Barnes arranged for him to conduct his experiments in larger quarters and personally accompanied him to New York to buy what he needed for his work. When Hille complained that he was not being properly compensated for his efforts—in a short time he had developed an iron tonic and a sleeping compound for Mulford—Barnes saw to it that his salary was raised, not once but twice. (Only later did Hille suspect that his salary had been kept low because his friend had double-crossed him by claiming that Hille had merely carried out his own [Barnes's] instructions in developing the products.)

Before long, Barnes felt that he, too, was being underpaid by Mulford. This led to a quarrel with the firm's director, and as a result Barnes suggested to Hille that they work together evenings on projects of their own. He would supply the ideas, and Hille would devise and carry out the laboratory experiments. Perhaps in that way they could both free themselves from Mulford.

Barnes's first ideas were not acceptable to his partner. He suggested making a cheese, but Hille talked him out of it, convincing him that cheesemaking was a special art, beyond their capabilities. Barnes, his mind still on food, then thought of developing a new kind of bread or biscuit mix. This time Hille tried, but the experiment, carried out on Barnes's mother's stove, was a disaster: the biscuits were rocklike and inedible. Finally, Barnes came up with a workable project—to search for a silver compound for use as an antiseptic, one that would not have the caustic qualities of silver nitrate but would retain its therapeutic effects. Various silver nitrate solutions had been used in the past to cure infection—above all, they had been used as eyedrops to prevent blindness in newborn infants—but these medications had frequently caused damage to living tissues, and their widespread use had been deemed inadvisable.

The idea was an intriguing one with enormous commercial possibilities, and this was not the first time Barnes had contemplated it. In a letter written almost a quarter of a century later, he claimed that the conception had come to him suddenly, mysteriously, in the midst of a lecture during a hot summer's day in Heidelberg, in 1900, after three years of brooding about it. But the idea alone, apparently, had not been enough. What was needed to bring it to fruition was a well-trained, highly skilled scientist. Obviously, Hermann Hille was such a man, for within a year after Barnes set him to work on the new project, the German chemist had found the precise formula for the silver compound they had sought.

To confirm their findings, the two young men turned to several well-respected specialists for additional testing. All were enthusiastic about the results of the tests on patients under their supervision, and a report on the newly developed substitute for silver nitrate was read at the third annual meeting of the American Therapeutic Society in New York on May 14, 1902. In the report, Barnes and Hille detailed the procedures followed in their discovery, noting that "our silver compound should be valuable in the treatment of genito-urinary diseases and in the various inflammatory affections of eye and nasal passages in which silver nitrate or one of its substitutes is indicated." To substantiate their claims, they quoted the opinions of the specialists.

Shortly after the report was read, and even before it was published (in the *Medical Record* of May 24), the two young chemists, encouraged by the acceptance of their findings by the medical establishment, reached an important decision: to go into business for themselves. They submitted their resignations to Mulford and soon afterward formed a partnership to manufacture and sell Argyrol—the name they had chosen for the silver solution—and other products they would develop in the future. The risks were small. Since the production of Argyrol was uncomplicated and inexpensive, and very few employees would be needed, little capital was required for the venture. The commercial possibilities were certainly promising enough to satisfy Barnes's desire to make money in a hurry. Basically it could remain a simple, two-man operation, and a contract was drawn up between the two partners, clearly defining their responsibilities. Hille was to perform whatever duties were necessary in the laboratory (this included the actual making of the products) and to work on the development of new ideas as they were conceived by Barnes or himself, while Barnes would be in charge of sales and promotion. All earnings were to be shared equally.

It would seem logical that the partners' very first step would be to take out a patent on their new product—a potential goldmine—yet Argyrol was never patented (though the name was registered as a trademark). Barnes's explanation for this differed from Hille's. According to Barnes's version, no patent was taken out because it would have expired in twenty years, after which his competitors would have been free to manufacture the medication. Hille, many years later, told another story, claiming that taking out a patent would have required revealing the precise contents of Argyrol, which neither he nor Barnes intended to do. The procedure described in their report was intentionally inaccurate, he noted, adding that if the correct formula had been published, there would have been no way of preventing other pharmaceutical manufacturers from imitating what he had worked hard to develop. Defending their actions, Hille told William Schack, Barnes's first biographer, that it had been "a harmless, self-protective camouflage" and a common practice, that the formula itself was of no importance to physicians who only wanted to know if the product did the work that was claimed for it. If they had given away the secret of Argyrol, there would have been no business at all.

This way there was a business, and it was soon a flourishing one. In the fall of 1902 the new firm of Barnes and Hille, Chemists, with a capital of sixteen hundred dollars borrowed from Laura Barnes's mother, established headquarters in a run-down three-story building at 24 North 40th Street, in the midst of a poor, predominantly black neighborhood. Their rent was twenty-five dollars a month. To keep costs down—Barnes estimated that their capital was only enough to last about three months if luck turned against them—only two employees, both women, were hired at four dollars a week. Barnes's father served as caretaker, and his mother kept the company's books. Neither partner drew a salary, and Hille used the third floor of the building as his residence.

Hille often worked until early morning, not only producing Argyrol but also washing, filling, labeling, and then mailing the containers of the medication to customers. Barnes was equally busy, looking after promotion and sales. "We never had a salesman," he later wrote, adding that the firm did not advertise in technical journals, "because we found in the psychology of William James principles which enabled us to dispense with those luxuries." He added, "From his and similar books we developed a business plan which in two years was financially profitable."

Whatever the source of his inspiration, Barnes's role in the success of the business was enormous. His marketing methods were aggressive, creative, and innovative. Instead of directing the promotion of Argyrol to pharmacists, as had been the common practice among pharmaceutical manufacturers, Barnes appealed directly to physicians. He obtained endorsements from a number of them and produced circulars containing these endorsements, which were mailed to thousands of doctors throughout the world. While Hille remained in the laboratory developing additional products for the firm (only one of them, Ovoferrin, an iron tonic, remained on the market for any length of time), Barnes traveled to London, Dublin, Glasgow, and Berlin, handing out Argyrol samples and receiving endorsements and orders in return.

As a result, the demand for Argyrol soared. Sales for the year 1904 were almost $100,000 and the company opened offices in London and Sydney to satisfy international demand for the medicine. Profits doubled the following year and by 1907 would reach more than $250,000, with a net profit of $186,188.53. Barnes and Hille were both wealthy men.

Though the business prospered, the partnership was not a successful one. The two men did not get along, and personal animosity soon led to mutual mistrust. Nonetheless, they needed one another. Hille knew how to make Argyrol but didn't know how to sell it, while Barnes, an expert at marketing the product, was unable to manufacture it. From the beginning, Hille jealously withheld Argyrol's precise formula from Barnes, while the latter refused to allow Hille to examine the company's financial records. Tension mounted; there were angry words and even threats of physical violence. Recognizing their interdependence, they tried to improve their relationship in April 1903 by drawing up a new, more detailed five-year partnership agreement. This included a clause which read "that each shall immediately make known to the other . . . all the formulae, methods, and processes for the manufacture of all the present and future products of their partnership . . . and that each of them shall from time to time when required give to the other all their knowledge, information, and contemplated acts touching the financial operations of their partnership. . . ."

Even this new agreement was of no avail. The sales of Argyrol continued to increase and the sale of Ovoferrin, too, began to pick up. Yet personal contact between the two men remained, at best, cold and formal. At worst, the relationship between the partners was marked by hostility and suspicion. Hille claimed that Barnes's father, whom he described as a drunk, spied on him and tried to force workers to reveal the processes that were used to make the company's two successful medicines. He admitted that he, in turn, had had Barnes followed, but all that he learned was that his partner kept assignations with various women, one of whom he took to Florida at the company's expense. According to Hille, some time in 1906 Barnes angrily asked for a greater share of the profits, charging that Hille had not contributed his share by discovering new products, a demand that the German chemist rejected. There were continued threats of physical violence, too, but the partners, evenly matched, never came to blows, content to stare each other down until one or the other backed off.

Finally, four years after their latest agreement had been signed, Barnes sought an end to what had become an impossible situation. On May 31, 1907, he presented his case in a Bill of Equity, which he brought against Hille in Philadelphia's Court of Common Pleas. Noting that the partnership could no longer be properly continued, he alleged that Hille had divulged secrets of the firm, left important phases of production in the hands of irresponsible employees, removed property from the building, refused to furnish him with records of research conducted for the firm, and even threatened his life. "Personal communications between the partners have become impossible owing to the threats and conduct of the defendant," he concluded. "The relations have become so hostile and inharmonious that the complainant cannot continue them consistently with his self respect."

As the only remedy to the situation, Barnes asked that the partnership be terminated, that an injunction be issued forbidding Hille from removing any property belonging to the firm, that a strict accounting between the partners be made, and that a sale of the firm's assets be held. One year later the court concurred, ruling that the firm would be dissolved and that each partner should have the right to bid against the other for the business until the highest bid was made. When the time for the bidding came, Hille was unwilling to offer more than half of his savings for the company, and, as a consequence, Barnes won. The firm was his for the sum of $350,000. Following this settlement, Hille, by his own account, was ordered by the court to make both Argyrol and Ovoferrin in Barnes's presence and then have the new owner himself make the two products under the German's supervision until Barnes was satisfied that he could make them himself. In this way the secret of Argyrol was revealed to the man who would later claim that he and he alone had invented it.

For the rest of his life Barnes dismissed all questions concerning Argyrol, never correcting those who gave him full credit for its development. Generally he brushed off the subject by stating simply that he had invented the medicine and had quickly made money from it. Occasionally he joked, as in his reply to one inquiry concerning his discovery: "I first made the product in 1778 while serving as a private in the Colonial Army at Valley Forge. The weather was severe, we had little food and less clothing, and we were devastated by disease. It was my ambition to relieve that suffering that prompted me to make the product and earn the encomiums of my glorious chief, General George Washington. . . ."

Hermann Hille, however, was no joking matter. For Barnes, after the termination of their partnership, the German chemist ceased to exist. "I invented Argyrol," Barnes stated under oath in 1929, completely ignoring the facts. Years later, he did acknowledge Hille's existence (without naming him) by confessing to a journalist that he had hired a German to serve as a technician to supervise the manufacture of the medication, but he insisted that the unnamed German (who he admitted, without explanation, became his partner) had only a technical hand in perfecting Argyrol. "An architect doesn't build the houses he designs," he noted. "An experimentally approved thing had to be adjusted to the mechanics of doing it on a big scale. I didn't know how to do that, just as a household cook wouldn't qualify as a chef in a large restaurant."

By wishing his disappearance, apparently, Barnes believed that Hille *would* quietly disappear. And in a sense, Hille did just that, remaining publicly silent about his relationship with Barnes until after Barnes's death, and never until then contesting his former partner's claim to be the inventor of Argyrol. Instead, Hille continued his career as a chemist and achieved considerable success as the president of Hille Laboratories in Chicago. Only an avid reader of *Who's Who in America* might have noticed that Hermann Hille, who described himself as a "lifelong student of science, philosophy, religion," also took sole credit for the discovery of Argyrol.

Barnes never wanted another partner. Though his experience with Hille had embittered him, it is unlikely that he could peacefully have shared responsibilities and decisions with any associate. By the age of thirty-six, when he assumed sole ownership of the company, he already displayed those characteristics that would intensify during the rest of his life. He was stubborn, strong-willed, doggedly opinionated, and totally unwilling to compromise. Then, as later, he found it impossible to see two sides to any question. He never doubted he was right, and those who disagreed with him were more than merely wrong—they were his enemies. Growing up in Philadelphia, he had learned to fight, and he would continue to do so.

Soon after the incorporation of the A. C. Barnes Company, he bought the firm's headquarters for $8,000 and organized the business his way, based on the writings of William James, the pragmatist who was his philosophical mentor. "In 1908," he later remembered, "we organized the business on a cooperative basis." The few workers he recruited among Philadelphia's poor—there were in the beginning five white women and three black men—were, he claimed, more than just a group of employees; they were part of a family. "The business never had a boss and never needed one," he added, "for each participant had evolved his or her own method of doing a particular job in a way that fitted into the common needs."

According to common definition, the business was not strictly a cooperative; though employees were encouraged to work together as a team and were rewarded with generous pensions, they did not share the profits or participate in decision-making. Nor was it a family, though the owner looked after his employees with something close to paternal interest and understanding. As for there being no boss, wherever Barnes was involved, there was one and only one boss.

Nonetheless, Barnes soon became an unusually enlightened employer. In the early days of the company, when a worker would get into trouble with the police for disorderly conduct, wife-beating, or assault and battery, Barnes would automatically fire him. Before long he realized that the all-too-frequent turnover was disrupting business. His best course would be to attempt to understand and get to the roots of each worker's problems. To do so, he began to pay special attention to their individual psychological needs, both at work and away from it, in an effort to integrate their personal interests into their duties at the factory. He would educate them according to a formula he put into words many years later. "Education," he wrote, "is the complete and harmonious development of all the capacities with which an individual is endowed at birth, a development which requires, not coercion or standardization, but guidance of the interests of every individual towards a form that shall be uniquely characteristic of him."

His system, for which he never failed to credit James, worked, and he frequently cited examples of his successes. Because one male employee was torn between the pleasure he found in his company job and his desire to work with machines—he had always wanted to become a chauffeur—Barnes allowed him to oil and repair the company car so that, as a result, Barnes commented, "his self became integrated." When a female employee proved temperamentally too energetic for the calm, routine job to which she had been assigned—labeling and packaging bottles—Barnes placed her in charge of stock and shipping, "where a new motor coordination was necessary nearly every minute."

Barnes found, too, that his personal involvement in an employee's after-hours interests could benefit both the employee and the firm. An example was Johnny, a black man whose hobby was boxing. He wasn't very successful at it, however, merely picking up small purses for participating in local battles royal—until Barnes took him in hand, again applying lessons he had learned from William James. Recognizing Johnny's potential, Barnes convinced him to quit the battles royal and begin training seriously; he even put on gloves with him to help get him into shape. Barnes also taught him three simple rules: size up the situation, decide what is proper, and don't do anything foolish. "That's all there is to William James," he noted. As a result of his employer's advice, Johnny's career took a turn for the better, and he eventually fought his way up to a championship bout. To Barnes's dismay, Johnny lost the fight. "William James backed up Johnny superbly on the offensive," Barnes explained, "but on the defensive he was inadequate." Johnny's defeat was not James's fault, according to Barnes. "The other fellow just happened to know the psychology of William James better than Johnny, although probably not by that name." In any case, Johnny became a satisfied, productive worker.

The case of Jake, another worker, was more complicated. Because he was one of the firm's best employees, he earned more money than did most of his fellow workers. These other workers became jealous. Jake was all right, they would say, but he beats his wife. Barnes explained that this was irrelevant, that what mattered was that Jake continued to perform his duties well. He advised the other workers not to worry about Jake's behavior at home. One day, however, they were forced to, because Jake didn't show up at the job—he had been arrested for beating up his wife. That posed a problem for the company, but upon investigation Barnes learned that there was still no reason to condemn Jake. He had not been arrested on the complaint of his wife but because the neighbors had complained that Jake's wife's shouting bothered them. Patiently Barnes explained to the other workers that if Jake beat his wife and the wife didn't mind, no matter how they felt about wife-beating, there was no reason to punish Jake. "And then I told them that Jake was a sadist and his wife was a masochist and it was a perfectly natural explanation to them, and when I said that they got interested in psychology. We took books and got right down to tacks and found these boys absorbed it."

In return for his sympathetic involvement in their lives, both at the job and away from it, Barnes demanded complete and unquestioning loyalty from his workers. It was then, as it would always be, an essential condition of their employment. In the case of two of these workers—the Mullen sisters, Nelle and Mary—his demands were amply met. Nelle E. Mullen joined the firm in 1902, at the age of eighteen. Barnes was her first and only employer; she remained with him until his death in 1951 and with the Foundation he later created until her own death in 1967. Born in 1884 near the town of Columbia, in the heart of Pennsylvania Dutch country, she came to Philadelphia with her family before the turn of the century. A tall, sturdy blonde with blue eyes and a fair complexion, she had not yet finished high school when she was hired by Barnes as a bookkeeper, at eight dollars a week. She must have been good at her job, for in time she ran the business and handled all of her employer's investments, and Barnes did his best to educate her throughout the years—he gave her books to read, sent her abroad, and advised her to build her own art collection, but she never became the intellectual he might have wanted. What she did come to learn, as the years passed, was that her survival depended upon her total devotion to her employer.

The same could be said of Mary Mullen, who joined the company several years after her younger sister and remained equally devoted to Barnes and his ideas until her death in 1957. Somewhat better educated than Nelle, Mary was put in charge of the firm's employees and conducted classes for them in psychology and aesthetics. Mary was also apparently more receptive to Barnes's theories of aesthetics than was Nelle, for in spite of her lack of academic qualifications, she became associate director of education at the

Barnes Foundation, taught several classes there, and was the author of the Foundation's first official publication, *An Approach to Art*.

Nelle E. and Mary Mullen are remembered above all for their total, slavish loyalty to their master. They had, according to those who knew them, no opinions apart from those of Barnes. In the eyes of one of their associates, they were like shadows—one thin and one fat.

By 1910 Dr. Barnes—later he was known simply as "Doctor"—was restless. The A. C. Barnes Company, staffed by a small number of loyal employees who efficiently performed what had become routine duties, no longer required his energy or imagination, or even, for much of the time, his presence. The manufacture of the company's most profitable product presented no problems; nor did Argyrol call for special handling or complicated packing. It was shipped from the factory in the form of small, highly concentrated crystals to druggists, who would then make it into a brown, odorless solution. Barnes's flair for innovative sales methods and promotion schemes was no longer required either, since the antiseptic had already gained wide acceptance throughout the world. (In America its acceptance was so complete that many states passed laws requiring that a few drops of the solution be placed in the eyes of newborn infants to prevent infant blindness.) In fact, its use was so widespread that it was sometimes used excessively in the treatment of sore throats and running noses, resulting in a brownish skin discoloration which became known as argyria or argyriosis.

As a result of the efficiency of his company's operation and the astounding popularity of its product, Barnes found greater challenge in tracking down and prosecuting the many jobbers and pharmacists in all parts of the world who sold bogus solutions under the name of Argyrol than he did in running his business. Most of the time he was bored, an intolerable condition for a man of his energy.

Not yet forty years old, Barnes had already achieved his first goal in life—he had made money. As an early consequence of his wealth, he had been able to establish himself firmly on the Main

Line, the home of Philadelphia's most distinguished citizens, and in 1905 had improved his position there by moving from his rented home in Overbrook. He purchased three acres of land in an undeveloped section of the nearby town of Merion, and he ordered the construction of a large family residence, which he put in the name of his wife and named, after her, Lauraston. Laura Barnes supervised the building of the twelve-room granite mansion, as well as the design of the furniture. There, too, Mrs. Barnes developed her interest in horticulture, planning and carrying out the landscaping and planting of the extensive grounds.

In 1910 Barnes further entrenched himself in Merion by buying the large property across the road from Lauraston, remodeling an old house on it and building four additional homes around it so as to create a neighborhood with a style which suited him. When he sold these new houses shortly after their construction, he did so at cost, forestalling any possible charge that he had indulged in real estate speculation.

Once settled in his new home, Barnes at first set about imitating the behavior and habits of his fellow Main Liners. Maids, a butler, and a cook were hired, and the home was stocked with the finest wines and liquors—Barnes always prided himself on his knowledge of vintage wines and rare Scotch. But while he enjoyed living in Philadelphia's peaceful suburbs, he was quickly bored by most Main Line activities, especially the quietly elegant dinner parties marked by witty, refined conversation. For a while, both he and his wife did show an interest in one Main Line sport, horseback riding; they bought horses, hired a groom, and maintained a stable, and Barnes himself went even further by joining the fashionable Rose Tree Fox Hunting Club. But his interest in riding and hunting waned when he came to the conclusion that man's body was not meant to be placed on the back of a horse. As a hunter, the doctor was known for his courage because of his willingness to get right back on a horse after his all too frequent falls, but he also gained a reputation as a "thruster"—one who, in the words of a man who observed him at the club, "thrusts his way in out of turn ahead of other people."

For most of the Main Line's well-bred citizens, Barnes was, and would always remain, a thruster. In their eyes, he was unacceptable—a self-made businessman of no breeding, an outsider who, with his gruff, unpolished manners, possessed none of the social graces that would have permitted him to become a part of their society. Understanding that no matter how hard he tried, he could never break the barrier that separated him from his well-behaved neighbors, Barnes reacted angrily. For the rest of his life, he played the role they had assigned to him, and he played it well.

CHAPTER

4

Since his work at the A. C. Barnes Company could no longer absorb his energy, and since he was temperamentally unsuited to a genteel life of leisure on the Main Line, Barnes turned his attention, sometime in 1910, to one of his earliest enthusiasms: art. He knew he could never be a successful painter (he reached this conclusion, he remembered later, after having completed 190 canvases), so he decided to do the next best thing—collect the works of other painters. "I collected my own pictures when I didn't have money," he wrote, "and when I had money I collected better ones."

Actually he had started a collection of sorts even before he had money, for he had returned from Germany with a number of paintings acquired there and elsewhere in Europe. They were undistinguished—decorative canvases which gave easy pleasure because of their technical proficiency—but it was a beginning. From 1905 on, after his business had begun to prosper, he made efforts to refine his taste. He began to visit New York galleries where he bought, among other works, rural landscapes and scenes of peasant life by recognized artists—second-rate paintings by masters of the then popular Barbizon School: Millet, Diaz, and Théodore Rousseau—and their imitators. (An Italian pastoral landscape by Corot, who was an important influence on these precursors of Impressionism, is the only known painting of this period with which Barnes never parted.) If his choices were conventional, the fault was not entirely his. With very few exceptions—and the novice collector was undoubtedly not aware of these—New York dealers were not interested in promoting the works of innovative, little-known painters. Even the Impressionists, whose works had been acquired by a handful of discerning American collectors, were too modern for most of them. Instead, they were content to cater to provincial American taste by selling facile portraits and imitations of classical or Renaissance art, seldom venturing beyond the Barbizon School, which had long ceased to be a revolutionary movement.

Barnes, who knew no better, bought what he was shown. He hung his paintings on the walls of his factory and filled his home with them. Much as he liked looking at them, he came to realize that his knowledge of art was superficial. He had put together his collection at random, without method or criteria. Driven by a scientist's curiosity, he now wanted to learn not only what was good but also why it was good.

With this in mind, he decided to seek the advice of the one artist he had known well, his high school friend William J. Glackens, from whom he had been separated for many years. "Butts," as he was known to his friends, had already made a name for himself as a journalist-illustrator, first in Philadelphia and then in New York. As a painter he had gained recognition as a member of the Eight, a group of American realist painters who had boldly proclaimed their independence from the all-powerful National Academy of Design, which had refused to show some of their paintings, by exhibiting together at New York's Macbeth Galleries in 1908. Though not a stylistically homogeneous group—the exhibition at Macbeth was their only joint one—the Eight were united in their desire to challenge the art establishment, as personified by the Academy, which had for many years imposed its standards of taste in art by means of its annual exhibitions.

Barnes's decision to contact his former classmate marked a

turning point in his career as a collector. Art was Glackens's life, and his world was peopled by those artists who, by defying the mainstream of American art, were changing its course. A generous man, he was willing to share his knowledge as well as this world with his old friend. When at their very first meeting, Barnes showed him his collection, Glackens quietly expressed his disappointment—much as he had many years before when Barnes showed him his own paintings. As a serious, intelligent artist, familar with current trends in both American and European painting, he told Barnes that his acquisitions, though respectable, were too conservative and conventional. He blamed New York dealers for selling him "safe" paintings—at what he considered exorbitant prices. Barnes listened attentively. Though suspicious by nature, he immediately trusted Glackens as a man and as an artist. He went even further. In the months following their reunion, he came to consider the painter, whose modest good nature apparently had a calming effect on him, as a member of his family. His affection even extended to Glackens's wife, Edith, and two children, Ira and Lenna, who soon called the Barneses Aunt Laura and Uncle Albert. The two families often exchanged visits—at the Barnes home in Merion, at the Glackens home in New York, and at their summer cottages in Long Island. It was a warm, informal relationship, unique to Barnes, who had found affection but little stimulating companionship from his own family.

During this period, which marked the beginning of what was to be a lifelong friendship, Glackens taught Barnes what he knew about art. Rather than impose his own more adventurous taste on his friend, the quiet, unassuming Glackens taught him to look at and to see paintings with a different, more discriminating eye. He patiently accompanied him to those few New York and Philadelphia galleries that showed the works of those modern European artists—the Impressionists and the Post-Impressionists—which he himself admired. In addition, he introduced Barnes to his friends and colleagues—Charles Demuth, Alfred Maurer, and members of the Eight, some of whose work Barnes began to acquire. By the end of 1911, Barnes had learned to see more acutely—if not to understand fully or admire what he saw. Through Glackens he had also come to realize that the capital of the world of modern art was not New York but Paris. Only in the French capital could he acquire the works of the future masters—still accessible at reasonable prices, an advantage that surely appealed to his sense of business. If he was to become a serious collector, he was convinced, he would have to turn his attention to Paris, and to acquire what was available there.

The idea might have been Barnes's, or it might have been Glackens's; in any case, in February 1912, the American painter was on his way to the French capital, authorized by Barnes to spend $20,000 to expand Barnes's collection. According to the collector's overzealous supporters, Barnes had given Glackens a precise shopping list of what to buy and how much to spend for each work. Given Barnes's limited knowledge and experience at the time, this would have been impossible; from Glackens's letters to his wife at home, it is even more obvious that there was no such list. The painter's assignment was to buy what he thought best—and of the best value—within the limit.

Glackens's stay in Paris, which lasted only two weeks, was exhausting. Accompanied by Alfred Maurer, who had studied in Paris and knew his way around Parisian art circles, he spent hours each day visiting the city's galleries and dealers in search of examples of modern art to enrich his friend's collection. He met collectors, too, among them Leo Stein, brother of the writer Gertrude Stein, who had been among the first to recognize the genius of Matisse and Picasso and whose collection of Renoir was remarkable. To Glackens's dismay, he soon discovered that Barnes would not get as much for his money as he—and Barnes—had hoped. Small Cézanne landscapes, of little commercial value in the past, were then selling for $3,000, with more important Cézannes bringing between $7,000 and $30,000. Nonetheless, he persevered and only a few days after his arrival was able to make his first purchase for his friend—a small Renoir portrait of a girl reading, for which he paid the equivalent of $1,400. Even at the time, this was considered a bargain. "Hunting up pictures is not child's play," the weary painter wrote to his wife.

By March 1, 1912, as he prepared to return to the States, Glackens reported again to his wife that he was "sick of looking at pictures and asking prices." Yet his mission had been more than successfully concluded; at the very end, after having spent the $20,000, he had found a fine Degas and cabled the news to Barnes, who authorized him, by return cable, to go beyond the limit he had set and make the purchase on his behalf.

Once back in America, Glackens presented Barnes with his new paintings. No official list of them is available, either from the Barnes Foundation or elsewhere. Ira Glackens, son of the artist, was told by Foundation officials years later—in an effort to minimize the importance of his father's purchases—that such a list would be of no interest, since most of the works had probably been minor ones, later sold or traded. Only the Renoir and one Van Gogh—a portrait of a postman—have been officially identified as part of this purchase. Evidence suggests, however, that among the other works Glackens acquired for his friend were paintings by Manet, Gauguin, and Cézanne, as well as the Degas.

Barnes was not as pleased with the results of Glackens's trip as the painter had hoped. He was puzzled and somewhat taken aback by works of art that seemed foreign to his as yet untrained eye. Even his contact with Glackens and his friends, and their art, had not prepared him for the light and color and the shimmering movement of the paintings which had been purchased on his behalf. Though enthusiastic about the Renoir—with whom, through Glackens, he was already familiar—he was doubtful about the others. When he expressed his reservations to Glackens, his friend suggested that he wait before rejecting them and offered to buy them back if Barnes still felt uncomfortable with them after living with them for a while.

Barnes took Glackens's advice. He lived with and studied the new paintings. At first, he thought their antique French frames were responsible for his inability to appreciate them. He ordered the frames removed and had them replaced with more conventional ones. Soon he realized that the frames had nothing to do with it. The original ones were put back on. Gradually, analyzing these works of art with the skill of a scientist, he came to learn what these painters had done and why, and to understand how their vitality had fired Glackens's enthusiasm. These dozen or so paintings opened up a new world to him, and he never again considered returning them to his friend.

Neither Glackens nor anyone else ever bought another painting for Barnes. The collector prided himself on making his own decisions and his own purchases. Naturally, he could be influenced. Dealers directed him to canvases they thought might be of interest, and he especially valued the opinions—if not the advice—of friends and artists. Jacques Lipchitz, for one, noted that Barnes carefully observed the responses of others to works he was considering for purchase.

Certainly Glackens encouraged the collector's passion for Renoir, the artist who had most influenced his own work. Yet even Glackens could not talk Barnes into buying anything; nor could he prevent him from buying the works of artists—Marsden Hartley is an example—that he did not admire. Their tastes usually coincided—most notably in their common esteem for William James and their distaste for most art criticism—but even when they didn't, Barnes and Glackens remained warm friends until the painter's death in 1938.

On the surface it seemed an unlikely friendship, for the two men's personalities contrasted sharply. Glackens was gentle, quiet, and unfailingly calm, in his wife's words, "a modest soul who spoke for himself only in the conscientiousness and beauty of his work"; while Barnes was quick-tempered, opinionated, and easily angered. If the painter, as Ira Glackens has written, could never hold an unpleasant thought, the collector seemed incapable of forgetting one and spent much of his energy seeking revenge over some slight or disagreement. "He never quarreled and would have been at a loss to know how," Ira Glackens wrote of his father, whose friend Barnes seemed to find special satisfaction in a good battle. Uncharacteristically Barnes granted Glackens the right to disagree with him, and granted it also to Glackens's wife, Edith Dimock, an artist of recognized talent and an independent, emancipated woman, who, since she feared no man, frequently took advantage of Barnes's dispensation. Because she was the wife of his friend, Barnes always forgave her, just as she always forgave Barnes's frequently outrageous behavior and his outbursts of temper. Their disagreements were, for both of them, family quarrels, which called for obligatory reconciliaton.

There was, however, never any need for a reconciliation between Barnes and Glackens. They never quarreled. Barnes felt protective toward his friend, and displayed toward him a tenderness and concern that he was rarely able to show to others. In 1914, when the painter was hospitalized for an appendectomy, Barnes—an M.D. again—put on a white coat and watched the operation. He wanted to make certain that nothing went wrong. Afterward, he paid daily visits to the hospital, on at least one occasion carrying with him a container of homemade chicken soup for his ailing friend.

Just as Barnes felt compelled to supervise his friend's appendectomy, he felt the need to defend his work during Glackens's lifetime and afterward. Though Glackens ignored the opinions of art critics, favorable or unfavorable, Barnes reacted angrily to even the slightest attack on his friend's painting. He knew that Glackens's art would speak for itself without the aid of promotion, and that his own esteem for the painter would be vindicated in time. "The important thing," he wrote the painter's widow after his death, "is that Glack is part of the future and the critics are just passing nuisances."

Even for the sake of a friend, however, Barnes would not deviate from his insistence that Glackens's masterpieces must remain part of the Barnes collection. In May 1937 Edith Glackens wrote to the collector of her concern that too many of her husband's works were hidden from the public—some hanging in the Foundation's seldom-visited gallery and others not displayed at all because of lack of space. As a partial remedy she asked to buy back one of her husband's most powerful paintings, *Armenian Girl*. Barnes answered that he would sell it—for $85,000 cash, then an exorbitant price which he knew would be unacceptable. As a consolation he assured her that he would donate major works to other galleries gradually, as they needed them to enrich their collections. (He never did so, though he did many years later give four Glackens drawings to the Blanden Art Museum of Fort Dodge, Iowa, as part of his only gift to a public institution.) He reassured her, too, of his friend's permanent place, not only at the Foundation, but in the great art of all time. "A hundred years from now," he wrote, "I'll let you peek down on earth with me and you'll be satisfied with the position he holds with the stars."

A year later, in May 1938, William Glackens died suddenly of a stroke while visiting the home of Charles Prendergast. Barnes was in Paris at the time; he was shocked and deeply saddened when he heard the news. In writing to Edith Glackens, he revealed not only the depth of his affection for Glackens but a side of himself that he rarely showed in public. "I loved Butts as I have ever loved but a half a dozen people in my lifetime. He was so *real* and so gentle and of a character that I would have given millions to possess. . . . He will live forever in the Foundation collection among the great painters of the past who, could they speak, would say he was of the elect."

In this instance, Barnes was true to his word. His friend's paintings and drawings are today among the treasures in the collection in Merion, which also includes works by Edith Dimock Glackens and Lenna Glackens. As Barnes's prominence as a collector grew—and especially after his death—many of his followers have tried to minimize the importance of Glackens in the early formation of his taste and of his collection. They have pointed out, correctly, that Glackens did not buy for Barnes as, for example, Berenson bought for Isabella Stewart Gardner, as Mary Cassatt bought for the Havemeyers, or as H. P. Roché bought for John

Quinn. Nonetheless, Barnes himself, too often wont to give no credit where credit was due, acknowledged his friend's influence when he wrote of him (in 1915): "The most valuable single educational factor to me has been my frequent association with a lifelong friend who combines greatness as an artist with a big man's mind."

Barnes's decision to become a serious art collector dates from his reunion with Glackens. Whether he was motivated by a genuine love of art, a desire to gain the power and social prestige his background and behavior denied him, or a combination of the two is unclear. "You bet I'm a social climber," the contemporary collector Robert Scull once said, "and I'd rather use art to climb with than anything else"—and Barnes might have said the same.

Whatever the reasons, it was a decision he did not take lightly—he took nothing lightly. He had never wanted to become just a chemist, but a millionaire chemist whose labor relations were based on the writings of William James. Now he was not content to be merely an accumulator of paintings by safe, recognized artists; his goal was to become a well-informed collector whose acquisitions would reflect his knowledge and experience. He understood that to gain that knowledge and experience would mean years of intensive observation and study, above all in Europe, but he was prepared to expend most of his energy—Argyrol still required some of his attention—in order to achieve that goal. In the summer of 1912 he was on his way to Paris, the first of his many visits to the French capital and to other European cities, as a collector rather than as a chemist.

He was a diligent student. Texts in hand, he methodically studied the masterpieces of European art wherever he traveled. These books proved to be of little use, however; most of them, including those by the widely respected art historians Julius Meier-Graeffe and Bernard Berenson, irritated, confused, or bored him. Only the paintings revealed to him what he really wanted to learn, convincing him that direct confrontation with a work of art was the only way of understanding it. "With a volume of Meier-Graeffe in my lap and a Cézanne, Van Gogh or a Bonnard propped on a chair, I have spent months in wading through his verbosity and froth hoping for a ray from it to reflect upon the painting and then to my mind carry with it the artist's message," he remembered in *Arts and Decoration* a few years later. "Finally, I did get the message, but I am not sure that it was what Meier-Graeffe wrote, but rather what Cézanne or Van Gogh said in paint, that created the light. . . . For several summers in succession, day after day, I carried a volume of Berenson to the Louvre, the National Gallery, the Kaiser Friedrich's Museum, and applied kindergarten methods in trying to learn the message of the really great in Italian art. It proved worthwhile in creating a strong liking for the Italian primitives to which I can attribute but little to Mr. Berenson's genius and hard work as found in his books."

Barnes's frequent visits to Florence, Madrid, Berlin, and London enabled him to examine the art of the past and to learn the essentials of aesthetics and of art history, sharpening his perceptions as he did. Only his visits to Paris, however, gave him an opportunity to study what Glackens and his friends had convinced him was the art of the future, and it was there that he made his earliest significant purchases.

The first decade of the twentieth century had been marked by enormous cultural vitality in the French capital, especially in the realm of the visual arts. In 1905, the works of Matisse, Derain, Vlaminck, and Rouault, among others, had been hung in one room at the annual Salon d'Automne. The distorted images and violent colors of these canvases had caused their creators to be known as the Fauves, the Wild Beasts, and though most went their separate ways in the years that followed, collectively they gained fame as a major force in the world of art. Likewise, following Cézanne's death in 1906 and the huge retrospective exhibition of his works held in Paris the following year, he had been recognized as the towering genius—and influence—of his time. And in 1906, Picasso, only twenty-five years old, was starting work on *Les Demoiselles d'Avignon,* which was to alter the course of art history.

In 1912, when Barnes arrived in Paris on his first buying trip, Parisians were recovering from the first Futurist exhibition held in the capital that February. The works shown there by the Italians Carrà, Boccioni, Severini, and Balla had scandalized the public, which was still debating the pros and cons of Cubism (then entering its final phase, which was to be known as Synthetic Cubism). But in spite of this extraordinary outburst of creative activity and controversy, modern art was still not easy to find—even in its birthplace. It was not hung in museums, which preferred to display the works of the old masters and still neglected even the Impressionists. And the few dealers and galleries—Durand-Ruel was offering the works of the Impressionists; Ambroise Vollard was selling the paintings of Cézanne and the Post-Impressionists from his small gallery on the rue Lafitte; and Kahnweiler was showing the Cubists—seemed reluctant to open their doors to outsiders.

Barnes, however, quickly made it known that he was no ordinary outsider. He had contacts—Glackens and his friends who had been to Paris—and through them was introduced to the men and women who made modern art. Armed with his newly acquired knowledge and brandishing his sizable checkbook, he was able to gain admission to their galleries and their studios.

Of all the addresses Barnes had been given, none was more important than 27, rue de Fleurus, the home of two expatriate Americans, Gertrude Stein and her brother Leo, who shared it with Gertrude's friend, Alice B. Toklas. Each Saturday evening the doors of their small, two-story pavilion were opened to writers, artists, and the merely curious. All were eager to meet their hostess, Gertrude, who had come to Paris in 1903, had championed the cause of Picasso (who painted her portrait), and had started to write puzzling, often incomprehensible books, which had won her fame if not many readers. All, too, were anxious to see the dazzling collection of paintings that hung two and three deep on the walls of the vast, somber studio—canvases by Renoir, Cézanne, and Matisse, as well as works by Picasso, Braque, and Juan Gris, artists whom Gertrude had discovered before they were well known. There was no museum like it in Paris or anywhere else.

It was through Alfred Maurer, a good friend of the Steins, that Barnes first came to the rue de Fleurus—though in *The Autobiography of Alice B. Toklas,* Gertrude wrote that Maurer disclaimed this responsibility, insisting, "so help me God, I didn't bring him." Barnes had little to say that first evening, but he listened and observed attentively. He never warmed to his hostess. At first, he was uncharacteristically intimidated and overwhelmed. Stein was often thought to resemble a Roman emperor, because of her noble, finely shaped head and her grizzled, short-cropped hair, and she enjoyed acting the part. Later, when he was a little more sure of himself, Barnes reached the conclusion that she was little more than a conceited exhibitionist.

Nor did Gertrude like the fledgling collector or his crude manners. She complained to her friend Mabel Dodge that he "did literally wave his cheque book in the air" and was taken aback when Barnes showed his lack of breeding by asking how much she had paid for Picasso's portrait of her. (He was stunned when she explained that the painter had given it to her as a gift.) Gertrude was not about to give any gifts to the rough-edged collector, though in 1912 she did sell him two of her Matisses, most probably the first to enter his collection. He wanted only one, but Gertrude insisted he take two or none, for which Barnes was later grateful.

Barnes made a similar impression on Michael and Sarah Stein, Gertrude's brother and sister-in-law, equally distinguished collectors, especially of their intimate friend Matisse. On Saturday nights, they, too, opened the doors to their home—a converted loft on the nearby rue Madame—to interested visitors. Barnes was among these, and Harriet L. Levy, a family friend, enjoyed telling the story of the Philadelphian's first visit there sometime in 1913. Like those of the rue de Fleurus studio, the walls of the apartment were covered by a myriad of canvases which the Philadelphian examined attentively. After completing a tour of the apartment, he pointed to a large Picasso and offered his host $5,000 for it. It was a generous offer, but Stein quickly turned it down, explaining that he was not a dealer and that nothing was for sale.

Barnes was incredulous. He asked Stein why he had hung all the paintings and invited visitors to see them if they weren't for sale. The answer was, quite simply, that they were there to be enjoyed. That reply was not good enough for Barnes, who gave his card to Stein in case he should change his mind.

Michael Stein did not change his mind. He never sold the Picasso to the brash collector, though an important Matisse canvas, *Red Madras Headdress,* which was part of Michael and Sarah Stein's collection at the time, did become part of the Barnes collection many years later.

Of all the Steins, the only one with whom Barnes felt an affinity was Leo. Two years older than his sister Gertrude (like Barnes, he was born in 1872), he had been her first mentor; in their early years, he was the family intellectual. A tall, thin, sensitive-looking man, his interests, which ranged from art to psychology and from aesthetics to the philosophy of education, coincided with Barnes's own. Though dazzlingly brilliant and with an enormous fund of knowledge at his disposal, he was chronically indecisive, unable to make constructive use of his considerable resources until late in life. "I think his primary weakness was a fear of responsibility— and, accompanying it, a fear of life itself," Mabel Weeks, who knew the Steins well, wrote of him.

Barnes and Leo Stein often parted company over matters of aesthetics and clashed because of differences of temperament; soon after they met, Barnes complained that while he was always willing to listen to Stein's lengthy expositions of his theories of aesthetics, the latter was rarely willing to listen to Barnes's own. However, they always made up, and theirs was a long, if occasionally stormy, friendship.

Throughout the first years of their acquaintance, Barnes was enormously active in Europe, traveling there at regular intervals and acquiring a large number of significant paintings. As his collection grew and began to take on a character of its own, he kept in close touch with Stein. Their preferences were remarkably similar: Renoir, Cézanne, and to a somewhat lesser extent, Matisse. If Stein didn't exactly tell his friend what to buy, he at least acted as guide, and Barnes's purchases of a prodigious number of paintings by these three painters, which formed the nucleus of his collection, clearly reflected Stein's taste as well as Glackens's and his own.

As he continued to buy at a dizzying pace, he enthusiastically wrote Stein of his new acquisitions. In March 1913, he reported that he had bought a dozen Renoirs since they had last met, commenting that he could never buy too many of them. He asked Stein to alert collectors—not dealers, whose prices were high—that he wanted to buy even more Renoirs, as well as Cézannes, when he next came to Paris. Less than a year later, in February 1914, he was able to inform Stein that his collection contained twenty-five Renoirs and a dozen Cézannes. (Only two years after that he had sixty Renoirs.)

In that same letter, Barnes wrote Stein that his collection also included twelve Picasso canvases. Though Stein had been among the first to recognize Picasso's genius, his interest in him had waned, and Barnes apparently bought the Spanish painter's work on his own—and at bargain prices. In 1913 he acquired the large *Composition* (also known as *Peasants and Oxen*), which he had first seen the year before in London, from Vollard, for three hundred dollars. At about the same time, he bought sixteen drawings from the artist himself, most of them of performers in the Cirque Medrano, for about a dollar a drawing.

If Stein played no part in these transactions, he nonetheless must not have disapproved of Barnes's purchases, for none of the works the Philadelphian acquired were from Picasso's Cubist period, which Stein deplored. "Picasso fooled first himself and then all the world with solemn nonsense," Stein wrote. Barnes, who had been initially intrigued by this revolutionary form of artistic expression but had soon tired of it, agreed. "Cubism: Requiescat in Pace" was the title of an article he wrote in 1916. For him, Cubism was "academic, repetitive, and dead . . . a typical commercial venture." Cubism did not meet the aesthetic principles he had formulated, and he was unable to understand it.

Stein's influence, however, must not be overestimated. Barnes, a newcomer to the Parisian art world in 1912, was a familiar figure there only two years later. He bought voraciously, and he did so on his own. He proved to be knowledgeable and well-informed; he knew what he wanted and quickly learned where to find it. In the eyes of many Europeans—and those who had recently become Europeans, like most of the Steins and their circle—his methods reflected a lack of breeding and culture. He not only liked to bargain, but he enjoyed boasting of the bargains he had acquired. Nonetheless, because of his eagerness to buy and his ability to pay, he found acceptance in most quarters. When the First World War began and travel to Europe was suspended, his collection was already an extraordinary one. Among the Europeans represented were works by El Greco, Goya, Daumier, Monet, Bonnard, Delacroix, Sisley, and Pissarro, in addition to those already mentioned. He had made no discoveries, and his acquisitions were neither daring nor adventurous—there were no radically modern works nor any examples of abstract art, which was then taking hold in Europe. Nonetheless, according to the critic and painter Guy Pène du Bois, writing in the June 1914 issue of *Arts and Decoration,* Barnes's was already "probably the most consistently modern collection in America."

Dr. Barnes's taste had been largely formed in Europe. Through his trips there—and his acquaintance with those Americans who had been most profoundly influenced by European painting of the past fifty years—he had developed the eye of a European. In spite of this, he did not ignore American art, though his relationships with American artists and dealers were, almost always, less than satisfactory. He bought from them, and he bought a great deal; but with the exception of Glackens they found his ungentlemanly demeanor even more unacceptable than had their European counterparts, who could excuse him on the grounds that he was an American and didn't know any better.

One example was Barnes's brief relationship with John Sloan, who had for one semester been his classmate at Central High and who was the most socially conscious member of the Eight. In 1913 Barnes bought the first painting the artist, then over forty years old, had ever sold. Sloan remained grateful to his earliest collector, but he found it impossible to like him. The two men spent time together on only two occasions—once when Barnes bought the painting and some prints (driving a very hard bargain), and again when Sloan and his first wife, Dolly, spent the night at Barnes's home. The painter's widow, Helen Farr Sloan, has explained what happened on that second occasion. "Sloan had a distaste for luxury and felt uncomfortable when surrounded by it," she wrote. "He remembered the wonderful pictures—which he was not allowed to study for himself because Barnes was busy 'conducting a tour.' And he was very unhappy that Barnes had such a possessive attitude about his collection. Sloan felt that a true collector should feel like a 'custodian' of works of art. The occasion for this reaction was this: They were standing next to an early Picasso. Barnes spat on his finger and rubbed a spot of paint off the picture. It was not so much what he said at the moment but the implication that he owned the work as a thing which he had the right to destroy if he chose." Sloan continued to respect Barnes as a collector and later declared that he "knew more about art than any artist needs to know," but he never cared to see the doctor again.

Barnes's relationship with another member of the Eight, Maurice Prendergast, the artist most directly influenced by the Post-Impressionists Barnes so admired, lasted far longer—until the artist's death in 1924. It survived only because of the collector's genuine affection for the man as well as his boundless admiration for his art. "In his joyful appreciation of the beautiful things of life he remained a child up to the time of his death," Barnes wrote of Prendergast. "To express that individual vision by the skilled use of plastic means represents one of the forms of consummate art."

Though Prendergast's feelings about Barnes were mixed—most often he found the collector to be a boor—Barnes forgave behavior on the part of the ingenuous painter which would have caused him to end a relationship with a less lovable figure, or one whose work he was less eager to collect. On one occasion, Barnes learned that the painter had told Edith Glackens that he, Barnes, was incapable of understanding an artist. Instead of erupting with rage, the short-tempered collector passed it off as a joke. On another occasion, Barnes showed even greater restraint. Ira Glackens has given a colorful account of the incident. "The Prendergast brothers (Maurice and Charles) were visiting Barnes, and the good doctor began holding forth on art and so on. Finally, Maurice got mad. 'You have no taste! Look at your house!' he shouted, and indicated the heavy, expensive furniture—Tudor-style tables with great bulges on the legs. 'You have no taste!' he repeated and seized a small chair, banging it on the floor in mounting rage. The small chair, an antique, and probably the only good thing in the room, collapsed from the strain—legs and rungs flying out in every direction." In spite of this, Barnes continued to buy Prendergast's work.

There was a far more serious incident, which should have caused a break between the two but didn't. This concerned the artist's role in a battle between Barnes and a competing collector, the Irish-American John Quinn. The occasion of the battle between the two iron-willed collectors—Quinn was just as rough as Barnes—was the first major showing of Prendergast's work, at New York's Carroll Gallery in February 1915. Quinn, a lawyer who was as much a patron of artists (and writers) as he was of art, and whose collection was more adventurous than Barnes's, had been an early champion of Prendergast, and he insisted that he be given the first opportunity to purchase the painter's major works. When Barnes disputed that right by attempting to bypass both Quinn and his gallery director, Harriet Bryant, and to buy directly from the artist, Quinn exploded. In a letter to Prendergast, he denounced Barnes as a brute and suggested that the artist authorize Bryant to notify "fertilizer Barnes" that she was Prendergast's only representative and that if Barnes wanted to buy any more Prendergasts, he would have to do so through her. That, Quinn concluded, would give Barnes a badly needed lesson in good manners.

The painter replied at once, unequivocally siding with Quinn. He was grateful for his suggestion, he wrote, which he felt would protect him from men like Barnes, whom he characterized as a bargain hunter. Furthermore, he assured Quinn that he had never really taken the Philadelphian seriously anyway.

Barnes, however, did take Prendergast—and his work—seriously, and he continued to fight for the right to purchase his work as he saw fit. The quarrel ended only after an avalanche of venomous letters—composed, on one side, by Quinn but signed by Bryant. Because of this subterfuge, the Philadelphian possibly never knew of Quinn's profound involvement in the quarrel. Almost certainly, he never knew of Prendergast's—for he continued, with undiminished enthusiasm, to consider him his friend and to add his works to his collection.

One of the few other American painters with whom Barnes was able to maintain a friendship was Charles Demuth, whom he had met through Glackens. Demuth, at the time Barnes met him, was known for his delicate still lifes and figure studies; he was a follower of Cézanne and French modernism. Over the years, Barnes bought some fifty of his paintings, watercolors, and drawings, and he urged his associates to buy them as well. The artist, a striking-looking man with bony cheeks and deep-set eyes, was worldly and well-educated. He had studied in Paris and had been befriended by the Steins. He seemed to combine the best of Europe with the best of America, and Barnes enjoyed his company, frequently inviting him to Merion, where he was always welcome to look at the collection. Demuth reciprocated, often inviting Barnes and his wife to visit him at his mother's home in Lancaster, Pennsylvania, where he lived.

Demuth was not unaware of the collector's eccentricities and was frequently angered by his behavior, yet he was always able to forgive him. "I like him and he has been nice to me," he wrote almost apologetically to his mother from Paris in 1921, as an explanation for his steady correspondence with the man so many other artists had come to dislike.

The two men had their disagreements—especially over the merits of Demuth's mentor and friend, John Marin, whose work Barnes refused to buy in spite of Demuth's efforts—but their friendship survived these disagreements. It survived, too, a mysterious quarrel—concerning a proposed trip to Bermuda, alluded to but not explained by the artist in a letter to his mother—which took place in the early 1930s and which only briefly interrupted their relationship, for by 1933 Demuth was again warmly welcomed at Merion. That quarrel was their last, and they remained friends until the painter's death in 1935. Eight years later, when Demuth's mother died, she paid tribute to that friendship by willing Barnes a set of dining-room chairs as well as a large Mayan stone toad, which had been especially valued by her son.

Barnes's rapport with artists was difficult—he seemed ill at ease with most of them—and his relationship with American dealers was equally awkward. The American public showed little interest in the upheavals that were taking place in European art and even less interest in the American modernists who were influenced by them. As a result, few New York dealers were concerned with the sale of contemporary paintings. Of these few, the undisputed leader was Alfred Stieglitz, who had opened his Gallery of the Photo-Secession (also known as "291") at the top of a Fifth Avenue brownstone in 1905. Stieglitz, a distinguished photographer as well as a prophetic, sensitive dealer and a courageous propagandist for contemporary art, had shown the works of Matisse, Cézanne, and Picasso before Barnes had started buying them, or perhaps before he had even heard of them. He had vigorously promoted the work of American painters who became known as the Stieglitz circle—among them Arthur Dove, John Marin, and Georgia O'Keeffe. Stieglitz's gallery quickly became the center of modern art in America and the gathering place and refuge of its artists. Yet, inexplicably, in his early years, Barnes made no purchases from it. Perhaps the collector was intimidated by Stieglitz himself, a towering figure who glorified the contemporary artist as no American dealer had done before him. Perhaps, too, Stieglitz, who was not primarily interested in selling but merely in showing the work of his artists, was simply offended by Barnes's style and was unwilling to cater to his wishes.

Barnes did, however, become a frequent, if not popular, visitor to the few other galleries willing to exhibit modern art. He got along with some dealers, notably William Macbeth, in whose gallery the Eight had shown as a group. Barnes not only bought from Macbeth but on occasion tried to sell through him—he never hesitated to sell a canvas when it ceased to interest him—and even advised him. On the whole, however, dealers found the doctor unpleasant and ill-mannered, far too eager for a bargain. But if they didn't like him, they were willing to sell to him. Buyers were not easy to find.

In these early years of his collecting, Barnes repeatedly demonstrated his independence. He showed no interest in the fashionable; nor was he influenced by public response to the sensational. Then, as always, he abhorred promotion of any kind. In Paris, he had rejected both Futurism and Cubism, which, in spite of the furor they caused, he considered merely fleeting artistic aberrations. He showed little perception in doing so. In New York he showed scant interest in what *Art News* hailed as "a bomb from the blue," the history-making Armory Show, which began in February 1913, attracted a quarter of a million visitors, and opened the eyes of the American public to modern European art and to the art of the future. While recognizing its enormous significance as a stimulus— "academic art received a blow from which it will never entirely recover," he wrote later—he found little in it that was new to him and bought only one painting, Vlaminck's *Les Figues,* for which he paid $162. What was genuinely new at the Armory didn't impress him, and he was unable to respond to the show's major attraction, Marcel Duchamp's revolutionary Cubist/Futurist study of motion, *Nude Descending a Staircase,* which he felt could as appropriately have been labeled *Cow Eating Oysters.* "To enjoy or understand such pictures there would be necessary not only new eyes, but new systems of psychology, metaphysics, geometry, and, especially, a new definition of aesthetic," he commented.

Barnes was not about to look at art with "new eyes"; nor would he apply "a new definition of aesthetic." He was rarely a pioneer collector, and he had none of the courage and foresight of John Quinn, Lizzie Bliss, Katherine Dreier, or Walter Arensberg, adventurous collectors who had been profoundly influenced by the Armory Show. Through his early acquisitions, he clearly demonstrated his predilection for the nineteenth-century Impressionists and Post-Impressionists and their descendants—above all, Renoir, Cézanne, and Matisse. His undeniably brilliant collection would expand and develop, but the masterpieces of those painters and of their contemporaries—not the work of their successors—would always remain at its core.

He had come a long way in a remarkably short time, and only three years after sending Glackens off to Paris to buy what would become the nucleus of the Barnes collection, the doctor felt sufficiently sure of himself to write his first work of art criticism. Published in the April 1915 issue of *Arts and Decoration,* it was titled "How to Judge a Painting." It is, in many ways, a naïve piece, poorly organized and frequently muddled. The title itself is misleading. Barnes devotes many pages to an explanation of how *not* to judge a painting: by paying attention to most art books, the judgments of moribund academies, or the words of verbose art critics, whom he attacks vigorously. But he uses only a few paragraphs to give his own formula for judging a work of art: simply looking at and reflecting upon the original. Nonetheless, the article is of value, for in it Barnes articulates clearly and with enormous enthusiasm his own personal credo as well as the joys and satisfactions he has experienced as a collector. The statement of a man passionately in love with painting, it reads, in part:

> What are some of the pleasures? The least is the mere possession, the best, the joy that one can feel but not express to others; between these two extremes are pleasures that may be

compared to the notes of a piano, limited in what can be produced only by the performer's skill and knowledge. Good paintings are more satisfying companions than the best of books and infinitely more so than most very nice people. I can talk, without speaking to Cézanne, Prendergast, Daumier, Renoir, and they talk to me in kind. I can criticize them and take, without offense, the refutation which comes silently but powerfully when I learn, months later, what they mean and not what I thought they meant. That is one of the joys of a collection, the elasticity with which paintings stretch to the beholder's personal vision which they progressively develop. And that is universal, for a painting is justly proportionate to what a man thinks he sees in it. As a substitute for other pursuits, collecting, living with, and studying good paintings—the enthusiast believes—offers greater interest, variety, and satisfaction than any other pleasure or work a man could select. . . .

A man with a house full of good paintings needs no subterfuge of excessive heat or cold to drive him north or south to get away from his own wearying self. Golf, dances, theatres, dinners, traveling, get a setback as worthy diversions when the rabies or pursuit of quality in painting, and its enjoyment, gets into a man's system. And when he has surrounded himself with that quality, bought with his blood, he is a King.

6

Dr. Barnes was not content to rest upon the fame of his growing collection. At heart he was, and would always remain, a pedagogue who wanted to share his ideas with—or, if necessary, impose those ideas on—those who, in his opinion, were inadequately educated. He had had this in mind when, over the years, he enlarged the experience in education initiated in the early days of the A. C. Barnes Company. At first he had sought to help his few employees to understand themselves, and to reach their own potentialities, both at their work and away from it. Later he undertook to broaden their capacities and to expand the range and accuracy of their perceptions by means of seminars, discussions, and readings, based largely on the recent theories of the philosopher and educator John Dewey, which stressed the importance of learning by doing and defined the aim of education as the development of a body of knowledge with which man might better deal with his environment and the needs of modern society. Since Barnes felt that six hours a day were sufficient to carry out the needs of the company, he decided to devote two hours—from 12:30 to 2:30—to this purpose.

It was a bold and unlikely experiment, he admitted. "The venture," he wrote, "was a shot in the dark, an experiment with very dubious material, namely, unskilled workers with but little early schooling." There were nine participants in the group. Only one of them had a university degree; three were high school graduates, four had gone no farther than primary school, and one man, already middle-aged, was illiterate. The leader of the group was Mary Mullen, who in spite of her limited education (presumably, she was one of the high school graduates) had, according to Barnes, "a flair for psychology," and was "thoroughly grounded in the principles of Dewey's methods." Her role was to suggest rather than to impose solutions and, in her own words, "to present knowledge stripped of its academic trappings, in a form relevant to actual problems."

Barnes himself described the program in some detail. It was one that might have daunted many a university student. Members of the group spent two years reading and discussing William James. They managed to get through *The Principles of Psychology, Pragmatism,* and *The Varieties of Religious Experience,* though they foundered on his *Essays in Radical Empiricism.* They learned from Dewey's *How We Think,* which is a statement of the principles of thinking and of the best methods for developing reasoning power, and they were enthusiastic about the writings of Bertrand Russell. They learned to appreciate art with the help of George Santayana's outline of aesthetic theory, *The Sense of Beauty,* and his *Reason in Art,* as well as through the writings of the British painter and critic Roger Fry. (Fry's books of art criticism were among the few such volumes that met with Barnes's approval.) And as a result of their reading, the many paintings that filled the walls of the factory were the subject of frequent, intelligent discussions.

Barnes was heartened by the success of the experiment, especially so because it proved to him the validity of Dewey's theories. When, in 1916, he read the philosopher's newest work, *Democracy and Education,* he had further confirmation that Dewey's views on education as growth toward more and better shared experience and his belief that the purpose of instruction was the creation of good thinking habits coincided to a remarkable degree with his own. He had never had the chance to talk to his earliest mentor, William James, who had died in 1910, but Dewey was very much alive and teaching at New York's Columbia University. In order to establish personal contact with the man whose ideas he so admired, he enrolled in the philosopher's weekly Columbia seminar for the academic year of 1917–18.

The presence in their midst of the sturdily built, gruff millionaire art collector may have intimidated the younger members of Dewey's class, but the seminar proved to be an immensely enriching experience for Barnes. Dewey, then almost sixty years old, was already a legendary figure in the academic world—he had laid the foundation for what would be known as progressive education—and, because of his unselfish devotion to liberal social causes, beyond it. Nonetheless, even his many admirers admitted that he seemed to lack all the essentials of a good teacher. He spoke slowly and unpersuasively, the train of his thoughts often wandering unintelligibly. "To most of the thousands, both on and off the campus, who over the years came to his classes," his biographer George Dykhuizen wrote, "Dewey's lectures were a boring experience; the wonder was how one who so stressed the role of interest in the educative process could himself fail so abysmally to create it in his own classes. But to those who tried seriously and faithfully to follow his thinking, who conscientiously took notes and studied them afterwards, Dewey's lectures eventually became an exciting educational experience."

Apparently the philosopher's seminars, such as the one attended by Barnes—"where the atmosphere was that of a group of thinkers cooperatively engaged in inquiry"—were more immediately satisfying. In any case, Dewey's influence on all those who came to know him was enormous. "For those who were his students," wrote Professor John H. Randall, Jr., one of his younger colleagues at Columbia, "and for many who were his colleagues throughout the University, Dewey became a part of their lives and selves. . . . It was not alone what he did and thought, it was what he was that drew men to him—simple, sturdy, unpretentious, quizzical, shrewd, devoted, fearless—a true Yankee saint."

Barnes was immediately drawn to Dewey—he admired the man as much as he had admired his ideas—and his warm feelings toward the philosopher were fully reciprocated. The two men quickly became friends. They frequently dined together following the seminar, and by November 1917, Barnes felt close enough to the philosopher to invite him and his wife to spend the weekend at Merion. It was the first of many such visits, during which the two men exchanged ideas, studied the works of art that filled the home, or simply enjoyed private afternoon chamber-music concerts.

In April 1918, as the Columbia seminar was about to end, Barnes proposed that he and other members of the group continue to work together by devoting their summer to a private inquiry—which he would subsidize—to determine why Philadelphia's large community of Polish immigrants continued to resist assimilation by remaining in their own neighborhood and retaining their own customs and language. It was more than an academic exercise. The Polish-American community had taken a position in favor of the conservative faction, led by the pianist-politician Ignace Jan Paderewski, in its struggle with the liberals for control of Poland's postwar government, and Barnes and Dewey, supporters of the liberals, wanted to know why. Barnes's stated aim was to work out a plan that would eventually "eliminate forces alien to democratic internationalism and promote American ideals in accordance with the principles announced by President Wilson in his various public communications." Dewey was enthusiastic about the project and in May agreed to act as its adviser and general supervisor.

The group that traveled to Philadelphia for the summer at Barnes's expense (he rented a house for them in the city's Polish section) was a distinguished one. It included Irwin Edman, later the head of Columbia's philosophy department; Brand Blanshard, who became the head of Yale's philosophy department; Paul Blanshard (Brand's twin brother), who became a well-known social critic; Mary Frances Bradshaw, who married Brand Blanshard and gained success as a writer; and Anzia Yezierska, who had been raised in the Polish ghetto and was to achieve fame as the author of stories of immigrant life.

Each member was assigned a special task. Edman was to study

the influence of the Polish press on the community; Bradshaw to investigate the roles of language and the schools in the life of the children; Brand Blanshard, the influence of the Catholic Church; and Yezierska to examine the role of women in the home and to act as translator for the group. Paul Blanshard didn't stay long enough to be given a special assignment. He left after a month— Barnes found him to be a procrastinator, and he felt Barnes was "temperamental and a bit crotchety," though Blanshard never felt that the doctor was responsible for his departure.

Barnes was dissatisfied with the methods of the investigation and with the unimpressive performance of its participants. He felt that the most competent member, Edman, was capable of replacing Dewey during the professor's absences and that Brand Blanshard was acceptable, but for him Bradshaw had the mentality of an undergraduate and Yezierska was basically an artist and not sufficiently scientific in her approach. He was probably right. Though each member of the young group would achieve prominence in his or her field in the years to come, at the time none had the experience or skills necessary to conduct a valid investigation of a complicated social and political problem. Nonetheless, by August, when the study was concluded, Dewey felt the findings were of sufficient interest to send their report to the Military Intelligence Bureau of the Army in Washington.

Though Washington apparently paid little attention to the group's findings, the experience united Barnes and Dewey in a fervent effort to gain American support for the liberal Polish forces. Barnes was almost obsessively preoccupied with this effort over a period of several months, and both men took their case to the public. In an article published in the August 14, 1918, issue of *The New Republic,* Dewey presented the results of the study. The isolation of Philadelphia's Polish community, he concluded, was due to a deliberate conspiracy of conservative, pro-Paderewski forces led by the Polish National Alliance, the Roman Catholic Polish Alliance, and local Republican politicians. By keeping these immigrants apart from the mainstream of American life, these forces could manipulate and exploit them for their own purposes. Their immediate aim, Dewey wrote, was to deliver their votes en masse at a forth-coming convention in Detroit called to express the sentiments of the four million Polish Americans concerning the future of Poland. By packing the convention, the conservative faction, whose magnetic leader would be in attendance, hoped to turn American policy definitively in their direction.

Four months later, Barnes published his first piece of political writing, a lengthy article in the December 28 issue of *The Dial*, accusing Paderewski of having deceived the new immigrants by forming an alliance with the Polish Roman Catholic church and "especially with that branch of the Polish clergy which openly opposes Americanization among the immigrants." Barnes had cause to be even angrier than Dewey had been, for the Detroit convention had been extremely successful, and American policy had shifted in favor of the Polish conservatives.

It was a cogent, effective statement, but it was flawed by its tone of almost childish indignation. In this and later quarrels, Barnes tended to be peevish and defensive, all too often watering down his otherwise valid arguments. He had been personally offended that the chairman of the Senate Foreign Relations Committee had ignored a letter "calling attention to the fact that a scientific study of Polish conditions in America was being made and that the organization and its data were at his disposal," as well as a subsequent telegram from Barnes suggesting that Dewey's report be consulted by the Committee.

He further complained that after both he and Dewey had been denounced at the convention as being pro-German (because of Barnes's presumed connection with German dye interests), they had been subjected to an investigation by the Department of Justice. Though he noted with satisfaction that "no arrests or warrants followed," the mere fact of the investigation offended him, and he felt it necessary to assure his readers of his impeccable credentials. "A minor irony of the situation," he added, "was the fact that one of the Americans investigated by the Department of Justice had furnished the total financial support to a private laboratory (presumably the A. C. Barnes Company) in which was originated the gas mask worn at that time by the American soldiers at the French front." (There is no substantiation of this extravagant claim, but it is known that Barnes did act as a consultant on the War Department's gas mask program.)

"Dewey's goodness was so genuine, constant, and sustained, even under provocation, that I sometimes found it somewhat oppressive," Sidney Hook wrote in *Commentary* following the philosopher's death in 1952. "It was almost with relief that I discovered a shortcoming in him. That was his indulgent friendship for Albert C. Barnes."

Dewey would not have agreed with this assessment of a long, uninterrupted friendship, equally important to both men, which began during the Columbia seminar and lasted until Barnes's death. Dewey, a shy, patient man who found no pleasure in arguing, was aware of his friend's failings. At times he complained—to Barnes himself and always good-naturedly—that the collector, in the midst of his many quarrels, lost perspective and overreacted. He explained to Hook that much of Barnes's frequently outrageous behavior was the result of an inferiority complex, an astute observation since the collector, apparently unsure of himself, almost always involved Dewey in his own controversies and reinforced his own position by citing the philosopher's support for it. (In the same way, Barnes in a sense hid behind his associates, real and fictitious secretaries, and even his dog, whose names were signed to many of the more scurrilous letters he wrote.)

In spite of his friend's shortcomings, Dewey was drawn to Barnes just as the collector had been drawn to him. They liked and admired one another, and they were congenial, meeting whenever possible and occasionally traveling together—once to the West Coast. It was after this cross-country trip that their previously rather formal relationship relaxed, and the "Dear Dr. Barnes" and "Dear Mr. Dewey" of their earlier correspondence changed to "Dear Al" and "Dear Jack."

This voluminous correspondence, which they kept up throughout the years, attests to a friendship of extraordinary warmth, intelligence, and mutual respect. In their letters, the two men candidly exchanged ideas on education and art, politics and people; their interests were similar, as were their inclinations. Barnes kept Dewey informed of the progress of his collection and of each detail of the countless controversies in which he was involved, and the philosopher kept his friend abreast of his own thoughts, activities, and travels. The collector consulted Dewey about almost everything—most often seeking his advice concerning his educational program—and the latter never failed to respond, frankly and sympathetically. Most important, perhaps, the two men were, at all times, loyal to one another, always available and supportive when needed.

Barnes profited immensely from his relationship with Dewey. The philosopher opened up new worlds to him, vastly increasing his range of interests, and Barnes responded with enthusiasm. In 1918, Dewey took him to a small theater on Macdougal Street, in Greenwich Village, to watch a performance by the Provincetown Players, the vigorous young group of authors and actors who had joined together a few years before and had distinguished themselves by presenting the early plays of, among many others, Sherwood Anderson, Edna St. Vincent Millay, and, above all, Eugene O'Neill. Barnes liked what he saw and returned there often. When the struggling group was in need of money, he came to their rescue with a generous gift of a thousand dollars.

Dewey also led Barnes to a greater awareness of social and political issues and involved him in the liberal causes to which he himself devoted so much of his energy. One of these was *The New Republic,* a magazine of liberal ideas which began publication in 1914. The philosopher introduced Barnes to Herbert Croly, its founder, and to other members of the staff, and as a result the collector frequently gave money—and occasionally contributed articles—to the magazine. In addition, Dewey was responsible for Barnes's interest in the New School for Social Research, a liberal institution for adult education founded in New York City in 1919 as an antidote to the restrictions of conservative academia. The school was interested in Barnes, too, and shortly after its founding he was invited to teach a course in psychology there. Dewey felt that his friend should accept the offer, but Barnes rejected it on the grounds that he was too busy elsewhere.

In the early years of their friendship, Barnes seemed to follow Dewey's lead in every direction. The philosopher even persuaded him to join in his own pursuit of what might be called body modification by becoming a patient of F. Matthias Alexander, an Australian who claimed that many physical and emotional ailments could be traced to the failure of modern man's body to keep up with his more highly developed brain and nervous system, and who suggested as a remedy that man alter his habits of posture and muscular control. (Barnes was ahead of his time. Alexander's book on the subject, *Man's Supreme Inheritance: Conscious Guidance and Control in Relation to Human Evolution in Civilization,* with an introduction by Dewey, is even more popular today, in holistic health circles, than it was when first published in 1918.)

It would be unfair, however, to give the impression that theirs was in any way a one-sided relationship or to imply that Dewey's ideas dominated Barnes's. Though the collector had based his educational theories on Dewey's, he was far more than a mere disciple. He learned from Dewey and was stimulated intellectually by his contact with him, but at the same time he also enriched Dewey's life, not only by responding intelligently to the philosopher's ideas with his own, but above all by leading him to an understanding and appreciation of his own world—the world of art.

When he first met Barnes, Dewey's knowledge of the fine arts was limited. Barnes immediately assumed the role of teacher. He took Dewey in hand and shared his experiences with him. He accompanied the philosopher and his family to galleries and museums, and to the studios of his friends, Glackens and Prendergast. On at least one occasion, the philosopher attended a class given by his friend at the Louvre, and during their weekends together in Merion, Barnes patiently explained the meaning of his collection to Dewey, who had never before been capable of seeing a work of art with the perceptions of an aesthetician. Apparently, Dewey learned from Barnes the importance of direct contact with a work of art; in 1928, on a visit to Leningrad, the philosopher's daughter-in-law, Elizabeth, was surprised at how long Dewey would stand before a painting, studying it with extraordinary intensity. If the philosopher Susanne K. Langer was correct in stating that Dewey was "enlightened, but also deeply confused by Barnes," Jane M. Dewey, his daughter, was also right in believing that contact with the collector "gave definite philosophic form to Dewey's previously rather scattered ideas of the arts."

In 1925 Barnes dedicated his first book, *The Art in Painting,* to Dewey. In 1934 the philosopher dedicated his *Art As Experience,* a summary of his philosophy of art, to his friend, writing in the preface:

> My greatest indebtedness is to Dr. A. C. Barnes. The chapters have been gone over one by one with him, and yet what I owe to his comments and suggestions on this account is but a small measure of my debt. I have had the benefit of conversations with him through a period of years, many of which occurred in the presence of the unrivaled collection of pictures he has assembled. The influence of these conversations, together with that of his books, has been a chief factor in shaping my own thinking about the philosophy of esthetics. Whatever is sound in this volume is due more than I can say to the great educational work carried on in the Barnes Foundation. That work is of a pioneer quality comparable to the best that has been done in any field during the present generation, that of science not excepted. I should be glad to think of this volume as one phase of the widespread influence the Foundation is exercising.

Privately Dewey acknowledged his debt to Barnes for allowing him to pick his brain and plagiarize his ideas. The dedication, he told Barnes in a letter, should have read: "To Albert C. Barnes, a genius and in affection also who often makes himself God damned uncomfortable by the way in which he expresses and suppresses it."

Barnes was deeply moved by his friend's words of appreciation. He was so used to harsh criticism that he often wondered if he deserved anything else, he wrote Dewey, adding that if it hadn't been for the philosopher he would probably have lived "the more intelligent life of drinking, yachting, fishing, and indulged in one of the other favorite indoor sports."

CHAPTER

7

The 1920s were years of feverish activity for Dr. Barnes—as a collector and as an educator. With characteristic zeal, he expanded and developed his collection, both in America and during many trips abroad. Based on lengthy and frequent consultations with Dewey, he worked out a systematic program of art education— far more precise than that applied less formally at his factory— and put it into practice. And he merged his two passions by establishing the Foundation that still bears his name.

There is, apparently, no detailed record of his purchases then, or at any time; if such a record exists, which is unlikely, it is among the carefully guarded secrets at the Foundation today. However, from the evidence available, it is obvious that his collection grew with astonishing speed, increasingly reflecting his expertise as well as the needs of his projected educational program. He became well known as a formidable presence in art circles wherever he traveled. Alert to every opportunity to enrich his collection, he bought from galleries and from friends and acquaintances. At the same time, he became a familiar figure at major auctions where, in America, he would often be seen in the company of Glackens. His tastes were catholic and subject to change, yet his interest in Renoir and Cézanne remained undiminished, and his pursuit of their work was relentless.

Because of this, Barnes must have been particularly pleased to receive, in early 1920, a letter from Leo Stein, then in Italy, telling him that his own Renoirs, sixteen of them, were for sale and asking his friend to make an offer. Barnes was intrigued. The price of Renoirs had soared since the artist's death in 1919—the doctor wrote Dewey that one canvas which had recently brought $28,000 in New York was similar to one he himself had purchased years before for only $3,200—and he sensed a bargain.

It seems that Stein might have been looking elsewhere at the same time, for there was no further mention of this proposed sale until December 29, 1920, when Stein again wrote to Barnes. This time, he had to sell his Renoirs—he needed the money—and he asked his friend's advice. "I don't know where to strike the balance between the rise in Renoir prices and the fall in francs," he wrote. "If you don't mind giving me some counsel in the matter as to whether there is a practicable market now or whether one had better wait; whether selling at auction gives a fair return or whether some other method were more judicious. . . ."

Barnes answered immediately, offering to examine the canvases before giving his advice. Stein replied in March. Grateful for Barnes's interest, he asked him to look over the pictures which he had shipped to New York, and do what he thought best with them. "I'm afraid that you think of them as more important than they are," he wrote apologetically. "Most of them are small and slight, and one lovely nude I cracked by foolish handling in the old days of my pathological impatience. . . ." As a postscript, Stein mentioned that besides the Renoirs, there were Cézanne watercolors, a Cézanne oil, a Delacroix, a Daumier, and a Matisse bronze sculpture available for purchase.

Barnes worked diligently at selling his friend's possessions. By May 21, he was able to report to Dewey that he had sold almost everything and had turned over $30,000 to Stein. Barnes had bought only the most important Renoirs and the Matisse for his own collection, at prices he believed were satisfactory to both of them. In the same letter, he proudly wrote Dewey that his personal collection of Renoirs now numbered over one hundred; he had bought more than a score over the past two years and had paid as much as $80,000 for one of them.

Barnes hadn't, however, bought all the Renoirs he wanted at the time, for one major work had been denied him—though for a while he thought it would be his. The painting was the artist's final masterpiece, *The Great Bathers,* completed shortly before his death. In 1921, when he had learned of its availability, Barnes had been quick to make an offer of 800,000 francs (then $48,000) for what would have been a major addition to his collection. He even hinted that he might be able to double the offer, but it was immediately rejected by the artist's heirs, who wanted instead to donate it to the Louvre. To the collector's delight, the museum was in no hurry to accept the gift. After two years of bureaucratic wrangling, the Renoir family almost gave up, and in 1923 Barnes was sufficiently encouraged to announce his imminent purchase of the painting. The announcement was premature; the family's threat to allow the canvas to leave France for America galvanized Louvre officials to action. After appropriate embarrassed apologies for the delay, they belatedly accepted the gift and deprived Barnes of one master-piece.

During this period Barnes had added an impressive number of Cézannes to his collection. In 1920 he acquired thirteen major works from a museum in Amsterdam, bringing the total number he owned to thirty. In early 1922, at New York's Plaza Hotel for an auction of 161 paintings and drawings belonging to the well-known antiquarian Dikran Kelekian, he bought still another, a landscape for which he paid $12,300—then considered a high price. By 1923 he owned fifty Cézannes.

Barnes didn't, of course, limit his acquisitions to Renoir and Cézanne. For example, in 1921, again at the Plaza Hotel in New York, he bought four Degas oils and four pastels at a sale of the collection of Jacques Seligman. On this occasion, he boasted to Dewey that he had been able to get one hundred thousand dollars' worth of paintings for thirty thousand.

The collector was also looking to the past in an effort to enlarge the range of his collection. In January 1924 he wrote to Glackens about the results of a trip to Europe, during which he had acquired a choice El Greco and an extraordinary Claude Lorrain from a private collector. Both were in such terrible condition that they would not have been recognizable at a casual glance. But his was not a casual glance. The Greco was, he felt certain, the best on the market at the time, and he considered finding it "a just act of God's kindness for the saintly life I've led." The Claude, in his opinion, was as good as any hanging in the Louvre.

During that same trip, Barnes met an elderly Greek with a superb collection of antique Greek and Egyptian sculptures. Barnes shook a check at him and came away with forty sculptures to add still another dimension to his collection. This latter purchase was particularly satisfying because he had started to study Greek and Egyptian art only one year before. During the same trip, he was able to buy one Italian painting and two Dutch fifteenth-century primitives.

Not everyone was pleased by the widespread reports of the fearsome collector's acquisitions. John Quinn was furious when news of his hated rival's activities reached him from Paris via H. P. Roché, his own adviser and representative. In July 1922 Roché, described by Leo Stein as "the great introducer," spotted Barnes at an important Parisian auction. He wrote Quinn that the Philadelphian, accompanied by his wife and a dealer, Durand-Ruel, had bought several first-rate Picassos. As consolation, he added that Picasso had refused to sign the drawings, and assured Quinn that he himself had never met Barnes and knew that if he did he could never get along with him.

In his reply, Quinn warned Roché of the "bully's" long purse and large appetite, agreeing that Roché couldn't possibly work with the Philadelphian. He also noted, with satisfaction, that one painter, Arthur B. Davies, had refused to let Barnes come to his studio and that when the collector boasted that he had three of Davies's works on approval from a dealer, the artist insisted that the dealer withdraw them at once.

. .

Though his greatest enthusiasm was reserved for European painting, Barnes did not totally neglect American artists in his quest for additions to his collection. In the fall of 1920 his search took him to Woodstock, New York, where he and Mrs. Barnes spent a few days examining the works of the many painters who had banded together there under the name of the Woodstock Art Association. He was greeted warmly by these artists, and as he visited their studios, he was friendly and good-natured, but, to their regret, noncommittal, buying nothing on the spot. He had, however, taken careful notes. About a week after his departure, he wrote to a few of these painters—among them Andrew Dasburg and Paul Rohland—expressing his desire to purchase specific works. He knew exactly what they were and where they had been hanging. To one other artist, he merely wrote a note of criticism, suggesting how his paintings might be improved.

It was around this time that Barnes finally bought works by one of Stieglitz's group, Marsden Hartley. For a short period, he was enthusiastic about Hartley's romantic, emotional canvases. In the spring of 1921, at a special auction arranged to raise money for the desperately poor artist at New York's Anderson Galleries, Barnes came to his rescue by buying a few small paintings for $115. Pleased with his purchases, he wrote a letter of gratitude to Hartley, telling him he had hung two of his works on the wall of his private office and inviting him to visit and see the wall whenever he came to Philadelphia. In the same letter, he mentioned that two of his associates—one of them was Nelle Mullen—were eager to buy two other small paintings which had recently been exhibited in Philadelphia. Though the asking price had been $350, the doctor offered $50. The painter turned the letter over to Stieglitz, who never replied. No more Hartleys entered the Barnes collection. Later Barnes, through the painter, Arthur B. Carles, offered $300 for a painting by another Stieglitz artist, John Marin, and Stieglitz again failed to respond, asking Carles to tell Barnes "to go to hell with his compliments"—and no Marins ever entered the collection.

. .

By the early part of the 1920s, Barnes's collection crowded every corner of his house. Paintings covered the walls of each room; they were hung along the stairways, in the bathrooms, and on closet doors. He was besieged with requests from visitors anxious to see them. "My collection of pictures got beyond me," he noted in *The New Republic* of March 14, 1923. "People wanted to come to see it from all over the world. And the teachers of art, and the painters, wanted to bring their classes there." It was time to expand—to build a gallery for his paintings, and to provide space in which to conduct the classes he envisioned.

For several years he had been trying to buy the twelve-acre property adjoining Lauraston—he had first shown it to Dewey in 1918—but the owner, Colonel Joseph Lapsley Wilson, a horticulturist, had rejected each offer, vowing that only the undertaker or the sheriff would get him to leave the land he loved. Finally, in 1922, Wilson, having been befriended by Laura Barnes, who shared his passion for plants and flowers, gave in—on the condition that Barnes preserve the plantings that formed the arboretum which he had carefully developed over more than forty years. Barnes agreed not only to maintain the arboretum, but to expand it under Wilson's direction and with the help of Mrs. Barnes. Barnes was to use a small part of the land for the construction of an art gallery, office, and a home; in return, he promised to build a new residence for Captain Wilson and his wife, for which they would pay an annual rent of one dollar.

In October 1922, Barnes selected an architect to design the new museum. Paul Philippe Cret, a native Frenchman, had come to Philadelphia as a professor of architectural design at the University of Pennsylvania. The style of the projected museum would be simplified French Renaissance; according to Cret, it would look more like a private home than a museum. It was an approach that appealed to Barnes, as did the architect's first concern—"to secure those conditions that the painter could wish for the display of his work." That meant a number of moderate-sized rooms, rather than the usual cavernous museum rooms, and studio lighting, similar to that by which works were painted, rather than top lighting. Useless corridors were to be avoided by having two series of small connecting rooms grouped around a large central gallery.

Cret knew what he was doing, and he did it well—he went on to design several other successful public buildings, among them the Detroit Institute of Art and the Folger Shakespeare Library in Washington, D.C. Barnes was entirely satisfied with the results, but he had been a difficult client—he knew little about architecture—and by the time the work was completed, the two men were on less than friendly terms. When, after the building was completed, a friend of the architect asked for a letter to Barnes which might help him get in to see the collection, Cret answered that such a letter would merely guarantee that he would never see it.

Once the problem of the site and the construction of the new building had been resolved, Barnes turned his attention to a more complex issue—the creation of a foundation that would, with the use of his collection, be the instrument through which his educational program might be carried out. He was insistent on two points: that the charter for this new foundation be granted to an educational institution and not to a museum; and that he remain in full control of that foundation, not only during his lifetime, but even after his death. Legally it was a difficult task.

Barnes discussed his plans with his friend, the lawyer Owen J. Roberts (later a justice of the Supreme Court), and after long nights at the lawyer's office, they came up with an acceptable plan. On December 4, 1922, a charter was granted by the Commonwealth of Pennsylvania to an educational institution, to be known as the Barnes Foundation. Two days later, an indenture of trust, providing an endowment of six million dollars, was executed.

The bylaws of the new Foundation had been worked out to the smallest detail, accurately reflecting the wishes of its founder. The over-all objective was clearly stated: "To promote the advancement of education and the appreciation of the fine arts; and for this purpose to erect, found and maintain . . . an art gallery and other necessary buildings for the exhibition of works of ancient and modern art; and the maintenance in connection therewith of an arboretum . . . together with a laboratory of arboriculture . . ." (this latter a concession to both Joseph Lapsley Wilson and Laura Barnes).

The Board of Trustees of the Foundation was to consist of five people—the original members were Barnes, his wife, the Mullen sisters, and Captain Wilson—yet only one of them, Barnes himself, was empowered to make decisions. Justification for this was contained in one provision which granted Barnes the sole power to sell or exchange any works in the collection, reserving to himself "this right, power and discretion for the reason that he has created said collection and best understands what may be necessary in the way of sale or exchange to complete it, perfect it, and render it more adequate." That right, it was made clear, extended even beyond Barnes's lifetime, for following his death it was specifically stated that the collection would be closed, and that no changes whatsoever could be made. In addition, after Barnes's death no picture could ever be loaned.

There were explicit provisions concerning the gallery's admissions policy. (These were frequently amended in later years.) During the lifetime of Barnes and his wife, the gallery would be open to the public on not more than two days a week, except during July, August, and September, but only upon presentation of cards of admission granted by the Board of Trustees; art students could be admitted during that time only by special arrangement with these same trustees. "Donor makes these provisions and stipulations," Barnes explained, "for the reason that said art gallery is founded as an educational experiment under the principles of modern psychology as applied to education, and it is Donor's desire during his lifetime, and that of his wife, to perfect the plan so that it shall be operative for the spread of the principles of democracy and education after the death of Donor and his wife."

In the next paragraph, Barnes spelled out in precise language the "democratic" admissions policy to be followed after his death and that of his wife, specifying to future trustees just who he believed should be admitted to the gallery and why:

> After the death of Donor and his said wife the gallery shall be open two days in each week, except during the months of July and August of each year, to students and instructors of the Pennsylvania Academy of the Fine Arts and similar institutions founded for the study of the fine arts. On three days a week (one of which shall be Sunday) the gallery shall be open to the public under such regulations as the Board of Trustees of Donor may make. It will be incumbent upon the Board of Trustees to make such regulations as will ensure that it is the plain people, that is, men and women who gain their livelihood by daily toil in shops, factories, schools, stores and similar places, who shall have free access to the art gallery upon those days when the gallery is to be open to the public. On those week-days on which the gallery is to be open it shall be open between the hours of 10 and 4 only, and on Sunday from one o'clock to five o'clock in the afternoon only. This restriction shall apply to the gallery and buildings connected therewith only, and not to the Arboretum. The Arboretum shall be open to the public and to students on such days and during such hours and under such regulations and administrative rules as the Board of Trustees of Donee may find necessary to protect the trees and plants constituting said Arboretum.

He foresaw and provided for every possibility. Because the purpose of his gift was "democratic and educational in the true meaning of those words," no "receptions, tea parties, dinners, banquets, dances, musicales or similar affairs" could ever be held in the Foundation's buildings, nor could the gallery ever be used for exhibitions of works not belonging to the Barnes Foundation. In addition, no artist would ever be permitted to use the buildings for the instruction of pupils who pay that artist for private instruction in art or any other form of education.

Within days after having been granted a charter for his new foundation, Barnes set off for Europe. The purpose of the trip was to purchase the buff-colored French limestone Cret had specified for the construction of the new building; in fact, it turned out to be one of the most extravagant buying sprees in the history of art collecting.

8

When Dr. Barnes arrived in Paris in late 1922, he was no longer the novice collector who, ten years before, had come to learn and to establish contacts. He knew his way around, and his visits to the French capital were avidly anticipated by artists, dealers, and other collectors—all those who had paintings to sell. Of these, none was more eager to greet him than Paul Guillaume, a young dealer who rapidly became the Philadelphian's unofficial man in Paris.

Guillaume's origins are obscure. He first attracted attention in 1913 when, at the age of twenty-one and apparently without money or family connections, he struck up a close friendship with Guillaume Apollinaire, the enormously influential poet and critic then at the height of his fame among the Parisian avant-garde. Initially their bond was a mutual interest in African sculpture—until then strictly the province of anthropologists and ethnologists—which they looked upon as art rather than merely as objects of religious or metaphysical significance. In time Apollinaire introduced the well-mannered, soft-spoken young man to the world of modern art, and before long Guillaume set himself up as an art dealer, first at his apartment on the avenue de Villiers and then at his small gallery on the rue Miromesnil. There he showed the works of Cézanne, Renoir, Matisse, and Picasso, as well as those of two artists who became his intimate friends, André Derain and Giorgio de Chirico. Success came quickly, and in 1917 Guillaume opened a larger gallery on the fashionable faubourg St.-Honoré, where he dazzled Parisians with the first comprehensive exhibition of African sculpture to be held in the French capital.

When Barnes first met him in the early 1920s, the dealer, though barely thirty years old, was firmly established at the center of French intellectual life. The collector took to him at once. Charming, sensitive, and intelligent, Guillaume was a man of good taste as well as one with the right connections. Barnes had bought from the city's well-established dealers—notably Durand-Ruel and Vollard—but the younger man could offer him something these older men couldn't, his full attention.

Guillaume recognized this and carefully cultivated their relationship. He handled Barnes with care. Understanding the dangers of attempting to impose his own ideas on the collector, he acted subtly as his knowing guide. He led the Philadelphian to museums and galleries and to the studios of promising artists whose work, not coincidentally, he was eager to sell. Though undoubtedly impressed by Barnes's keen mind and stimulated by his companionship, he also realized that Barnes was a rarity—an enthusiastic collector who had money to spend and was willing to spend it.

Under Guillaume's guidance Barnes developed a passionate interest in African sculpture—a number of important pieces, most of them originally owned by Guillaume, became part of his collection. At the same time, Guillaume helped Barnes to increase the number of Renoirs, Cézannes, Matisses, and Picassos in the collection and introduced him to the paintings of the Douanier Rousseau. Barnes's collection of the French "primitive's" works is now among the finest in the world. Most important, Guillaume led the collector to the discovery of a totally unknown artist, Chaim Soutine—a discovery that would make the painter famous and add immeasurably to the doctor's reputation.

Soutine's own story is a remarkable one. Born in 1894, in a small *shtetl* in Smilovitchi, near Minsk, he had tenaciously made his way to Paris in 1912, equipped with nothing but a burning need to paint. His enormous talent had gone unrecognized, and he had been saved from starvation only through the kindness of Leopold Zborowski, a bearded, ascetic Polish poet who had protected him and tried, without success, to sell his paintings. Barnes's discovery of the anguished, moody Lithuanian has become a legend. According to one version, the Philadelphian first saw Soutine's work hanging on the wall of a café, immediately sought out the artist, and bought up all of his work on the spot. According to another version, Barnes merely caught a glimpse of a Soutine hanging in the window of an obscure gallery while riding in a taxi. Excited by what he saw, he jumped out of the cab and traced the artist to his home—likewise buying the painter's entire output.

The most reliable version, however, is that given by Guillaume and substantiated by some of the artist's own friends. According to this, it was Guillaume who first saw a Soutine canvas while visiting a studio to examine the works of still another artist, the Italian Amedeo Modigliani, who had been a friend of the Lithuanian's. The dealer, fascinated by the painting—a portrait of a pastry cook—bought it at once and took it to his gallery. It was there that Barnes saw it and recognized the unknown artist's genius. "It's a peach," he reportedly told the dealer, who, knowing little English, replied that there was no peach, but only a pastry cook.

Taking advantage of the collector's spontaneous enthusiasm and his eagerness to see more Soutines, Guillaume led him to the home of Zborowski, to whom Soutine had consigned most of his completed paintings. Barnes was overwhelmed by what he saw: the distorted figures, chaotic landscapes, and tormented flowers so moved him that he immediately offered to buy everything in sight. Estimates of the number of canvases vary from fifty to a hundred; what is certain is that Barnes paid 60,000 francs ($3,000) for his acquisitions.

The following morning, Zborowski relayed the news to the incredulous Soutine, adding that this new patron was anxious to meet him. The notoriously ragged, ill-shaven, and unwashed painter—he had a chronic fear of water—reluctantly dressed in his one acceptable outfit and followed his friend to his modest home, where Barnes awaited them. The meeting was an awkward one. Years later Soutine gave an abbreviated account of it to his friend Chana Orloff: "Barnes was seated, looking at me, and he said, 'Ah, Soutine. Good.' " They went no farther; both men were hopelessly ill at ease and unable to make conversation. Soutine told Orloff that Barnes was a boor and complained of having had to dress for such an occasion. "I'll never forgive myself for having been an idiot enough to go to such trouble," he told her, and for the rest of his life he felt an implacable contempt for the man who had first recognized his talent. "He gave my paintings to the blacks," Soutine often said contemptuously.

Nonetheless, the "boorish" American had radically changed Soutine's life, transforming him from a penniless artist to a successful one. When the startling news spread throughout Montparnasse, the Lithuanian became a hero. He was, literally, an overnight success. Immediately following the sale, he took some of his newly earned money and hired a taxi to take him from Paris to his home in the south of France, a ride of at least fifteen hours.

For Barnes, it was a tremendous coup—his first and only major discovery—yet he was as ungracious about it as the painter had been. "As soon as I bought some of his work, his stock went up like a skyrocket," he told a reporter when he returned to the States with his purchases. Years later he bragged to an acquaintance, "I caught him when he was drunk, sick, and broke and took the contents of his studio for a pittance." In spite of the antipathy he felt toward the painter, Barnes continued to take pride in recognizing Soutine's genius and in being the first, in his books and articles, to proclaim it to the world. He never changed his mind. Twenty years later, in 1943, in a foreword to a catalogue of an exhibition held in New York, Barnes wrote of Soutine: "He ranks with Matisse and Picasso as one of the painters whose experiments and ideas have had the most profound influence upon contemporary painting."

Though Guillaume had only inadvertently led Barnes to the discovery of Soutine, he was directly responsible for introducing the collector to the work of several other young artists during this extraordinary visit to Paris. All of them were outsiders—expatriates who had been drawn to the French capital from other parts of Europe and had brought a new vitality to the Parisian art world. One of these was Soutine's good friend Modigliani. Modigliani was not exactly unknown, since word of his brilliant talent had spread following his death in 1920, but he was far from famous when Barnes first saw his paintings. According to another artist, the sculptor Jacques Lipchitz, Barnes bought several of Modigliani's voluptuous nudes and gentle portraits on the same day he purchased his Soutines and deserves credit for Modigliani's discovery as well as for that of the Lithuanian painter. "I remember the day very well," Lipchitz wrote later, "this day which caused a lot of noise in Montparnasse and will remain forever in the annals of art history. It was at this point that the two friends, Modigliani and Soutine, began to win international recognition."

Lipchitz, who had come to Paris from Lithuania in 1909, also credited Barnes with changing his own destiny during the same visit to the French capital. Lipchitz, too, met the collector through Guillaume, but in spite of him, for the dealer and sculptor had recently quarreled, and it was only at Barnes's insistence that their introduction was arranged. It was an enormously successful meeting—surprisingly, because Lipchitz's work was greatly influenced by the very Cubists Barnes had earlier scorned—and in the course of it Barnes startled the artist by purchasing eight of his sculptures. Lipchitz was further stunned when, at a dinner following their meeting, Barnes not only paid for his purchases in full but also asked the sculptor to design five reliefs for the niches on the façade of the museum he was having built in Merion. It was an exciting and challenging offer, but after examining the designs for the building which Barnes eagerly showed him, Lipchitz declined. His style, he felt, would not suit Cret's classic French Renaissance architecture. Barnes, however, was insistent, and in the end the sculptor agreed—on the condition, to which the collector readily agreed, that he be allowed full freedom in executing the designs.

Lipchitz's first meeting with Barnes had been far more pleasant than had the collector's first encounter with Soutine and equally beneficial to the artist. The Philadelphian's generosity had provided him with the opportunity to develop his art, free from the financial pressures which had plagued him until that time; and the mere fact of having sold his work to the astute collector enabled him to sell to other collectors, both in Paris and in America. Furthermore, it seemed—for a while at least—to be the beginning of a valuable friendship.

Though conversation between them was difficult—Lipchitz spoke no English and had to rely on his knowledge of Yiddish to communicate with Barnes, whose German was fluent—their friendship flourished in the beginning. Each time Barnes came to Paris, he called upon Lipchitz, and together they visited galleries and museums—just as the collector did with Guillaume. The dealer represented one point of view and Lipchitz another—that of an artist— and Barnes benefitted from both. Aware of the doctor's reputation, the sculptor scrupulously kept to the rules which he had learned governed a successful relationship with him. He kept his opinions to himself and was especially careful not to take advantage of their friendship by seeking favors for himself or for other artists, many of whom begged the sculptor to introduce them to the affluent collector. When, however, after two years, Lipchitz broke this latter rule he learned, as would many after him, that one transgression was often enough to end a friendship with Dr. Barnes.

The incident that shattered this warm relationship involved one of Lipchitz's friends, an artist who desperately needed money to pay for a lifesaving operation for his wife. The sculptor, moved by the man's pleas, presented his case to Barnes, asking that he visit the artist's studio and perhaps buy some of his work. At first Barnes balked at the idea, but he finally agreed on the condition that Lipchitz have his friend's paintings brought to his own studio so that he would not have to meet the man, and possibly be influenced by his tragic plight.

All was arranged according to the collector's wishes. The following day, he examined six canvases which had been brought to Lipchitz's studio. Without a word, he pointed to two of them, handed the sculptor a check, and left. The check saved the life of the artist's wife, but it ended Barnes's friendship with Lipchitz. Six months later the sculptor was surprised to learn from outsiders that the collector was again in Paris. Unable to understand why his friend had not contacted him at once, he patiently awaited word from Barnes, certain that he would offer an explanation for the delay.

Shortly afterward, without warning, Barnes arrived at the sculptor's studio. Lipchitz was delighted, but when he opened his arms to embrace his friend, the latter stiffly backed away, pointing his finger in rage while proclaiming that he would never forgive Lipchitz and never wanted to see him again. The reason: Lipchitz had "used" him and had been responsible for his confusing philanthropy with art.

The two men never met again, and in 1925 Barnes ceased being Lipchitz's patron. The sculptor, however, remembered his benefactor with affection. "Barnes was a marvelous man, extraordinary but extremely difficult," he wrote in his autobiography. "He was a self-made man and had a tremendous desire for power. Nevertheless, he deserved what he got because he had an excellent eye and was extremely courageous in his gambles on young and unrecognized talent." For his part, Barnes once again did not confuse friendship with art. He retained his esteem for the artist if not his affection for the man. Lipchitz's works remain among the few sculptures in the Foundation's gallery, and his reliefs continue to adorn the façade of the building which houses the collection.

Soutine, Modigliani, and Lipchitz were but three of the younger artists whose work Barnes bought in those few memorable weeks in the French capital. Among the others were the Italian surrealist Giorgio de Chirico and Jules Pascin, born in Bulgaria of Spanish parents. Barnes came to know and to befriend both artists. His friendship with the Italian, who had been presented to him by Guillaume, was a formal one, based largely on intellectual affinity and mutual convenience. They were not close companions, but Barnes's admiration for the artist's work was such that he agreed, in 1926, to write the foreword to a catalogue of an important exhibition held at Guillaume's gallery. In it he praised the artist's ideas as those of a sage and a scholar, characterizing him as a mystic, a poet, and an independent man. De Chirico returned the compliment. That same year, he executed two portraits of Barnes— a drawing, which hangs in the Foundation's gallery, and an oil, which is in its library and is thus visible only to those few who have access to this corner of the Foundation.

Barnes's relationship with the warm-hearted, generous Pascin was far closer, but his 1922 discovery of the artist's work was a belated one. He had missed his first opportunity to buy Pascin's work several years before.

Pascin had first come to Paris in 1905. A colorful figure, known for the wild Saturday-night parties at which he played host to the artists, models, and prostitutes whose lives he chronicled in his art, he made a good living in the French capital, largely through his brilliant drawings, which were published regularly in a German satirical weekly, *Simplicissimus*. In 1914, the advent of war, together with his insatiable love of travel, brought him to America. Life for him there was far less agreeable and, because of the problems involved in transferring funds from Europe, he experienced poverty for the first time in his life. Through mutual friends, he made contact with Barnes. The collector looked through his portfolio of drawings, but he was unmoved and bought none. Ironically the painter was saved by Barnes's enemy, John Quinn, who had started collecting his work in 1913 and in 1917 agreed to give him a regular allowance in return for his art.

In 1920, Pascin returned to Paris where, in late 1922, Barnes finally "discovered" him, making the first of many important purchases. (The painter, then successful, was no longer in desperate need of money.) When Pascin visited America several years later, he was lavishly entertained at Merion. According to George Biddle, the American artist at whose home the painter was staying, the evening at the Barneses' proved to be an embarrassment for the guest of honor. After a splendid dinner, the table was cleared and champagne was served. "Then Pascin, whose inner being had been mellowed, noticed that servants had trooped into the room and were standing at attention in grateful silence," Biddle wrote in his memoirs. "Barnes formally addressed them: 'Tonight,' he said, 'we have with us an artist who, in Berlin, in Tokyo, in Paris is equally famous for the sensitivity of his line and the dynamic, three-dimensional pregnancy of his composition. M. Pascin, a great dessinateur of all time, will now honor us with a few words.'

"Pascin rose slowly to his feet and started once or twice to speak," Biddle continued. "The sweat poured down his brow, and the faces about him melted away. It was the first and only speech of his career."

Barnes watched with satisfaction as Pascin's reputation grew throughout the decade, and he continued to buy his work enthusiastically. Pascin, however, in spite of his success, his many friends, and his apparently carefree life, was a deeply troubled man. In 1930, at the age of forty-five, on the day of the opening of a major Parisian exhibition of his work, he committed suicide. Barnes, in Paris at the time, was profoundly saddened. The usually undemonstrative collector joined the enormous procession that slowly accompanied the artist's body on the long walk to the cemetery; he was seen crying as the rabbi spoke his words of blessing at the grave. At the funeral, he delivered a moving eulogy to the man who had become his friend and whom he believed to be one of the most vital of contemporary artists.

Though he managed to acquire works by Soutine, Modigliani, Lipchitz, de Chirico, and Pascin during this phenomenally successful visit, even Barnes couldn't buy everything he wanted at the time. According to Gilbert Seldes, who heard the story in Paris, the collector met with failure in the studio of Russian émigrés Nathalie Gontcharova and her husband, Michel Larionov, both known for their stage sets as well as their paintings. Larionov, who had been ill, looked on silently as Barnes, taking careful notes and putting aside what especially interested him, carefully examined Gontcharova's work. At one point Barnes spied what Seldes thinks was a painted screen. Intrigued, he asked how much it would cost. Gontcharova answered that it was a present she had made for her husband and was not for sale. Undaunted, Barnes made a large offer—one hard to refuse, for the couple needed the money—but the artist repeated that it belonged to her husband and was not for sale. Barnes doubled the price, Gontcharova again rebuffed him, and Barnes raised his offer once more. Larionov fled from the room, unable to bear it, but Barnes seemed not to notice, piling up offer after offer, until the distraught Gontcharova finally drove him out of their studio.

In spite of this minor setback, Barnes had good reason to be immensely pleased when he prepared to return to America in early January 1923. Guillaume, too, was more than satisfied with the collector's visit; it was said at the time that the Philadelphian's purchases accounted for almost three-quarters of his entire business. In the January 1923 issue of the dealer's magazine, *Les Arts à Paris,* he paid fulsome tribute to the man he called "the Medici of the New World" and gave an account of his recent visit to the French capital.

> Dr. Barnes has just left Paris. He has spent three weeks here, each hour devoted not to social calls, soirées, or official receptions, but rather as this extraordinary, democratic, ardent, inexhaustible, unbeatable, charming, impulsive, generous, unique man must. He has visited everything, seen everything shown by dealers, artists, patrons of art; he has bought, refused to buy, admired, criticized; he has pleased, displeased, made friends, and made enemies. The gold-bearing jingle of money preceded his steps. The covetous rose up before him like apparitions—they followed him, plagued him, pursued him. . . . Like gnomes, a whole population of petitioners, having something to sell, surrounded him, encircled him. . . .

Ignoring the possibility that he himself might be considered prominent among the petitioners, Guillaume noted that the doctor could not be fooled. Though besieged, he was as free and independent as a "Mohican." Guillaume was overwhelmed and exhausted by his client's energy. He recalled that at two in the morning on New Year's Eve, the doctor informed him that they had to study a painting at ten that morning. They left the party, and at eight o'clock Barnes called to say he was up and on his way to do something for the Foundation. In awe, Guillaume reported: "I've never seen such a man. And he offers his whole collection and the building simply for educational purposes."

Addressing himself to the "Painters of the Rotonde," he concluded: "You've lived through feverish weeks. You've had the feeling that a golden prince was, benignly, sharing your destiny, and you were right. He bought works from many of you. . . . That's not all: this distinguished ambassador of French art will fight for you . . . against those who laugh, the imbeciles, the ignorant, the impotent of the New World. . . . He remembers your names, the stories of your lives—all in minute detail. Dr. Barnes is gifted with a prodigious faculty of judgment; he will use it to help you over there."

CHAPTER

9

Barnes arrived in New York on January 13, 1923, on the S.S. *Paris*. His trip had been stunningly successful. He had accomplished his primary purpose in ordering nine hundred tons of limestone to be used in the construction of the Foundation's new buildings. He had also, according to the press, bought more than one hundred paintings, valued at the time at over half a million dollars.

Shortly after his arrival, his ambitious plans for the Foundation were announced—for the first time publicly—by Forbes Watson in his influential magazine *The Arts*. The magazine attached such importance to the event that it devoted a large part of its January and February issues to the new Foundation and the man behind it. Watson's two-part article was generously illustrated by reproductions of paintings from Barnes's collection—works of Renoir, Cézanne, Matisse, Manet, Puvis de Chavannes, Lawson, and Prendergast. (The magazine devoted an entire article to Glackens a few months later, with illustrations from the Foundation's collection.)

According to Watson, the importance of the news could not be overestimated. "What it means," he wrote, "is that we are to have, at last, a public museum of modern art—that is, some of the most vital art that has been produced since about 1870 to the present day." Included in the January issue was a piece by Cret

89

concerning the design of the new gallery as well as an article by Barnes, entitled "Some Remarks on Appreciation."

Following the official announcement, things moved quickly. On February 7, the first shipment of French limestone arrived, and shortly afterward the building contract was awarded, with work to begin as soon as the winter ended. In early February, too, it was announced that the Foundation's director of education would be John Dewey. The appointment of the most influential figure in American education to this position constituted a tremendous coup for Barnes; it was a valuable endorsement of his program. It was also announced that Laurence Buermeyer, a member of the philosophy department at Princeton, would be joining the Foundation as associate director of education. According to the *Evening Bulletin,* Philadelphia would soon become the "radical art centre of the country."

Before then, however, Philadelphians would be given a chance to evaluate at least a part of the Barnes collection, for, at the urging of his friends Arthur B. Carles and Henry McCarter—among the few Philadelphians who recognized the vitality of contemporary art—Barnes had agreed to show some of his recent acquisitions at the Pennsylvania Academy of the Fine Arts.

The exhibition, to be held between April 11 and May 9, was to include seventy-five works in all: seven Lipchitz sculptures, nineteen paintings by Soutine, seven by Modigliani, five each by Matisse and Derain, four by Pascin, four by Moise Kisling (a Polish-born painter who had come to Paris), two each by Picasso and Utrillo, as well as single examples of the work of de Chirico, Marie Laurencin, and a sample of canvases by painters little known today.

Barnes was a realist; he knew that Philadelphia was not Paris and had never been hospitable to innovation in the arts. Though his pride in his collection was enormous, it did not blind him to the realization that the tradition-bound Philadelphia public, especially those who attended exhibitions at the conservative Academy, would find it difficult to accept his latest acquisitions.

He had, in 1921, already had a taste of what the reaction to his own paintings might be. The occasion then had been a comprehensive exhibition of modern American paintings, held at the same Academy in April and May of 1921. The exhibition had attracted large crowds and generated much discussion. It had also been the subject of a virulent attack by a group of prominent physicians who, at a meeting of the Philadelphia Art Alliance, charged that many of the modernists exhibiting were insane and that their paintings were degenerate. Prominent among the speakers was Dr. Francis X. Dercum, a well-known specialist in mental diseases whose daughter later studied at the Academy. "I can only infer that, in a large degree, the pathological element enters into these paintings and drawings, both in the representation of colors and of forms," Dercum stated. "I believe, also, that a certain number of the people who paint these curious pictures are merely shallow tricksters who try to achieve prominence by coming in on the wave and floating into the public eye, getting some sort of reputation which they could not get by legitimate hard work. . . . I think the main feature, however, is the disease of the color sense and of a great many other mental faculties."

Barnes did not let these charges go unanswered. His reply was published in the June-July issue of *The Arts*. In it he suggested that the psychiatrists knew as little about mental illness as they did about art. These doctors were "men who had arrived at positions of eminence by conforming to the traditions of a bygone age, standing pat on somebody else's thinking, and vociferously denouncing the work of men who have devoted their lives to research work in art and science."

Barnes had no kind words for the organization that provided a forum for the doctors, either. "The Art Alliance," he wrote, "is composed largely of what may be classed as 'social climbers,' who look upon art as a step in the ladder that leads to the kind of prominence that everyone is familiar with who reads the society columns of the daily press. . . . So I think if you put the background and speaker-doctors together you will see that they unify into a typical example of the unfortunate situation so prevalent in Philadelphia as regards intelligence and art. . . ." It was notable as the first of Barnes's many stinging attacks on the Philadelphia establishment.

A few months later, Barnes had again come to the defense of modern art against what he called the Philadelphia doctor's "loose thinking." Dercum's opinions concerning the degeneracy of modern artists had been quoted in an anonymous pamphlet attacking still another exhibition of modern painting, this one at New York's Metropolitan Museum of Art. Once again, Barnes was enraged. This time he issued an infantile, peevish challenge—he would do so frequently in the course of his public quarrels. He offered to donate his entire collection, as well as a gallery in which to house it, to the city of Philadelphia—if Dercum could prove himself qualified in the field of psychology by satisfactorily answering eight questions put to him by the collector. When Dercum ignored him, Barnes raised the stakes, this time proposing to build an addition to his new gallery that would be large enough to house the distinguished collection willed to the city by John G. Johnson. Dercum, who had not spoken out specifically against the Metropolitan exhibition, said he was not interested in the pamphlet, nor in accepting Barnes's challenge, and let the matter rest.

Barnes, however, never let the matter rest and never forgot. Nonetheless, in granting the Academy permission to show his paintings, he decided to give Philadelphians one more chance. His introduction to the exhibition's catalogue was a long and carefully reasoned one. He first explained the scope of the exhibition:

> Most of the exhibit is of the work of artists now living in Paris but who were born and spent their youth in other countries—Russia, Poland, Italy, Spain, Bulgaria, Lithuania, Belgium. The work is a product of the influence of French environment upon cultures and endowments racially and radically foreign to France. Perhaps that explains why the exhibit differs in certain significant phases from any held previously in this country. All of the artists represented, except Modigliani, are living and all are under thirty-five years of age,

except Matisse, Picasso, and Derain. Every one of them knows
the great masters of the past—Rembrandt, Titian, Tintoretto,
El Greco, Renoir, Cézanne—through enraptured, assiduous
study in the galleries of Europe. These moderns are as individual in their expressions of what they believe constitute the
essentials of plastic art as are any of their predecessors. That
entitles their work to respect and attention for what it is in
itself.

He knew what he was up against. He reminded the public that
eight years before, a performance by the Philadelphia Orchestra of
Arnold Schoenberg's first *Kammersymphonie* had been greeted with
snickers, jeers, and scoffs, but that the same work, recently performed before practically the same audience, was listened to with
respect and loudly applauded at its conclusion. The change in response, he wrote, could be traced to the audience's gradual education. "We were led to Schoenberg by easy, not too-long steps,
at not too-long intervals," he wrote.

He asked for a similar understanding and patience on the part
of Philadelphia's art lovers. Warning that these new works of art
would most probably seem as strange to most viewers as Schoenberg's music had to listeners several years earlier, he reiterated that
all the artists represented at the Academy's show were legitimately
working in the traditions of great art of the past. One example
was Modigliani. "If the long, attenuated necks of the Modigliani
figures seem absurd or grotesque, go to the University Museum
and look at the even longer necks on the pieces of ancient African
sculpture, so rich in art values," he wrote. "Then you will see that
Modigliani's inspiration came from his devotion to the spirit of
negro art and that that experience did something to him and he
did something to it by his imagination and reason."

In conclusion, he wrote of these modern painters: "These young
artists speak a language which has come to them from the reaction
between their own traits, the circumstances of the world we all live
in, and the experience they themselves have had. . . . To quarrel
with them for being different from the great masters is about as

rational as to find fault with the size of a person's shoes or the shape of his ears. If one will accord to these artists the simple justice of educated and unbiased attention, one will see the truth of what experienced students of painting all assert: that old art and new art are the same in fundamental principles. The difference lies only in the degree of greatness, and time alone can gauge that with accuracy."

Though he had feared the worst, official reaction to the exhibition was even more devastating than Barnes had anticipated. Most critics refused to grant the artists the educated attention that he had requested. They were offended and troubled by what had been presented to them as serious art—especially so since the paintings in Barnes's exhibition, many of them anguished and tormented, were shown at the same time the Academy mounted an exhibit of portraits by members of Philadelphia's illustrious Peale family as well as a collection of modern Japanese paintings, all of them undisturbing and pleasing to the eye. The contrast was simply too great.

One writer, the *Public Ledger*'s Edith W. Powell, whom Barnes had considered a friend and who had often seen the collection before the doctor's most recent European buying splurge, was particularly upset by Soutine. In her review she wondered what the Peales would have thought about his "portraits of the dregs of humanity." Her answer was that they would have found them to be "the creations of a disintegrating mind with a cheated abnormal outlook." Eager to show that she was no reactionary, she tried to understand and excuse the artist. "He may be mad, he may be an outcast, and being a Russian he may be morbid, emotional, unliteral, but he presents life as he sees it," she wrote. "He is said to be a genius," she conceded. Nonetheless, echoing Dercum, she wondered, "Are we willing to look at the world with his eyes? Are we willing to give careful attention to what actually exists for him, even if it seems to us diseased and degenerate? Is it a good thing to visit morgues, insane asylums, and jails?"

Soutine came in for harsh criticism, too, from other reviewers.

For C. H. Bonte of the *Inquirer,* he "was represented by a series of seemingly incomprehensible masses of paint, known as landscapes, and by some other pictures which only by an exercise of vivid imagination could be termed similitudes to plausible human beings." For Edward Longstreth of *Art News,* the painter quite simply "glorified the ugly."

The rest of the artists fared little better. Powell was generally unhappy about all the "unabashed presentation and even flouting of the unmentionable," concluding that "confession in paint or in stone may be as good for the soul as confession to a priest or a Freudian," but wondering if public confession should be countenanced. Bonte was somewhat kinder, admitting that Picasso's *Composition* (*Peasants and Oxen*) was "by no means unattractive, especially in color and design and would make an impressive splash of color against a darkling wall of time-toned wood," and conceding that at least one Matisse was "by no means without a certain charming appeal." Modigliani, however, held no such appeal for Bonte, who labeled him a "compressionist, since he usually sees the human head in an oddly flattened shape, as if some frightful pressure had been applied to the skull." This pressure, he noted, "also seems to have had its effect upon the intelligence of his subjects."

Francis Z. Ziegler, writing in the *Record,* was more than disturbed—he was angry. Taking note of Barnes's statement that most of the artists represented were foreigners who had come to France, he suggested that they should have stayed home. "These pictures are most unpleasant to contemplate," he commented. "It is debased art in which the attempt for a new form of expression results in the degradation of the old formulas, not in the creation of something new. . . . It is hard to see why the Academy should sponsor this sort of trash."

Dorothy Grafly of *The North American* was both emotionally and physically sickened by the uncleanliness of it all. "It is as if the room were infested with some infectious scourge," she wrote. "Unclean thoughts crowd into the mind—thoughts utterly untrue to oneself. . . ."

Barnes's immediate reaction to this collective assault on his collection and on his judgment was predictable for a man of his temperament. He wrote furious letters—among the first of those ill-tempered missives for which he became famous—to all of those who criticized the exhibition, reserving special contempt for his old friend Powell. The only way she could become a good art critic, he suggested, was by having relations with the iceman. Unsettled by the suggestion, Powell asked her colleague Grafly if perhaps Barnes, whom she acknowledged to be an expert in psychology, might not have had a good idea. Shortly thereafter, she left Philadelphia for an extended stay in Paris, presumably to study modern art at its source.

The experience had been a bitter one for Barnes. He had been hurt and stunned by the ignorance and insensitivity of the men and women who called themselves art critics, and he never forgave them. For the rest of his life, he closed his gallery to most of these so-called experts. There were a few exceptions, but as a rule even those art historians and critics who could understand and intelligently appreciate and profit from an examination of the masterpieces he brought to Merion were prevented from seeing them.

Undaunted, or perhaps even stimulated by the critical fiasco of the Academy exhibition, Barnes returned to Paris in June 1923. News of the establishment of the Foundation had been first published there in *Les Arts à Paris;* the same issue had announced Paul Guillaume's appointment as foreign secretary of the Foundation, and the magazine soon came to represent the Foundation's interests as well as Guillaume's. Not surprisingly the dealer was effusive in his praise of the doctor's plans. By that time, anything that was sold to Barnes in Paris passed through his hands. In an article illustrated with a sketch of the front view of the new building in Merion, he paid tribute to an achievement of extraordinary beauty, brought to fruition through the efforts of one man, "to take root on American soil and dedicated to the greatest good of humanity for the purest glory of the genius of France."

Most other French reaction to Barnes's plans was equally enthusiastic. In an article published in *L'Esprit Nouveau*, Maurice Raynal acclaimed the doctor's collection as well as his method of judging a painting, which he summarized as "Don't look at what's behind a canvas, but what's on it." Georges Marlier, writing in *Selection*, called the new gallery the most important of its kind in the world and concluded that "Europe would do well to meditate on the example that this nation of salami salesmen, as some journalists call it, offers us." Waldemar George, in *L'amour de l'art*, wrote that the new museum represented "the most beautiful homage, rendered in America, to French art of which it is the temple . . . revealing the highest expression of our artistic genius."

There were a few dissenters; not everyone approved of Barnes's activities. H. P. Roché, who knew better, wrote Quinn in early 1923 that although Barnes was "ravaging" Paris, he was buying nothing of real importance. But this was merely an effort to placate the man for whom Roché was buying at the time. More significant—and more amusing, given the nature of the attacks on Barnes by American conservatives—was the criticism leveled at Barnes by members of the Parisian avant-garde, who, involved in Dada and Surrealism, found the doctor's taste too conservative. Under the title (in English) of "Hallo, Boys, Cheer Up," the French revue *Montparnasse* published an article ridiculing Guillaume for having led the Golden Calf to the ateliers of the wrong artists, and criticized Barnes's choices—especially Soutine, Lipchitz, and Pascin. It concluded: "Between us, *old chap,* it would have been better if you had sent us a cheque of fifty thousand francs to help us launch a magazine of aesthetic creation and real criticism, which we intend to publish next year."

Harsher words came from the pen of the Parisian artist Francis Picabia. Writing in the *Paris-Journal,* he attacked the Philadelphian for collecting too many Renoirs and Cézannes. "Why place these two painters at the top of an epoch when they are only at the bottom, the decrepitude of the preceding one?" he asked, answering his own question by noting that during the last years those painters had been big business for Parisian dealers, and that Barnes had paid!

In anticipation of Barnes's next visit to Paris, Picabia addressed himself to the collector. "Dear Mr. Barnes," he wrote. "You're going to come back, you're awaited impatiently, you're talked about in the shops as well as the cafés of Montparnasse, and the second cargo that will embark with you to free America, under the supervision of Guillaume the First, is already being prepared. . . .

"I'm afraid that once there, when, all alone, you open the crates, you will find in them mildewed merchandise instead of the truly youthful works of art, expressing our epoch, that you would have wanted and should have chosen. . . . I have the feeling that as a souvenir of a visit to the Barnes museum one will take away nothing but a head cold."

The collector paid no attention to these minority opinions; he was far more interested in countering American attacks on his collection. He had returned to Paris to look at paintings and to add to that collection, and he set about his task with his customary vigor, usually accompanied by Guillaume. The dealer had been the first to show some of Barnes's recent acquisitions—before they were transferred to Philadelphia—at his gallery in January and February, and as a consequence had firmly established him as the foremost American collector of modern art. He was eager to protect his interests. In an article published after Barnes's visit, Guillaume wrote of the secrecy and anxiety, the air of mystery that surrounded the arrival of "the Mohican," and of the plots hatched to capture him and gain his patronage—plots which he himself, undoubtedly, foiled. He wrote, too, of the surprising impression that Barnes made during his visit: he was not the naïve ingenuous sitting duck Parisians had expected. "A meeting with Dr. Barnes is an unforgettable experience," he wrote. "Those who wanted to took the measure of his brain—American, yes, but above all, cosmopolitan, worldly, universal."

Even during that short stay, Guillaume was again astounded by Barnes's inexhaustible energy, as was Waldemar George, who described, in a letter to William Schack, a typical day with the Philadelphian. It began at nine in the morning: "We would take in five to ten museums and private collections. . . . We would then make the rounds of antique dealers . . . and galleries and studios. . . .

"Paul Guillaume and his young wife were always with us. . . . Towards eleven o'clock at night Barnes would ask them to open up their gallery on the rue La Boétie, which had long been closed and which we got into via the service entrance. We stayed there till a late hour of the night looking at the African Negro sculptures and the paintings of Soutine. Sometimes Barnes asked Guillaume to call up some young artist and have him come over to explain his picture, to justify certain color relationships or some linear rhythm. I didn't care for his pedantry, but I did admire his boldness."

Barnes thoroughly enjoyed his busy days in Paris. Removed from the irritating controversies which marked his activities at home, he was able to relax in the French capital, where he found enormous satisfaction not only in buying paintings but in looking at art and discussing it with congenial, knowledgeable companions. For this reason, the hours he spent at Guillaume's headquarters, which had been transferred to the rue La Boétie, were especially memorable. He celebrated both the gallery and its owner in "The Temple," an article published in the May 1924 issue of *Opportunity* magazine. "I have named it 'The Temple,' " he wrote, "because in no other rendezvous have I witnessed so much devotion by so many of the painters, sculptors, composers, writers, connoisseurs who have made the art history of our epoch; and they are there to worship works of art and to commune with kindred spirits."

He characterized Guillaume as the high priest, "a creator in the greatest of arts, life itself," and he described his own experiences there in glowing terms:

> I have seen six chiefs of African tribes there at the same time with four principals of the Russian ballet. . . . In a single week, I have met at Paul Guillaume's English, Japanese, Norwegian, German, American, Italian artists—painters, sculp-

tors, composers, poets, critics—whom I had known only by name. I have heard there criticism more penetrating and more comprehensive than I had ever heard or read elsewhere, for a glance of the eye, a quality of voice add much to the transfer of what we mean. Practically all important French painters and sculptors visit the temple with regularity. Stravinsky, Satie, Auric, Poulenc, Milhaud, Honegger have long been worshippers there of the Negro art which has inspired so much of their fine music. One summer afternoon when the heat was intolerable outdoors, I called at the temple and found Roger Fry and Paul Guillaume discussing Negro art. I listened for a while and then took possession of Roger Fry and had a talk on Renoir and Cézanne, which I shall remember for the rest of my life. The atmosphere of the place is imperturbably peaceful, for no matter how keen the discussion it is never desecrated by a personal quarrel between artists of even widely diverging opinions. One instinctively and always respects a sanctuary.

The discussion habit is contagious in that milieu and I soon fell a victim. How many discussions I have had there with artists, connoisseurs, directors of museums from all parts of the world I could not say because I have visited the temple a hundred times and nearly always found interesting people there. One memorable argument with Waldemar George lasted an entire afternoon. Before it was finished I had learned something about one phase of modern painting that I had never been able to understand from volumes of writing. On another occasion Jacques Lipchitz and I became so completely engrossed that I did not know until Paul Guillaume informed me later, that for a part of the time we sat on the floor of the gallery.

Though Barnes would clearly have preferred to spend his time at "the temple," Guillaume on two occasions during this visit convinced him to observe some of the social amenities. The first arose when the dealer learned that the United States ambassador to France,

Myron T. Herrick, as much a Francophile as Barnes, expected the patron from Philadelphia to pay him a call—other great collectors, such as Morgan, Carnegie and Rockefeller, had paid similar official visits to the American Embassy. Barnes had always balked at the idea, but one day when he appeared at Guillaume's gallery in a good mood, Guillaume took him off guard by announcing that the ambassador expected him there in a few minutes. To Guillaume's delighted surprise, Barnes smiled, left the gallery, and jumped into a taxi. He returned two hours later, enthusiastic. He had found a soul mate in the ambassador. Barnes had told Herrick the story of his life, and Herrick had told the collector the story of his own. In a short time they had become friends. It was an immensely successful encounter, and when they parted, Herrick presented Barnes with a sample of his own art.

Encouraged, Guillaume set up a second official meeting, this time with Paul Léon, the director of the Beaux-Arts in France, who he felt certain would express his gratitude to Barnes for his interest in promoting French culture in the United States. This time he was wrong. The meeting was to take place at six in the evening; because Barnes and Guillaume were to attend a premiere of the Swedish Ballet following it, they were wearing evening clothes. Léon took one look at the inappropriately dressed visitor and concluded that Barnes was just one more provincial American. As a result, he paid little attention as the collector explained how he would use his money, energy, and intelligence to introduce French culture to his fellow Americans. Soon, to his horror, Guillaume noticed that their distinguished host was falling asleep. It was time for him to intervene. Rising from his chair as noisily as possible in order to awaken him, the dealer explained to Barnes that Léon already knew of Barnes's worthy accomplishment, that he was obviously tired, and that, under the circumstances, it was best that they take their leave. The dealer arranged no further official visits for his client.

"Dr. Barnes has returned to Merion," Guillaume wrote following the collector's 1923 visit to Paris. "The construction of the magnificent buildings goes ahead quickly. The inauguration will take place next year. Intellectuals have their eyes on this corner of American soil which will become a center of French culture."

Refreshed by his Parisian experience, Barnes was prepared to proceed with the practical implementation of his plans for not merely a center of French culture but for the embodiment of all his ideas—the Barnes Foundation.

The formal opening of the Barnes Foundation's new buildings took place on March 19, 1925. The invitation to the ceremony announced that John Dewey would at that time "dedicate the Foundation to the Cause of Education." It was to be accepted by representatives of the University of Pennsylvania, Columbia University, the county, the state, and the neighborhood, and, on behalf of the artists of America, by Leopold Stokowski, the conductor of the Philadelphia Orchestra.

At the beginning of the afternoon's program of speeches, which emphasized the Foundation's function as an educational institution and not as a museum, a number of congratulatory telegrams were read. Two of them came from Europe, one calling the new enterprise "monumental" and one referring to it as "epoch-making." In his discourse, written with the help of suggestions from Barnes (who worried that the absent-minded philosopher might not arrive in time and implored Mrs. Dewey to make certain that he did), Dewey agreed with these assessments. He concluded his remarks by telling the audience of several hundred:

> I feel confident we can open our eyes and look into the
> years ahead, to see radiating from this institution, from the
> work of this Foundation, influences which are going to effect

education in the largest sense of that word: development of
the thoughts and emotions of boys and girls, youths, men and
women all over this country, and to an extent and range and
depth which makes this, to my mind, one of the most important educational acts, one of the most profound educational
deeds, of the age in which we are living.

There were many more speeches, including one by Mrs. Barnes
concerning plans for the arboretum, and a lengthy one by Barnes
himself. It was a ceremony worthy of the event, and the doctor
was justifiably proud. The only known dissenter was Stokowski,
who was annoyed by Barnes's stubborn insistence that he didn't
want people to visit Merion merely to enjoy the paintings, and that
the Foundation's aim was a far loftier educational one. On his way
home, the conductor complained to his companion that he found
it impossible to like a man who didn't want the public to enjoy
the arts for their own sake.

The ceremony itself was somewhat anticlimactic—none of the
Philadelphia press reported on the proceedings—since the Foundation was by that time a functioning educational institution. It
already had a teaching staff—for the most part, a distinguished
one. Following Buermeyer's appointment, Barnes had added two
more associate directors of education. One of them was a talented
young scholar, Thomas H. Munro, a former student of Dewey's
who had left a teaching position at Columbia to join the Foundation
in 1923. The other was Mary Mullen, neither a scholar nor an
educator, whose experience consisted solely of her years of faithful
service to Barnes. These three associate directors would benefit
from consultations with Dewey and would teach, under the close
supervision of Barnes.

The Foundation had also already started its own press. Its first
publication, in 1923, had been a short pamphlet, *An Approach to
Art*. Its author was—surprisingly, given her qualifications—Mary
Mullen. Praised by no less an expert than Havelock Ellis as "a
most helpfully instructive volume," it was a tentative, preliminary

attempt at explaining what would later be known as the Barnes method. The second book of the Barnes Foundation Press, published the following year, had been Buermeyer's *The Aesthetic Experience*. In addition, starting with the issue of April 1925, the press planned to publish on a regular, continuing basis the official journal of the Foundation, which would serve to disseminate the ideas developed there.

Both Mullen's and Buermeyer's small books were to be used as texts for the Foundation's courses, but by 1924 Barnes was eager to summarize and put together in a far more comprehensive volume the ideas he had formulated throughout his long researches and studies. Uncertain that he himself could do the job adequately— his own recent writings on art had been too frequently rejected by *The New Republic* and *Dial*—he initially turned to professional writers he believed would be better qualified than he was. First among these was his friend Waldemar George, the Parisian critic, but George turned down the offer on the grounds that he was not in complete agreement with Barnes's ideas. Next, he turned to a painter, Thomas Hart Benton, and an art critic, Thomas Craven, then a reviewer for *Dial*. He was encouraged when both men accepted his invitation to come to Merion to discuss his ideas, and that first visit went so well that he suggested they spend several more weekends together. In the course of these long visits, spent in serious discussion of the problems and meaning of art, Barnes confessed to Benton that he needed a skilled writer for a book on painting and implied that Benton—or possibly Craven—might be just the man to do it. In his autobiographical *An American in Art*, Benton described how their relationship came to an end:

> After a few visits, trying to clinch my employment, I brought some of the cubistic drawings I had made for my sculptures and told Barnes that similar diagrams might serve to explain the designs of many works of art. Barnes asked how I would handle the Impressionists with such drawings. I was impolitic enough to say that the Impressionists were not notable in

matters of compositional form and that it would be useless to
approach their work with that in mind. Barnes, who was then
avidly collecting Impressionists, unfortunately took what I said
to be a slur on the school, and a few days later wrote me one
of his famous letters, which broke off all relations between
us. He got rid of Craven at the same time.

Barnes never forgave Benton, or even Craven, who participated
in all the discussions. Nonetheless, the painter retained a certain
amount of respect for the collector. "He was the one collector I
ever knew who had something of the painter's technical view of
painting," he wrote in another autobiographical volume, *An Artist
in America*. "In addition, he was an informed and ingenious thinker
and a hard man to down in an argument. He could not stand
opposition and used to pace the floor like a caged animal when
Craven and I got him in a corner. His temper was always well
controlled when we were in his presence but in his letters, which
were frequent, he went into gutter manners which made dealings
with him finally impossible."

During that same period, Barnes also failed to enlist the services
of Francis Hackett, the influential critic of art and literature for
The New Republic, but this time he came closer to succeeding.
Barnes greatly admired Hackett's thoughtful essays, and on the
basis of them summoned the critic to Merion. Hackett agreed to
come—with his wife, Signe Toksvig. After their arrival, it was made
clear that the two men would talk about serious matters, and that
Hackett's wife, also a writer, would spend her time with Mrs.
Barnes discussing trivialities. The two men got along famously.
Hackett was impressed by his host's quick intelligence, his seri-
ousness, and his stimulating conversation. He enjoyed talking to
Barnes and was flattered by and willing to accept the generous offer
the collector made to him, to study at the Foundation, at Barnes's
expense, in order to put Barnes's ideas into writing. His wife,
however, had not been impressed. She didn't like Barnes and deeply
resented his high-handed, condescending manner toward women.
As far as she was concerned, her husband would have to choose

between the two of them. It was no contest. Hackett, happily married, chose his wife and turned down the doctor's offer.

Barnes was livid at this rejection of what he believed to be a unique offer. He threatened reprisals against Hackett and against *The New Republic*. He carried out neither, but he never forgot the incident. Many years later he found himself at a dinner seated next to a former member of the magazine's staff.

"I tried once to take one of your fellow editors into my establishment, Francis Hackett," he said. "I'd have made a man of him. And he knew it. He wanted to come. But he had a wife, a bitch, a damn bitch, who yanked him around by the balls. It was a sin and a shame, a real man yelling with a clutch on his balls. At first I meant to blow Francis and *The New Republic* sky high. I could have done it."

Realizing that it would be impossible to find anyone to do the job for him, Barnes decided to write the book himself. It was an enormous project, one that took all of his energy and skill, but he is said to have completed it in six months. He had help from members of his own staff—from the Mullen sisters, from Laura V. Geiger (another recruit from the Argyrol plant), and especially from Laurence Buermeyer, to whom, he noted in the book's preface, he was indebted for his knowledge of the psychology of aesthetics as well as "for his fine services in bringing into orderly arrangement my scattered notes relating to the paintings in the galleries of Europe and in our own collection." Yet, the book is unmistakably Barnes's own. *The Art in Painting*—he felt the title was of special significance—remains today the definitive statement of the principles which were the basis of his formal, scientific approach to the analysis of painting. Whatever else may be said of the book, it is without question the result of meticulous research and staggering erudition.

Acknowledging the author's debt to Santayana, and dedicated to John Dewey, "whose conceptions of experience, of method, of education, inspired the work of which this book is part," *The Art in Painting* was first published by the Barnes Foundation Press in early 1925. (It was later published in a trade edition by Harcourt, Brace and Company.) That first edition—there were subsequent revised and expanded versions—was already a massive tome of 530 pages, including 106 illustrations and well over 100 pages of detailed analyses of individual works of art. Because Barnes's disciples complain that his ideas are too often misunderstood by outsiders, it is best to allow the doctor himself to explain the scope of his book, as he did in the flier announcing its publication:

> This book sets forth a method by which an understanding and appreciation of paintings may be secured. It aims to furnish a guide for discovery of the essentially plastic, that is, pictorial qualities in painting, and so to disengage what is central in art from the narrative and antiquarian aspects which in ordinary academic criticism and instruction are all that receive attention.
>
> Alleged appreciation of art, especially of plastic art, is usually preoccupation with qualities which are irrelevant and distracting. A painting, so far as it is a work of art, is not a literary document, an archaeological specimen, or a mere exercise in craftsmanship. It is an independent creation, the materials of which are color, line, mass and space, and appreciation is genuine only when it is directed to these plastic essentials. THE ART IN PAINTING is an explanation of these essentials, and of their organization in the complete work of art. The method employed in the book seeks to combine objectivity with due regard for the factor of personal and individual taste. It is offered in the hope that it may aid in the replacement of mere whim and idiosyncrasy by a rational enjoyment of demonstrable realities.
>
> The book contains a general account of aesthetic principles, a specific statement of those principles in the field of plastic art, and an appreciation of them to the more important schools and individuals in painting, past and present, as well as to a large number of particular paintings. The conclusions are, so far as possible, reinforced by illustrations, of which there are more than a hundred. From the discussion as a whole the conclusion emerges that the essential values of plastic art are

the same in all periods of painting, that the qualities that made Giotto, Titian, and Rembrandt great painters are to be found also in Renoir and in Cézanne, Picasso, and Matisse. Indifference to either the great men of the past or their successors of today brands supposed aesthetic appreciation as illusion and self-deception.

Barnes's ideas as expressed in *The Art in Painting* were not entirely original ones. He borrowed liberally from the British aestheticians and critics Clive Bell and Roger Fry, who believed that aesthetic satisfaction derives primarily from an understanding of the formal qualities of a work of art—the relationship of line, color, and volume—rather than from its subject matter or its moral or narrative content. Today *The Art in Painting* is generally regarded as a ponderous and dated study. It is used almost exclusively by students at the Foundation in Merion, and even they are asked to read only brief excerpts from it. Nonetheless, when first published, it was received with respect and enthusiasm by most critics. Joseph Wood Krutch, in *The Nation,* wrote: "Mr. Barnes's book seems to me as one interested in the methods of criticism in general, a distinct and important contribution. . . . Mr. Barnes furnishes a method of approach in consequence of which one may talk about a picture and be sure that one is, indeed, talking about the picture and not about archaeology, literature, the physics or physiology of vision, or merely vague impressionistic reactions."

Alfred H. Barr, Jr., then a young art professor and not yet director of the Museum of Modern Art (which didn't open its doors until 1929), writing in the *Saturday Review of Literature,* was equally enthusiastic, noting:

This is an important book because it presents a systematic and confident statement of what is central in the "modern" attitude toward painting. Its five hundred pages are the expression of an energetic critic, of an experimenter in the education of art-appreciation, and of the owner of the finest collection of modern paintings in America.

According to Raymond Weaver, of the *New York Herald Tribune,* the book's publication was an important event. "It offers something scholarly, sound and real to replace the sentimentalism, the antiquarianism, which make futile the present courses in universities and colleges generally," he wrote. "*The Art in Painting* is an original and impressive book. And what is more, it is interesting and clear."

Praise came later, too, from what must have been an unexpected source, Ezra Pound, who not only lauded the book but the Foundation's educational program and Barnes himself. "Not only has Monsieur Barnes spent a great deal of money on paintings by dead and living painters, and spent it with great intelligence," he wrote, "but he has put these pictures in a gallery open to serious members of the public, and provided instructors for those who are bewildered by being introduced to so much all at once.

"He has also written that very rare thing THE RIGHT KIND of book about painting. . . . He wants to augment the visual faculty, or at any rate augment the efficiency of the eye by coupling it with the efficiency of the perceptive intelligence. . . . And as his gallery is open as a school, he obviously does not intend it simply as cold storage: Any fool can see that he wants painting to exist in America, on a par with, and ultimately above the level of painting in Europe.

"Such a man is worth more to the country than 6000 Calvin Coolidges."

Not all the reviews were favorable, but only one of them, published in the December 2, 1925, issue of *The New Republic,* drew the force of Barnes's wrath, not only because of its criticism but even more because of its source—Leo Stein. Stein was, after all, Barnes's friend; the doctor had earlier told Dewey that Stein was the only one fully qualified to review the book. Stein had also furnished the Foundation with a blurb, quoted in an early issue of its official journal, in which he praised *The Art in Painting* as "something fresh and new and thoroughly worthwhile . . . very well written, comprehensive, systematic without pedantry, and as intelligible as a thing of that kind can be made." Because of this, Stein's major reservation, that Barnes mistakenly imposed his own evaluations upon the reader, expressed in an otherwise favorable review, came as a shock. "I believe that there is in this a serious defect of method," Stein wrote. "Mr. Barnes's scale of value points very clearly the direction of his own interest but it would be a great mistake on the part of any student to direct his effort towards a similar vision."

Barnes felt betrayed. He was unable to allow Stein's words to go unanswered. His angry response was published in the April 1926 issue of the Foundation's journal as part of an article titled, "Day-Dreaming in Art Education." Labeling Stein's criticism "a perfect example of the aesthetics of the ivory tower," he went on to say that it was "inefficacious practically, not because it is too fine for the real world, but because it is too feeble; its sterility is an indication of its inner emptiness." He concluded his attack on a personal note, a low blow aimed at a man who had long and painfully suffered from a neurotic inability to conclude any task he set for himself. "It explains why," Barnes wrote, "the book on aesthetics which, fifteen years ago, Mr. Stein announced as forthcoming, has never materialized."

Stein never replied publicly to Barnes's attack. His own book, however, *ABC of Aesthetics,* was published in early 1927—that might have been sufficient response. In any case, it was several years before the two men spoke to one another again.

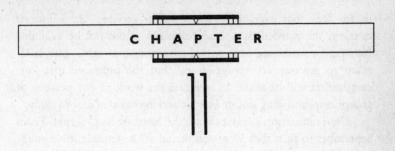
The first issue of the *Journal of the Barnes Foundation* contained an article by Mary Mullen outlining the Foundation's present activities and its plans for the future. Its program was an enormously ambitious and generous one. In addition to its classes and its publishing plans, it already included an active department of arboriculture (making use of rare trees found on its twelve-acre property) and a department of floriculture, in which research was being conducted in the development of new species of flowers and trees.

In the future the Foundation would continue to foster research in the arts and in other topics "related to the application of scientific method to life." It would actively defend "individuals manifesting intelligence, progressiveness, and public spirit in the art world" through its journal and elsewhere, and it would attack, through public discussion, "the enemies of intelligence and imagination in art, whether or not those enemies are protected by financial power and social prestige." It was also prepared to offer the services of its trained personnel to educational institutions throughout the country—to give advice on the organization of art instruction and the selection of equipment, and to provide counsel for the acquisition by institutions of worthy works of art. "In general," Mullen concluded, "it will make its collections, its buildings, and its personnel available for educational purposes to the people of America, in any way that may be found of public service." As a note of caution, she warned that these resources would not be available for "persons desiring only casual amusement or other ends irrelevant to genuine art appreciation," but she promised that "arrangements will be made to facilitate the work of any persons or groups demonstrating sincere interest and intention of serious study."

The Foundation's classes were the heart of its program. From September to June they were conducted at the Foundation's buildings in Merion, utilizing Barnes's own collection. During the summer months, the Foundation's activities were transferred to Europe. It was the doctor's belief that to understand modern art it was essential to trace the fundamental traditions, and this could only be accomplished by visits to European museums and not through the study of imperfect reproductions. Summer headquarters were at Guillaume's gallery on the rue La Boétie. Buermeyer led one group through the museums of Paris, Madrid, and Toledo; Munro took his students to the Louvre, the Luxembourg, several private Parisian galleries, and to the major museums of Italy; Mullen taught a group of advanced students in the museums of France, Spain, Italy, and England. Copies of *The Art in Painting* in hand, each class acquired an objective method for evaluating art, based upon observation, experience, and reflection.

Classes in Merion were small, and the admissions policy was haphazard. Among those admitted were writers, teachers, non-professionals, and students from a number of nearby institutions. At least two of them achieved prominence in the years to come. One, Dorothy Norman, a distinguished photographer, writer, and editor, attended a class in 1924, while studying at the University of Pennsylvania. Then nineteen years old, she felt the whole modern-art movement come to life during her hours in the gallery. Though she paid little attention to the lectures or to Barnes's theorizing, she never forgot the lessons she learned from the collection itself. Another, the Precisionist painter Ralston Crawford, joined the Foundation's classes while studying at the Academy. He was not only stimulated by the unparalleled collection—above all, the Cézannes—but also deeply influenced by Barnes's formal analytic approach to art which helped free him as an artist and shape his own approach to painting.

Barnes's vision extended far beyond the physical boundaries of the Foundation itself. Merion, of course, was to be the center of his activities, but he hoped that his educational theories would be accepted and applied wherever art was taught. From the very beginning he understood that his ideas could be most effectively spread by actively cooperating with already existing institutions. Toward that end, in 1924, he subsidized a Columbia University course in applied aesthetics, conducted by Munro. At the same time, but on a larger scale, he made his first efforts to combine his program with that of the University of Pennsylvania.

Barnes's alma mater had always been part of his plans for the Foundation. According to its bylaws, the university's board of trustees was empowered to name two trustees of the Barnes Foundation following the death of Barnes and his wife. In addition Penn was authorized, if feasible, to supervise the curator of the Foundation's arboretum. Penn, too, was to benefit from any excess income received by the Foundation for "the creation of scholarships or otherwise encouraging and enhancing the study of aesthetics"—subject to the approval of the Foundation's own trustees.

An alliance with Penn, Barnes believed, would be advantageous to both institutions. By making use of the peerless resources of the Foundation, the university's School of Fine Arts could develop into the country's leading center of art instruction. For Barnes, Penn would be the ideal testing ground for his own theories of art education.

An official agreement between the two institutions was announced in May 1924 by Warren P. Laird, dean of the School of Fine Arts. Under its terms the Foundation would offer three courses to the university's students. Munro would teach two of them, and a third, "The Aesthetic Experience," was to be conducted by Buermeyer. Using the facilities of the Barnes Foundation, notably its collection, the program was to be subsidized entirely by the Foundation. In an effort to forestall any adverse criticism of the plan on the part of the conservative Philadelphians who supported the university, the announcement was deliberately cautious. Laird made it clear that Munro would be considered an exchange professor and not a member of Penn's faculty. He emphasized that the program, sanctioned by the university's provost, Josiah H. Penniman, was an experimental one, no more than an attempt to strengthen Penn's art department. Obviously some far-sighted official of the university must have envisioned a permanent relationship which could result in the annexation of the Barnes collection, just as Barnes must have hoped that their relationship might lead to a solution of a problem he foresaw—determining the eventual fate of that collection. Nonetheless, for the moment the collaboration was labeled an experiment.

In spite of the low-key announcement, a burst of anger that equalled or exceeded the reception given to the Academy exhibition a year before greeted the plan. "It will lead to anarchy," said Theodore M. Dillaway, director of art in the city's public schools, who noted that many paintings in the collection made him physically ill. "If we keep on with that sort of thing, people of culture will lose all interest in art, and there will be a growing distaste for pictures."

Harriet Sartain, dean of the School of Design for Women, was aghast. "I am not a conservative in art matters," she commented, "and I have always been open to new ideas, but from what appeared as part of the Barnes Foundation collection at the Pennsylvania Academy last spring, I cannot appreciate the stand of the university in instituting a course with such art as source material. It is a bad thing to put any such ideas before susceptible minds." Huger Elliott, principal of the School of Industrial Art, was also stunned, denouncing what he considered the Foundation's "Bolshevist art."

Perhaps the most infuriating criticism was delivered by Charles Grafly, professor at the Pennsylvania Academy, a sculptor and brother of the critic Dorothy Grafly. Angered that the arrangement with the university would legitimize the Foundation as a serious institution of learning, on a par with the Academy itself, he wrote: "If the exhibition of modernist art held at the Pennsylvania Academy of the Fine Arts in 1923 as a part of the Barnes collection is representative of the type of rot students in the department of fine arts at the university will be transported to the Merion gallery to study, I cannot imagine a greater calamity, either in the world of art or of education."

Few voices were raised in defense of the plan, but Barnes could find some consolation in the words of Arthur Carles, who was having his own problems with Philadelphia's conservative forces. "Philadelphia does not appreciate, as it should, what Dr. Barnes is trying to do," he commented. "I dislike the distinction constantly being made between so-called 'modern paintings' and the old conservative masterpieces. There are only two kinds of paintings, good and bad, and those of Dr. Barnes happen to be good."

Barnes himself also, naturally, rose to his own defense, lashing out against the institutions represented by those who had denounced his collection. He took on three of them in an article in the April 1925 issue of his Foundation's journal. The School of Design, he wrote, was concerned solely with industrial art, guided by rules which were the antithesis of true art. The School of Industrial Art was "an institution in which the mechanical repetition of absurdities and technical tricks masquerades as instruction in art." He was even angrier at the entire Philadelphia public school system and specifically at Dr. Dillaway, particularly since his recent offer to make the Foundation's facilities available to the schools had been rejected. Barnes wrote that Dillaway was guilty of "the counterfeit thinking and threadbare conceptions of art which have never been regarded by educated people as anything but the unintelligent, ritualistic mummery attendant upon a total confusion of educational and art values. . . ."

Barnes's harshest reaction, however, was reserved for another institution, the Academy as represented by Grafly, whose faculty members he threatened to bar from his gallery on the grounds that certain of them came there "habitually in a state of profound alcoholic intoxication." Officially the Academy expressed surprise and bewilderment. Its president refused to comment on the accusation, and its executive secretary could only say that he was unable to understand Barnes's charges. Frustrated, Barnes sent a letter to each of the officers, trustees, and members of the Academy. In it, he attacked not only the institution but, once again, the mentality of Philadelphia's ruling class:

> . . . Intelligent Philadelphians are wondering why a collection of paintings which many people—including the director of the Louvre, and the director of the Pinakothek, Munich—have said is one of the most important in the world, should be condemned by a teacher in your institution, which is generally referred to as the "morgue." Is your spokesman's attack the result of my refusal to allow certain members of your faculty to continue to use my house for purposes of instruction because they went there habitually in a state of profound alcoholic intoxication? Isn't the attack just the familiar lament of the country school teacher whose pupils have deserted him for the college where life and reality are offered instead of death and imitation?
>
> I have on file the duplicates of every point in your alleged spokesman's attack: they were published in 1874 by the fossils of that age concerning twenty-two masterpieces now in the Louvre. The fact seems to be that your director-Neros are still fiddling and your senile, befuddling faculty are producing vituperation instead of intelligent, sober instruction. Outsiders say that Philadelphia is noted for its abysmal ignorance of and hostility to educational and artistic movements that are recognized everywhere else as sound and progressive. They deride our outworn institutions, laugh at our fatuous egoist who pins medals on the popular burlesque actor of the moment, wonder at our toleration of corrupt, cowardly journalism. But a new era has arrived and it will be the job of a group of modern Philadelphians to try to remove the stigma from our city and to analyze those public men and institutions that are incurably ignorant, indecent and unfair.

Despite the opposition to their plan, Barnes and the university went ahead. From the very beginning, however, it was clear that

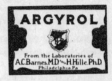

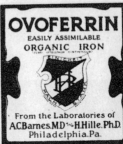

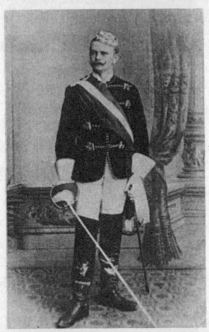

LEFT: Hermann Hille in 1895 (Courtesy Mona W. Hille)

ABOVE: Argyrol and Ovoferrin made Dr. Barnes a rich man.

BELOW: Barnes and Glackens (Courtesy Ira Glackens)

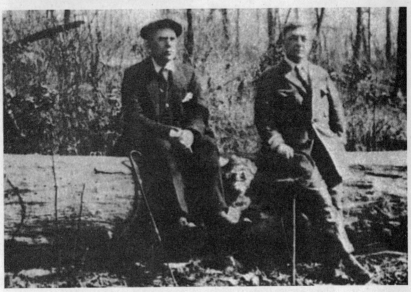

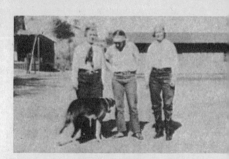

RIGHT: Laura Barnes (*left*) with friends (Courtesy Ira Glackens)

BELOW: Illustrators' Ball, 1917. *Standing, from left:* Maurice Prendergast, Charles Prendergast, and Glackens; *Seated:* Mrs. Lillian E. Travis and Edith Glackens (Courtesy Ira Glackens)

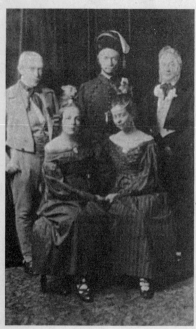

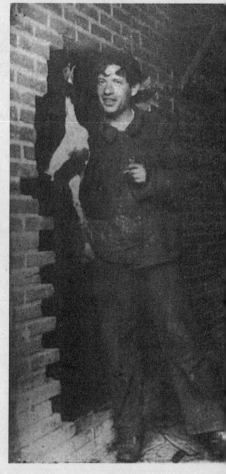

Chaim Soutine (Roger-Viollet)

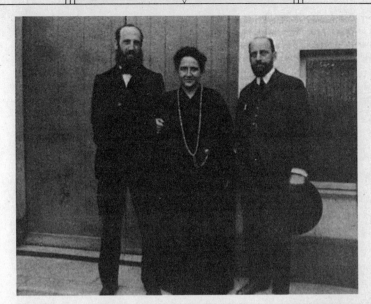

Leo, Gertrude, and Michael Stein in the courtyard of 27, rue de Fleurus, Paris, early 1906 (The Cone Archives of the Baltimore Museum of Art)

Studio of Leo and Gertrude Stein, 27, rue de Fleurus, Paris, c. 1913 (The Cone Archives of the Baltimore Museum of Art)

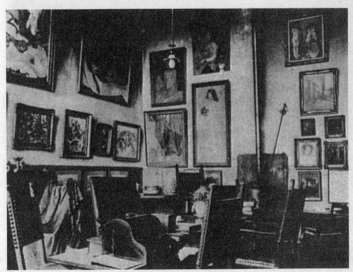

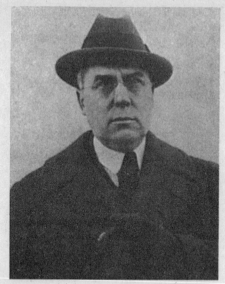

RIGHT: **Dr. Barnes arriving in New York on January 13, 1923, following his hugely successful trip to Europe** (*Inquirer*/Temple Urban Archives)

BELOW: **Barnes (with Fidèle) and Dewey in the Foundation's gallery** (The John Dewey Papers, Morris Library, Southern Illinois University, Carbondale)

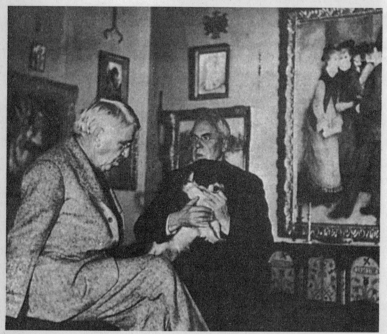

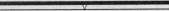

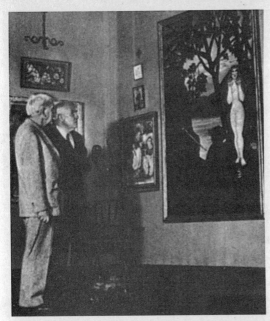

LEFT: Barnes (*right*) and Dewey in the Foundation's gallery, studying a masterpiece by the Douanier Rousseau (The John Dewey Papers, Morris Library, Southern Illinois University, Carbondale)

BELOW: Charles Laughton admiring his friend's collection of Renoirs, 1940 (*Bulletin*/Temple Urban Archives)

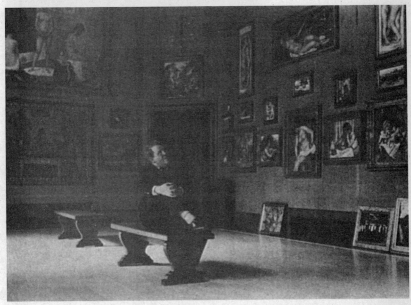

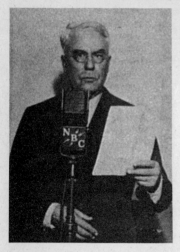

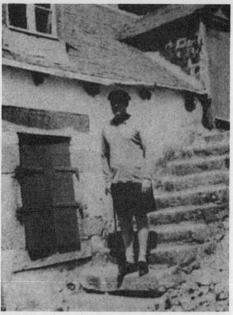

ABOVE: Dr. Barnes addressing the nation, May 10, 1936 (*Inquirer*/Temple Urban Archives)

RIGHT: Dr. Barnes relaxing in Brittany (Courtesy Henry D. Mirick)

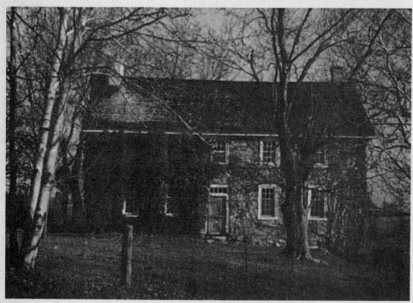

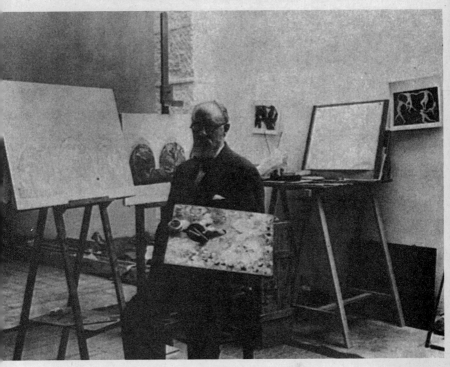

Matisse working on *La Danse*, 1929 (Photograph, Pierre Matisse)

LEFT: **Ker-Feal (Courtesy Henry D. Mirick)**

Renoir, *Mussel Fishers at Berneval* (*Bulletin*/Temple Urban Archives)

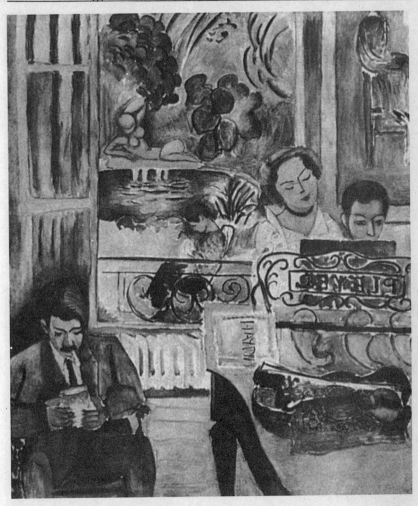

Matisse, *The Music Lesson* (Photograph copyright © John Condax)

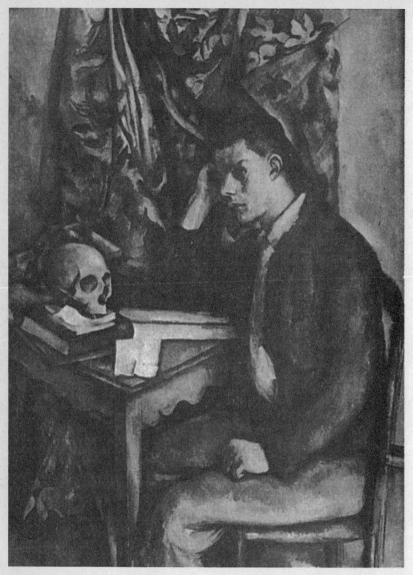

Cézanne, *Man with Skull* (Photograph copyright © John Condax)

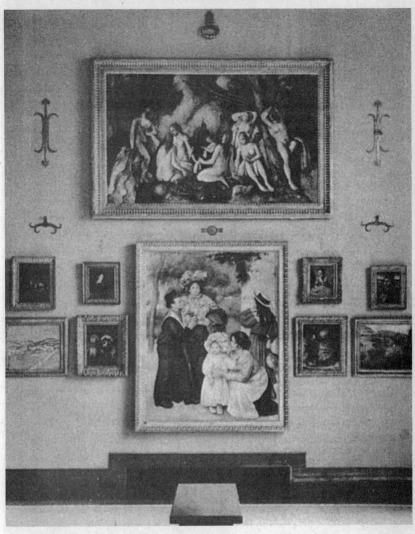

East wall of the main gallery of the Barnes Foundation, 1942 (Photograph copyright © John Condax)

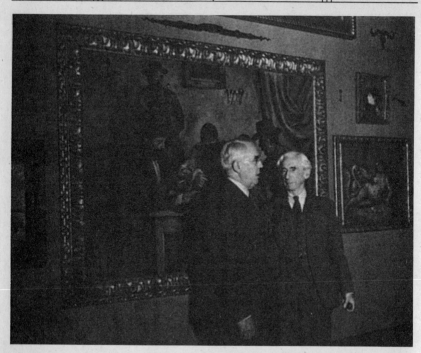

ABOVE: Barnes with Bertrand Russell on January 3, 1941, the philosopher's first day as an instructor at the Foundation (*Bulletin*/Temple Urban Archives)

RIGHT: Alexander Woollcott as Sheridan Whiteside, March 10, 1940 (AP/Temple Urban Archives)

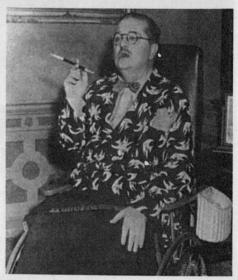

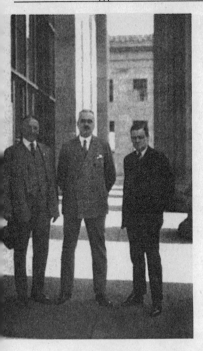

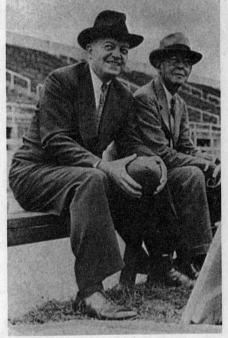

LEFT: Stodgell Stokes, Fiske Kimball, and Horace Jayne of the Philadelphia Museum of Art, 1929 (Philadelphia Museum of Art)

RIGHT: Harold E. Stassen and George W. McClelland of the University of Pennsylvania, September 23, 1948 (*Bulletin*/ Temple Urban Archives)

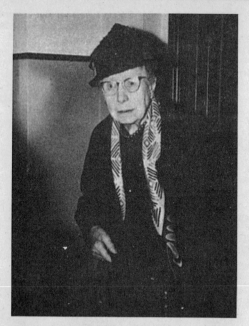

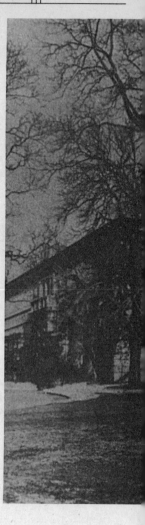

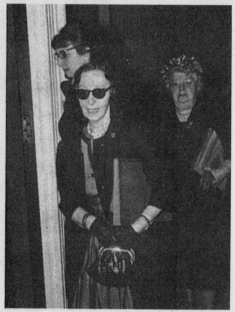

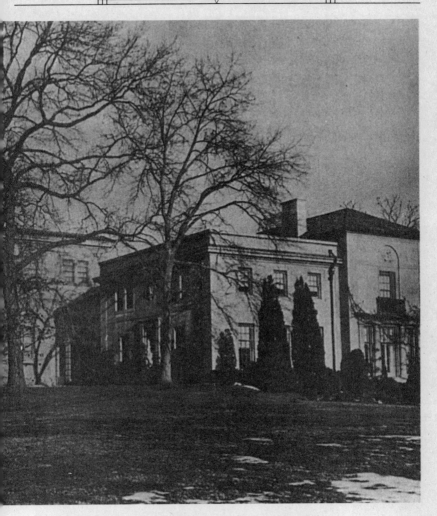

ABOVE: The Barnes Foundation, 1967 (*Bulletin*/Temple Urban Archives)

OPPOSITE, TOP: Laura Barnes arriving for court hearing in Norristown, April 6, 1962 (*Inquirer*/Temple Urban Archives)

BOTTOM: Violette de Mazia (*front, left*) and Nelle E. Mullen (*right*) in Norristown, April 6, 1962 (*Inquirer*/ Temple Urban Archives)

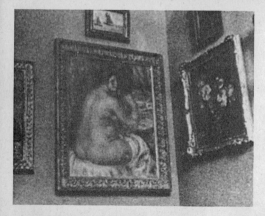

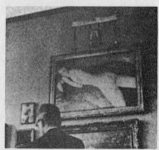

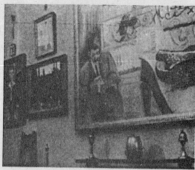

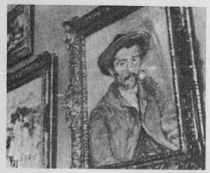

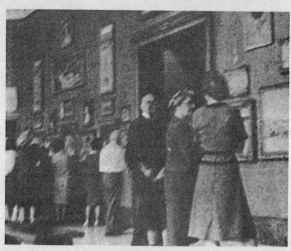

Photographs taken secretly in the Foundation's gallery, June 1969 (Philadelphia *Inquirer*)

Penn was not nearly as committed to the program as was the doctor. Throughout their relationship, the behavior of the university's officials was marked by indifference and, at times, hostility, while Barnes was, on almost every occasion, uncharacteristically willing to turn the other cheek.

At the outset the doctor had been optimistic. There had been some problems: the university had rejected his suggestion that Buermeyer teach a course in aesthetics so that Penn's students might be better prepared for the Foundation's courses, and he had been dismayed by what he considered Penniman's general lack of imagination in dealing with the program. Nonetheless, his hopes for the future of the alliance led him to overlook these problems. Only a few months after initiating the program, he was even prepared to expand it to other areas.

On March 17, 1925, he wrote a letter to Dr. Edgar A. Singer, Jr., a professor of philosophy at Penn, suggesting that the two institutions, already cooperating in the instruction of art and aesthetics, join in another, equally exciting venture. This would assure the university's preeminence in the fields of arboriculture and horticulture. A seventeen-and-a-half-acre tract of land, adjoining the Foundation's twelve-acre park and arboretum, was for sale, he informed Singer. If the university was willing to raise the estimated $450,000 to buy the land, he would commission and pay for the construction of a new $300,000 building there, which would belong to Penn. Furthermore he promised to pay the salary of a new professor and allow Penn the free use of the Foundation's own facilities, with the active cooperation of the staff of its arboretum. He was so eager to bring the plan to fruition that he agreed to grant the university complete autonomy in all matters concerning the project and personally guaranteed the upkeep of the new center following his death.

It was an unprecedented and extraordinarily generous offer. Singer knew it and was as excited as Barnes was. Singer responded immediately, promising to relay the offer to Penniman that same day. It seems, however, that Penniman did not share Barnes's or Singer's enthusiasm. Apparently busy with more pressing matters,

Penniman never replied, and nothing ever came of Barnes's offer.

Nor did anything lasting emerge from the temporary alliance between the university's art department and the Barnes Foundation. For two and a half years, in spite of his strong determination to make the plan work and his willingness to overlook rude treatment from university officials, Barnes made no progress in his efforts to make his alma mater a center of art education. His suggestions were repeatedly rejected or, even worse, ignored.

It was a frustrating experience for a man accustomed to having his own way. At regular intervals he warned that students of the School of Fine Arts—"debauched" by faulty education in the past— were not adequately prepared for the Foundation-sponsored classes and urged that they be offered background courses in general culture. University officials paid no attention and, as a consequence, students frequently found the Barnes lectures difficult to follow. These same officials did little to promote interest in the new courses— prospective students were hardly aware of the advantages of the resources of the Barnes Foundation—and the courses were poorly attended. When it was learned that even those few fine arts students who did enroll in the classes were overloaded with other studies and therefore unable to devote sufficient time to their new course in modern art, the classes were opened to students from other departments of the university. Even this failed because of Penn's indifference; few students took advantage of the unique opportunity offered to them, for no effort had been made to convince them to do so.

Finally in an attempt to remedy this seemingly hopeless situation, Munro asked that a faculty committee be formed to look into ways of improving cooperation between the two institutions. The committee was formed, but it never met. Its members were invited to come to the Foundation as a group, and they never came. The college's faculty advisers were also invited to come to the Foundation to discuss the program, but only two or three of them appeared. In the spring of 1926, invitations to visit the gallery were sent to the entire faculty of the college, the postgraduate, and education departments. Only six members attended the meeting, during which Munro outlined his new plan, invited criticism, and pleaded for cooperation. Nothing resulted. In spite of repeated invitations to come to the Foundation and to listen to Barnes's plans for the present and the future, Penniman never even paid a casual visit to Merion.

During this entire period Barnes was remarkably patient. He wanted, almost desperately, to link his Foundation's future with his alma mater and remained determined to go to any length to do so. On May 21, 1926, he made one last offer to the university. In a letter to Penniman, he requested a chance to explain to the board of trustees a plan whereby Penn would ultimately have control of all of the Foundation's resources, with an income ample to support it in perpetuity, provide instruction, and award scholarships. Though he coupled his request with suggestions concerning a reorganization of the School of Fine Arts, he assured the provost that no attempt would be made by the Foundation to usurp any of the university's powers.

Even this letter, containing a proposal which would have been of lasting benefit to the university, was never answered by Penniman, nor was its receipt acknowledged until many months later. By then it was too late. On November 27, 1926, Barnes wrote again to the provost, formally suspending all formal arrangements with the university. Penn's students would still be allowed to attend classes at the Foundation, but no academic credit would be given them. He still kept the door ajar, however, adding that this new policy would be followed "as long as conditions at the University seem to discourage the hope of intelligent co-operation."

Years later, Barnes was able to joke about his experience, noting that he had once been introduced as the only man who had ever expelled an entire university. Nonetheless, he had been deeply hurt by the failure of his efforts to build a permanent relationship between his foundation and Penn. He had, once again, been rejected by the establishment. He had offered everything—his full cooperation, his experiments in education, and his entire collection—and had received nothing in return, not even a show of good manners.

· ·

At the same time that Barnes was struggling to form an alliance with his alma mater, he was trying to build some kind of relationship with another Philadelphia institution—its museum, then known as the Pennsylvania Museum of Art, not yet officially born and not yet situated in its present quarters. Barnes had had no official dealings with the museum, but he frequently accompanied his students there to study its collection. After one such visit in May 1925, he received a warm letter from Dr. Samuel Woodhouse, the acting director, regretting that Barnes had not made his visit known and offering to assist him personally in any way possible the next time he came to the museum. He added, "We are very glad that you should find the collection of the Museum useful to your educational purposes."

It wasn't much, but it was at least an opening—a note of official recognition of his educational program—and it pleased Barnes, who was not accustomed to kind words from the Philadelphia art establishment.

A few months later Barnes had further reason to be pleased when the museum announced the appointment of Fiske Kimball as its permanent director. He would lead the museum when it moved to its new site on Fairmount Hill. Kimball, who had enthusiastically praised *The Art in Painting,* was apparently a man with whom the doctor could establish a personal as well as a professional rapport. Superficially, at least, the two men had a great deal in common. Most important, Kimball was, as was Barnes, an outsider, in no way connected with Philadelphia society. A New Yorker, Kimball had served as chairman of the art department of New York University. Over six feet tall, with short hair and a commanding physical presence, he was known as a man of enormous energy, with a single-minded dedication to the arts which equaled Barnes's. Intellectually as arrogant as Barnes, he showed no pity toward those who lacked his drive and mental agility, and he believed, as did the doctor, that only he was entitled to make long speeches and lengthy pronouncements. Furthermore he shared Barnes's penchant for ribald humor and good liquor.

There were differences, too, between the two men. Kimball's academic credentials were impeccable. He had studied architecture and art history at the very institutions Barnes believed were responsible for educationally "debauching" students. His tastes, unlike Barnes's, were conservative. Though aware of modern art, he planned to begin his work as director of the new museum by concentrating on the decorative arts and the period rooms which were uniquely suited to the architecture of the new galleries that were to house the museum's formal collection. It was clear that, at the beginning at least, he had no intention of taking the risks necessary to educate the Philadelphia public.

Conceivably, these differences between two intelligent men, otherwise bound together by a passion for art, could have been reconciled. Nonetheless, a fundamental difference of purpose was sure to emerge: Barnes wanted to use the museum as a forum for his own ideas of art education, and Kimball, a singularly able negotiator for gifts as well as purchases—he was to acquire a number of great private collections—envisioned it as a home for the Barnes collection.

The relationship between the two men began on a friendly note at their first meeting in October 1925, at Kimball's office in Memorial Hall, the site of the old museum. Though the new director expected the worst—he was aware of Barnes's reputation for irascibility—the two men found wide areas of agreement. Barnes prefaced their talk by admitting that few people would listen to him because they considered him a "wild man," but Kimball listened attentively as the collector expounded his ideas concerning modern art and the problems of running an art museum. Before he left, Barnes warned Kimball that his would not be an easy task, especially in view of the nature of the museum's trustees, but he generously offered to advise the new director whenever he wanted to share his problems and his plans. Kimball was delighted; at no point had there been any sign of Barnes's eccentricities. On the contrary he felt confident that he and the museum had made a valuable new friend.

Barnes too was optimistic, and soon after that first meeting he took advantage of the friendly rapport he had established with Kimball by suggesting that Thomas Munro be included in a series of public lectures to be held under the museum's auspices. After listing Munro's academic credentials, Barnes added: "His personality has none of the sharp edges which have cut into the art luminaries of this city as mine have done, so he would be able to give the good of the Foundation minus the bad." Furthermore he offered to admit students from the museum's art school to the Foundation's own classes at Merion.

Though inexplicably nothing came of either of these offers, Barnes and Kimball remained on good terms. Though Barnes was irritated by the museum's rejection of his suggestions, he in no way showed it at the time. On the contrary, in the spring of 1926, Kimball received his first formal invitation to visit Merion. It was a typical Sunday afternoon at the Foundation. There were speeches by Barnes and two members of the Penn faculty (the audience consisted of students from the university), a concert of Negro spirituals, and carefully measured cocktails, after which the guests were permitted to examine, freely, the treasures of the Foundation. Kimball was disappointed by Barnes's two-hour talk, wondering how the author of a book he found so fascinating could be so boring a lecturer, but he was enthralled by the gallery itself and by its incomparable collection.

When the two men parted company that afternoon, Kimball felt confident that it had been only the first of many visits he would pay to the Foundation. The afternoon there had served to confirm his belief that he knew how to handle the reputedly difficult collector and that their relationship would remain a stable, warm one—one that would eventually benefit the new museum.

Somehow, however, Kimball had miscalculated. Though he had no reason to suspect it at the time, this first visit was also his last. In spite of his proven ability to flatter and get along with the rich, he had misjudged Barnes, as had Lipchitz and others before him. He had been unaware of Barnes's almost paranoic fear of being used. Specifically, Kimball's sin, committed repeatedly during the months following his own visit to the Foundation, was that of taking advantage of what he supposed was their friendship in order to gain admittance to the gallery for his friends. At first, Barnes had granted Kimball's frequent requests, but by the fall he had tired of them. Without warning he sent off the first of many scathing letters to Kimball. Significantly, it was mailed at the same time Barnes was finally losing his patience with Penn's officials. Dated October 27, 1926, it read:

> Repeated applications, similar to that which you made this morning, seem to indicate that you share a very prevalent idea that the Foundation is a place for more or less conspicuous Philadelphians to entertain their friends. When you assumed your present position, more than a year ago, I told you that the Foundation would cooperate with you as an official in any move that could be intelligently interpreted as educational. Also, one of our staff called on you with a plan to help those students of painting at the Institution of which you are the head, by a systematic course of study in our gallery. Not a thing intelligent came of these proposals; what did happen was a series of requests to have your friends and acquaintances use the Foundation as a diversion. . . .
>
> The Foundation has a charter as an educational institution and it intends to live up to its stated purposes. It provides for all classes of people who show sufficient interest to enroll in and attend the classes organized for systematic study. If you have any persons who meet that description, we can take care of them. But for casual visitors, whatever their alleged qualifications or under whatever local prestige they may be proposed, there is absolutely nothing doing. I am writing you frankly so that we shall be spared the nuisance of further "phone calls, pleadings and arguments."

Kimball was stunned, but he refused to accept defeat. He wrote Barnes an abject apology at once, pleading that he had failed to understand the Foundation's policy concerning visitors and expressing delight that he would from then on be freed from having to act as intermediary for those who wanted to gain admittance to the Foundation. He was sorry, he wrote, that Barnes had not told him of his annoyance before then. "Rather than have that, and especially rather than injure our first friendly relations," he added, "all those people can go to the dickens." It was, however, too late—for the museum as it was for the university. No apology was sufficient, and even Kimball's request for a meeting to straighten out their differences went unanswered.

Kimball made one last attempt to gain Barnes's cooperation, but it too failed. The occasion was the eagerly anticipated opening exhibition at the newly christened Philadelphia Museum of Art in March 1928, for which Kimball wanted to discuss the possibility of borrowing some of the Foundation's paintings. In a letter to the collector, Kimball explained the layout of the new museum's galleries, one of which would contain a long wall filled with nineteenth-century French painting from Renoir onward. "I should like to give these modern masters the very finest representation possible," he wrote. "We could readily secure loans of certain fine pictures elsewhere, but I should prefer to recognize here the commanding position of the Barnes Collection in this field." Kimball went even further, expressing the hope that this initial loan was to be "the first step in a co-operation which could go much further when we secure additional gallery space and the floor specifically devoted to active educational work is finished and put into operation." If the director believed that his flattery and his references to education, so dear to Barnes, could achieve his ends, he again miscalculated the reactions of the man who despised flattery and was now his implacable enemy. The doctor, understanding Kimball's real aim, did not even answer the letter. Instead Kimball received a letter signed, but surely not composed, by Nelle Mullen, asserting that the proposal "would make a horse laugh" and "would be offensive to the intelligence" were it not "so provincial and embedded in the matrix of the stereotyped blah which comes to us so often from performers who would like to annex us as a sideshow to their circuses."

At this point, Kimball gave up, but the museum did not. Only two years later, Henri Marceau, its curator of fine arts, tried to succeed where Kimball had failed. The story of his relationship with Barnes parallels in many ways that of Kimball's. At first Marceau had reason to be optimistic. He and the collector had been on good terms. Marceau had generously assisted the doctor during the preparations for a book on French primitives, and Barnes had graciously returned the favor, inviting Marceau and his wife to visit Merion, not once but twice. As a result Marceau, like Kimball before him, could not help believing that stories of the collector's intransigence and eccentricity were exaggerated. Then he made his mistake. He asked the man he considered a friend a favor—to lend an El Greco to the museum. Marceau had written an article on El Greco which had been published in the museum's *Bulletin* and hoped to follow it up with a large exhibition of the artist's works. His letter asking for the loan was a warm one; the reply was not. Barnes was furious, and in a letter of December 29, 1929, he launched a savage attack on both Marceau and the museum. The letter read:

> Your letter of December 18th indicates that the same mis-understanding of our collection exists as two years ago when, in a reply to a similar request from your director, a letter was written of which a copy is enclosed. In other words, you ask me to deprive an educational project which is in daily oper-ation, of pictures which are indispensable to that plan, in order to further what would be essentially a grotesque parody on art and education.
>
> The only purposes your proposed El Greco exhibition would serve would be to entertain an uninformed public and continue to discredit the intelligence of Philadelphia by the pretentious parade of "society" people and *fonctionnaires*. That prediction is assured of realization by your own recent article on El Greco in which you eulogize two pictures which every well-informed person knows are fakes. In its general aspects, your article is a repetition of the published clichés on El Greco and what you write about the particular pictures is psychological proof

of lack of individual experience. The exhibition would be as offensive to a cultivated intelligence as was a recent lecture by one of your staff, which I heard at your Museum, and which consisted of a recital of the article on the painter as published in the Encyclopaedia Britannica.

The institution which I serve is dedicated to the development of an understanding of art through the medium of education and we work in harmonious cooperation with other institutions that have the same purpose. If the Art Museum of Philadelphia ever attains to that level, as contrasted with what is represented by the incidents above mentioned—and many more analyzed but not herein stated—we shall be pleased to grant the "cooperation" that you ask. . . .

CHAPTER 1

Dr. Barnes's list of enemies was growing. It included journalists, art critics, dealers, other collectors, and other millionaires, representatives of the world of conservative academia, and now museum officials—all those who had offended him in the past. This was reflected in his response to those who sought admission to the Foundation's gallery. Officially the admissions policy was a rigid one, stated unequivocally on a printed card sent to those who asked to see the collection. "The Barnes Foundation is not a public gallery," it read. "It is an educational institution with a program for systematic work, organized into classes which are held every day, and conducted by a staff of experienced teachers. Admission to the gallery is restricted to students enrolled in the classes." Unofficially it was less rigid. Barnes never closed the doors to his Foundation as has been frequently charged—either after the angry reaction to the Academy exhibition or after his break with Penn. Individuals and even groups were permitted to view the peerless collection, but they could do so only with the doctor's permission, and no one knew exactly why or to whom that would be granted.

With rare exceptions, members of the establishment, those on his blacklist, were out. If they enclosed a stamped, self-addressed envelope, they received the standard rejection form. If not, their requests were usually ignored. Walter P. Chrysler, Jr., had two strikes against him—he was a millionaire and a collector. His letter to Barnes was modest and polite. "We have so many mutual interests in connection with modern art which are as deeply rooted with me as they are with you," he wrote, "that I feel confident you will not think me too presumptuous in writing you to ask if it might be possible for a close friend of mine and myself to take advantage of your hospitality in seeking your permission to view the magnificent group of pictures you have collected in the Barnes Foundation."

Barnes's reply was signed by a fictitious secretary, "Peter Kelly." In it he wrote:

> It is impossible at this time to show to Doctor Barnes your letter . . . because he gave strict orders that he is not to be disturbed during his present efforts to break the world's record for goldfish swallowing. However, since I take it from . . . your letter that you are very important and also a punctilious observer of the social amenities, I shall assume the responsibility of breaking a universal rule and enclose a statement of the regulations concerning admission to the gallery of the Barnes Foundation. The rule I break is that the card is sent only to those who enclose a stamped envelope for reply.

Lizzie Bliss, another millionaire collector and founder of New York's Museum of Modern Art, was treated with even less respect. Her request was granted, on the condition that she arrive at the Foundation at eight o'clock in the morning. When she did so, she found the gates to the Foundation closed, and no effort on her part could rouse anyone to open them.

Other, less prominent personalities usually fared better. Apparently, the doctor, true to his democratic principles, favored struggling artists and workers; the uneducated and the underprivileged, without connections, posed no threats to his sovereignty. James Michener applied three times as a student from fashionable Swarthmore College and was ignored. After he sent a letter from

Pittsburgh claiming to be a poorly educated worker in a steel mill, permission was granted by return mail.

Michael Ellis, an unknown young Philadelphia painter and football player had learned of the Barnes collection through his interest in Cézanne, whose work he had discovered in 1925. He wrote Barnes a simple, straightforward letter and was invited to come to the Foundation. Barnes, who Ellis thought looked like a tough tycoon, greeted him warmly, gave him a copy of *The Art in Painting*, and advised him to go to Paris if he really wanted to become a painter. He also invited him to join his class at the Foundation, which Ellis did the following year. Barnes liked him, the young man felt, because his lower-class background was similar to the doctor's own.

Ben Shahn, not yet a well-known painter, managed to visit the Foundation's gallery not once but several times in the 1920s. Eager to see the collection, he had sought but failed to obtain letters of introduction to Barnes. Finally he took the bold step of going directly to the Argyrol factory and asking for the doctor himself. To his surprise he was admitted to Barnes's office, where the collector asked him if he had read his recently published book. Shahn hadn't—he didn't even know Barnes had written one—but he bluffed answers to several questions, after which Barnes ordered a car to have him taken directly to Merion. Somehow Barnes himself reached there before Shahn did and personally conducted the young man on a two-hour tour of the gallery. As Shahn was about to leave, he mentioned that he would like to return another time. "Are you rich?" Barnes asked him. Flabbergasted, Shahn replied, "Moderately." It must have been the right answer, for Barnes told him that he would arrange for a car to pick him up at the station if he would arrive on a certain train on each Thursday. Shahn, delighted, did this for several Thursdays . . . until he committed the unpardonable sin of arriving in the company of a friend—not just a friend but one who dared to suggest to their host that the collection wasn't really up to date. That was too much. In no uncertain terms Barnes ordered the two men out of the gallery. Shahn never saw it or the doctor again.

Another future notable, the journalist Joseph Alsop, got into the Foundation in 1929, when he was a nineteen-year-old student at Harvard. He used, in his own words, "shameless flattery and sheer persistence" in order to do so. Barnes himself, "alarming even in carpet slippers," opened the door. Alsop never forgot Barnes's words as he pointed him toward the gallery. "Just remember, young man," he said, "these pictures you're going to see are the old masters of the future, *the old masters of the future*."

Though applicants for admission were carefully screened, Barnes occasionally made mistakes, and in 1925 Jeanne Robert Foster, an intimate friend of John Quinn, was allowed to view the collection in the company of H. P. Roché. They had been refused permission before, but on this occasion they presumably used pseudonyms. They were greeted at the door by a man who described himself as a Virginia mountaineer and explained that he was in charge of the building. He followed them on their tour of the galleries and told them Barnes had said they could remain in the building until five o'clock. Though Foster admired several of the canvases, she felt the collection on the whole was inferior to Quinn's. Above all, she found there were too many paintings, most of them badly hung. She took careful note, however, of just what the collection lacked, for the Quinn collection (he had died in 1924) was about to be put up for sale.

At four o'clock Barnes entered the gallery with a party of female sightseers, including Mrs. Barnes and her sister. The doctor greeted Foster and Roché, who found him to be cordial if not friendly, and apologized for the arrangement of the paintings, which he said was only temporary. In the course of their conversation, Foster was impressed above all by Barnes's imposing physical presence—his bushy eyebrows and deep-set eyes in which she detected a reddish gleam which she likened to that found in some animals, particularly black bears. The red, she noted, brightened when he was animated or disturbed, as when he spoke of rival art collectors.

Not every visitor found Barnes so intimidating. A member of a class of high school students from the Oak Lane Country Day School, admitted to the gallery with their teacher, Grace Gemberling, herself a former Barnes student, remembered the doctor as being gràcious and charming. Other visitors were also warmly received and often were given a tour of the gallery by Barnes himself, who was not only proud to show off his collection but also curious to hear visitors' reactions. According to some reports, Barnes was so eager to know what his guests thought of the collection that on at least one occasion he wore workman's clothes, so that he might freely wander through the gallery and listen to their unguarded expression of their thoughts. Those who expressed criticism were ejected.

Of all the guests at Merion, none was more welcome than Paul Guillaume, who, accompanied by his wife, came there in April 1926. Madame Guillaume, a strikingly beautiful, flamboyant Frenchwoman, had reservations about the visit. She vociferously complained to friends that she almost starved while there—there was plenty of food, but it wasn't French. Her husband, however, expressed no such reservations and enthusiastically described his visit in the May issue of *Les Arts à Paris*. If his own gallery on the rue La Boétie was, for his American host, "The Temple," the Foundation in Merion, for Guillaume, could only be compared to the institution founded centuries before by Ptolemy Philadelphus, who made Alexandria the center of Hellenistic culture.

The Parisian's official duties, as foreign secretary, included a speech before an invited audience at the Foundation on April 4— the subject was "The Discovery and Appreciation of Primitive Negro Sculpture"—and attendance at Barnes's Sunday morning lecture. These lectures had become a regular part of the Foundation's program, and Guillaume effusively praised his host's performance. By ten o'clock the distinguished audience of university professors, students, collectors, and artists had filled the gallery. "Barnes appears," Guillaume wrote. "He has no notes. He stands, unpretentious. His glance envelops the audience, he speaks at once. He goes directly into his subject. . . . His dialectics are insinuating, adroit, compact, direct. He makes use of syllogisms and poses dilemmas. His speech is, by turns, tender, angry, musical, harsh. He holds his audience's attention, takes care not to tire them—he pauses, begins again. The faces before him show understanding, joy, enthusiasm. Dr. Barnes has spoken in this way for thirty or forty minutes. He has finished, but he asks for questions, asks that someone raise a controversial issue. After a few seconds' hesitation, a listener gets up and ventures a weighty question. Dr. Barnes answers, develops the question himself, studies it, clarifies it, folds it, unfolds it, turns it over, twists it, plays with it and gives a satisfying answer to the questioner and to the audience who, the time having come, leaves the hall regretfully, as if the charm of the words, whose echo still resound under the high vaults, refuse to break off."

Guillaume also joined his host on two less official occasions, which he also described in *Les Arts à Paris*. The first involved what turned out to be a rather hair-raising visit to the doctor's colleagues at the nearby Narberth fire department. Barnes, who had retained his childhood interest in fire companies, was an honorary colonel and benefactor of the department. The visiting Frenchman was warmly greeted by the firemen—the doctor had told them of his accomplishments—and was shown their imposing equipment. Afterward he was invited to take a ride on one of their trucks, an honor he couldn't refuse. Guillaume rode seated between Barnes and Fire Chief Albert Nulty (formerly Barnes's chauffeur, Nulty had become the Foundation's restorer as well as one of its trustees). The Frenchman, "used to the moderate oxygenation of the air of the rue La Boétie," was terrified of the speed at which the engine raced through town. When he asked Nulty to slow down, the fire chief accelerated. Guillaume survived, however, and at the end of the ride was rewarded with an appointment as the company's honorary captain.

Guillaume's second outing with Barnes was less dangerous and more spiritually rewarding. As part of a group which included the Barneses, the Mullen sisters, Laura Geiger, and Madame Guillaume, he traveled to Bordentown, New Jersey—"on the other side of the strange Indian river, the Delaware"—for a concert given by the chorus of the Manual Training School for Negroes. Attendance at the concerts had become a ritual for Barnes, and he derived enormous pleasure from them. Guillaume, too, was moved. He and the other guests were seated on the stage and listened, enthralled, to a program of traditional Negro songs led by the chorus's distinguished director, Frederick Work. "Their sweet, warm voices were raised in song," Guillaume wrote, "expressing the nostalgia, the grief, the anguish, the despair, and the hopes of the wretched slaves, their ancestors, who, brutally uprooted from their African homes, suffered so long in the Carolinas, in the plantations of the South. They sang for more than an hour. We were very moved, charmed, transported." Following the concert, Barnes addressed the students, telling them that their ancestors had an art of which they could be proud and thanking them for the aesthetic pleasure they had just given to him.

Guillaume's visit offered Barnes a welcome respite from his feuds with both the museum and the university. He had been gratified by the Frenchman's praise, and the French government had, in 1926, recognized his achievements by naming him Chevalier de la Légion d'Honneur, but he was receiving no such honors at home. Though he continued to add to his collection—during this period he often boasted that paintings he had acquired for a pittance had soared in monetary value, giving proof of his sound judgment— much of his energy was expended in time-consuming and increasingly bitter quarrels.

In the spring of 1927 Barnes was embroiled in still another one, provoked this time by a threatened invasion of his carefully preserved neighborhood. It began with the announcement that 126 houses would be constructed on land adjoining the rear of the Foundation's property. The new homes, built of stone and stucco, were to be sold at between $17,000 and $25,000 each. Barnes reacted angrily. He charged that "Merion will have an incipient city slum on its hand" and that the construction of the new houses would cause his property to be surrounded by the same urban conditions he had sought to escape and would destroy the atmosphere of seclusion he had tried to establish. He vowed a fight to the finish to defeat the scheme. If he lost, he declared, he would move his priceless collection to the Metropolitan Museum in New

York: "I shall be an humble and unworthy follower of great people like Stokowski, Mary Cassatt, Abbey, Henri, Sloan, Glackens and many others who leave Philadelphia to get a breath of fresh air and never come back." Even worse, he stunned Main Liners by stating that the Foundation's buildings in Merion would be used in the future as a center for the study of black culture under the direction of the National Urban League. Though enrollment in classes would not be limited to blacks, he noted that most of the students coming to Merion would be from black colleges in the South.

It was not, he insisted, a new, hastily devised plan. He had long contemplated establishing such a center in New York or Washington, but the removal of his art collection from Merion would leave the Foundation's buildings there empty and, as a consequence, the ideal site for his latest experiment in education. In a pamphlet accompanying an open letter which he sent to all residents of Lower Merion Township, he gave further details of the project and the reasons for it:

> For 20 years the founders of the Barnes Foundation have conducted scientific experiments to determine the artistic and intellectual endowments of the ordinary, uncultured Negro. The results of these experiments have been published in the leading magazines of America and Europe and have been endorsed by authorities as of epoch-making significance.
>
> In order to make the native qualities of the Negro contributory to a richer and more intelligent civilization in America, plans are being prepared to have the Barnes Foundation property serve as a national center for the development, by scientific educational methods, of the rare artistic and mental endowments of the Negro.
>
> Comfortable living accommodations, freedom from oppression, and instruction by skilled educators of both races, all supplemented by the art resources available, cannot fail to be conducive to important creative work in art and social life. Only prejudice would deny that the Negro has social gifts

which enable him to live in harmony with his white neighbors, and only lack of information would dispute that the best hope for the artistic salvation of America lies in systematic development of the extraordinary native artistic endowments of the Negro.

Barnes's startling threat mobilized the citizens of Lower Merion and divided them into two camps. Some, who supported the doctor, did so because they did not want Merion to lose the collection; the majority, less concerned with art, were frightened that their Main Line enclave would be invaded by blacks. Those opposing Barnes challenged his right to take such steps and threatened to take legal action against him. He responded by warning that his swan song to Merion would be "a pamphlet on Who is Who in political corruption, and a copy of it will be mailed to every voter in the Township." He offered to bet, at odds of two to one, that a disinterested inquiry would prove conclusively that the construction of the new homes was the result of political skullduggery.

Nobody took the bet—nobody ever paid attention to these bets—but angry charges were exchanged by both sides. Barnes leveled accusations of racism, political corruption, trickery, and deception at the Township and at several of his neighbors. His opponents called him a crackpot, labeled his new plan outrageous and ridiculous, and accused him of using "intemperate and offensive language" in the battle.

In the end Barnes lost—there was no legal way to stop the construction of the new homes. Frustrated, he ordered completion of the building of a ten-foot-high gray stone wall, extending over a distance of five blocks (work had begun as soon as ground had been broken for the new houses) to separate the Foundation from its new neighbors. At the end of May, just before leaving for Europe, he put a good face on his defeat by announcing that due to the pleas of the citizens of Merion and an agreement that every effort would be made to "purify" local politics, his collection would not be moved.

• •

The entire episode could be dismissed as a typical Barnesian tantrum—much ado about very little. The new homes, not inexpensive ones, could not possibly—and did not—turn his neighborhood into a city slum; nor could they endanger the sanctity of his foundation. His threats of reprisal, too, were without substance. There is no evidence that Barnes ever seriously intended to move his collection to New York—there is no record of his ever having talked to the Metropolitan about such an important matter. And the archives of the National Urban League contain nothing that would indicate that he ever discussed with its officials the possibility of establishing a center for black studies in Merion.

Nonetheless, the idea for establishing such a center might well have been a serious one, for during the 1920s Barnes's interest in black culture and history was intense. There were no blacks on his list of enemies, and had there been a list of friends, they might have headed it. Since his childhood, his concern for the black people, the underdog with whom he conceivably identified, had developed into a passion. His understanding of their social plight had grown as a result of the educational experiments he had carried on in his factory, and his enthusiasm for black traditions and culture had been stimulated by Guillaume and had resulted in one of the Foundation's first books, *Primitive Negro Sculpture*, written by Guillaume and Munro and published in 1926.

During this period, Barnes's interest went beyond mere rhetoric. He was prominent among the American whites who actively supported the New Negro movement (also known as the Harlem Renaissance), which proclaimed the affirmative values of the heritage of the blacks and demanded for them full social and political equality in the democracy for which they had fought in the First World War; and in 1926 he contributed to *The New Negro*, an anthology of historic importance which set forth the ideals and goals of the movement. Edited by Dr. Alain Locke, professor of philosophy at Howard University and chief mentor of the Harlem Renaissance, the book covered every phase of recent black cultural and social achievement. Among the black contributors to the volume were Countee Cullen, James Weldon Johnson, W. E. B. DuBois, Walter F. White, and Langston Hughes. (Hughes met the doctor in Paris through Locke and was unimpressed. According to Arnold Rampersad, Hughes's biographer, Barnes on art reminded Hughes of his own father on mining.) Barnes's contribution was a chapter entitled "Negro Art and America." Praising Negro art, music, and literature, Barnes noted that "through the compelling powers of his poetry and music, the American Negro is revealing to the rest of the world the essential oneness of all human beings." The Negro's achievements, Barnes went on, had been accomplished without the help of the whites, and his hope was that the Negro would be forgiving and "consent to form a working alliance with us for the development of a richer American civilization to which he will contribute his full share."

During the twenties, too, Barnes was actively involved with the National Urban League, the interracial organization which sought to better the living conditions of urban blacks, with an emphasis on the elimination of racial barriers in hiring and the subsequent broadening of employment opportunities. In addition to making generous donations to the League, he vigorously supported its monthly magazine, *Opportunity* ("Not Alms, but Opportunity" was its motto), which had begun publication in 1922. "I can see in the journal abounding evidence of the high intellectual and aesthetic status of the Negro," he wrote in a flier soliciting subscriptions. "Moreover, I see it presented and arranged in a way that is sure to get the commendation of discriminating readers of both races as a milestone on the road to the high conception of intelligence and culture that is the goal of all fine living."

Barnes and his associates also contributed articles to the magazine. Its issue of May 1924 included essays by Barnes and Guillaume, reprinted from *Les Arts à Paris*. The issue of May 1926 might well have passed for a special issue of the Foundation's own journal. Largely devoted to Negro art, it was prepared with the full cooperation of the Foundation. Among its contributors were

Barnes himself, Guillaume ("The Triumph of Ancient Negro Art"), Munro ("Primitive Negro Sculpture"), and Mary Mullen ("An Experiment in Adult Negro Education").

The doctor's contribution, "Negro Art, Past and Present," was a reprint of a speech he had delivered at the Women's Faculty Club of Columbia University on March 26, 1926. A later contribution, first broadcast over radio station WABC (on the magazine's radio program), was published in the May 1928 issue of *Opportunity*. Both articles traced the history and tradition of black culture, emphasizing its influence on modern European and American art, music, and literature. Earnest contributions toward an acknowledgment of the vitality and potential of the black people, they were written by a man who was both well informed and genuinely concerned. His threat to establish a center for black studies in the heart of the Main Line was made in a fit of peevish anger. He had used a legitimate cause as a ploy to get his own way in the housing issue, and he never made a serious attempt to put his plan into practice in Merion or elsewhere. Nonetheless, the sincerity of his desire to further an understanding and appreciation of a race he deeply admired, for whatever motivation, cannot be questioned.

13

All this time Barnes's hopes for expanding his educational program and proliferating his ideas through already existing institutions were fading. The hardest blow had been his failure to form a permanent alliance with Penn, but plans to work with other schools were equally unsuccessful, and these were soon abandoned as well. In the beginning students and professors from a number of institutions—among them the Pennsylvania Academy and New York's Art Students League—were welcomed at the Foundation, but the results proved disappointing. From Barnes's point of view, these academic groups were inadequately prepared to appreciate the Foundation's collection and were handicapped by what they had been taught in the past, victims of what Barnes called "intellectual disorder." In other words they had not been indoctrinated in the Barnes method. These professors and students benefited from their visits no more than did the groups of lawyers and bankers who were also welcomed at the Foundation periodically. When Barnes suggested to one member of the Academy's faculty that they might work out a plan whereby its students would be guided toward an intelligent approach to paintings by members of the Foundation's faculty, he was told that even the suggestion of such a plan would result in the instructor's dismissal. As a consequence classes from the Academy were no longer permitted to study the

Foundation's collection. Similarly, classes from the Art Students League were barred from the gallery, since they too were unwilling to submit to supervision by the Foundation's faculty and refused to make use of its texts.

It was the end of Barnes's dream of mass education in the arts. In the future, he announced, the Foundation would close its doors to those who had been inadequately prepared to appreciate its paintings—"aimless wandering in a gallery is about on a par with the daydreaming furnished by attendance at the movies," his spokeswoman Mary Mullen wrote in the *Journal*—and that included most prospective students. Classes would be open only to those few who met with Barnes's personal approval, and all courses would be taught by members of the Foundation's faculty.

That faculty had, in a short time, lost its most distinguished members. Soon after its inauguration, Dewey severed his official ties with the Foundation by resigning his post as director of education. This represented no break with Barnes. Dewey continued to act as a consultant; he had served his purpose by lending his name and prestige to the new enterprise when such prestige was important, but he wanted to be free to travel and pursue his other activities. In June 1926, too, Buermeyer left for the more traditional world of academia to become assistant professor of philosophy at New York University. He also remained on the best of terms with Barnes, collaborating with him and contributing his services whenever called upon.

In the same year Thomas Munro also left the Foundation. His departure was also amicable, though he had been fired. As early as the spring of 1926, Barnes had begun to suspect that the young professor was too firmly set in his old-fashioned pre-Barnes ways and had warned him that his days were numbered. Munro asked for another chance, and Barnes granted it, sending him to Europe for a third time to teach the Foundation's classes during the summer. The following winter, however, Barnes informed Munro that his contract would not be renewed after its expiration in June. It had become clear that he was not sufficiently involved in the Foundation's activities. As an example Barnes complained that during his own month-long winter visit to Europe, Munro had come to the gallery only to pick up his mail. The doctor was genuinely disappointed. He liked Munro and respected him, but he was unable to excuse his lack of total devotion to the cause. Before Munro left, Barnes offered him good references as well as sententious advice concerning his future; as a sign of his esteem, he never mentioned to outsiders that he had fired him, explaining instead that Munro had left voluntarily. For his part Munro, who went on to Rutgers, Long Island University, and Western Reserve (he later became curator of education at the Cleveland Museum of Art), continued to speak of Barnes with affection and to remember his time at Merion as a valuable step in his career.

The departure of university-trained, professional instructors from the Foundation's staff was accompanied by a curtailment of its official activities. Its publications program, originally aimed to reach a wide audience, was greatly reduced. Few additional books were published in the years to come, and all of them—admittedly monumental studies—were coauthored by Barnes himself. Its official journal, too, ceased publication with its issue of April 1926. The doctor had apparently lost interest in sending his message out into a world which didn't understand it. He was becoming increasingly isolated behind the Foundation's walls, surrounded by a group of loyal, nonthreatening employees, teachers with little or no educational background whom he himself trained and raised to positions for which they were at least initially unqualified. Of these there had been one recent and most significant addition, Violette de Mazia, who learned her lessons well and is worthy of special attention.

Miss de Mazia has been and remains a deliberately mysterious figure, and information about her background and personal life has been one of the Foundation's best-kept secrets. According to *Who's Who of American Women*, she was born in Paris, the daughter of Jean Jules de Mazia (thought to have been born in Russia of Italian parents) and Fanny Franquet, a Frenchwoman. When Miss de Mazia was a child, the family moved to Brussels, where she was educated at the École Superieure de la rue des Marais. During the First World War, the family again moved, this time to London, where their daughter (her date of birth has never been given) attended the Priory House School and the Swiss Cottage Conservatory. According to that same official biography, de Mazia came to Philadelphia in 1926 and began teaching at the Barnes Foundation the following year.

Other evidence suggests that this "biography" might not be altogether accurate. De Mazia's own testimony at a trial several years later, according to the attorney who questioned her, appeared "to be lacking in candor" concerning her educational background, perhaps for fear that "candor" might expose her lack of preparation for her job. Whether deliberate or not, her testimony was unquestionably contradictory. Considering that she was known for her unusually keen memory (her ability to remember names of students after only one meeting is astounding) and was also known as a meticulous researcher, she found it surprisingly difficult to remember just where she had studied and when. The date of her arrival in Philadelphia seems uncertain. According to seemingly reliable sources, she arrived in Philadelphia in 1921 or 1922 and stayed for a while at the home of wealthy relatives on North Broad Street. While there she earned her living teaching French both privately and at a fashionable girls' school. It was in this capacity that she entered the Barnes Foundation, hired to teach French to members of Barnes's staff. From that time on, she remained an integral part of the Foundation. After auditing the Penn classes held there, she was personally trained by Barnes. According to the information in *Who's Who*, she became an instructor in 1927. Again, her memory seems to have failed her, for as early as 1926, when she contributed a translation from Blaise Cendrars's *Anthologie Nègre* to the May issue of *Opportunity* magazine, she was identified as an instructor at the Foundation. Furthermore in January of that year, Barnes gratefully acknowledged her help in the preparation of the first trade publication of *The Art in Painting* (she had not been mentioned in the 1925 edition).

As a true Barnesian—and the doctor had no more faithful

disciple—Violette de Mazia might well complain that such information—or misinformation—is irrelevant. What counts is who she is and what she has contributed to the Foundation, not what's behind the canvas but what's on it. Throughout Barnes's lifetime, she was his first assistant in every way, as well as his collaborator on four of the Foundation's books. Always available, always loyal to the man and his ideas, she never failed him.

Laura Barnes was steadfastly in charge of the doctor's personal life, his hostess in Merion, and his social companion away from the Foundation (though de Mazia often accompanied him on his trips abroad, presumably to assist in the research for their books). She and her husband were both strong-willed people, a fact Mrs. Barnes did well to hide under a mild, polite, genteel manner—and the bond between them, if difficult to explain even by those who knew them well, was unbreakable. Violette de Mazia, however, soon assumed another and perhaps equally important role which inevitably conflicted with that of Mrs. Barnes. The two women were barely on speaking terms, and those who met Laura Barnes rarely met de Mazia—and vice versa. Increasingly the Foundation became the latter's home and its gallery her salon, where she reigned as hostess throughout the doctor's life. Upon his death, she assumed responsibility for the collection. Her appearance has changed little since that time. A small, slight woman, her eyes shielded by sunglasses (which she wears because of an allergy), she habitually wears a flower in her hair or on her dress, and a ring on her thumb tinkles as she points, analytically, to a picture she describes. Today, as vice president and director of education of its art department, she completely dominates the Foundation. They are now inseparable in the eyes of most observers. Violette de Mazia has become the Barnes Foundation, and the Barnes Foundation is Violette de Mazia. It is hard to imagine them apart from one another.

Barnes's declaration of noncooperation with the educational establishment quickly became a declaration of independence in every way. He had no experts on his staff, and by 1927 he felt he could dispense with experts of any kind. With very few exceptions he found art historians especially unreliable and their advice misleading. He deplored their enormous influence on dealers as well as on collectors. He enjoyed telling the story of an El Greco he almost bought on the advice of a friend, Professor Mayer of the University of Munich, director of the Pinakothek and a renowned Greco authority. On the advice of his doctor—who had told him he needed a couple of weeks in the sun—Barnes and his wife had planned to leave Paris for a holiday in Sicily when word came from Mayer that an enormous and uniquely important Greco had just come on the market. A wealthy German banker had bought it to give to the Kaiser Friedrich's Museum, but the banker had died before he could do so, and his heirs had decided to sell it. Certain it could be his because it was too large for a private home and too costly for a museum, Barnes lost no time. He immediately made an offer of $150,000—the asking price had been $200,000—and decided to cancel his trip to Sicily, a four days' journey from Paris, and to wait for news in Vence in the South of France. His European trip had already been a very expensive one; he had just bid $150,000 for an Ingres and had recently purchased a Corot and a Manet, but he badly wanted the Greco. In a letter written to Dewey in America, he made light of the matter, asking the philosopher to lend him the $150,000 for three months; in return Dewey would receive 6 percent interest and be given a chance to look at the painting once a week until the debt had been paid.

The stay in Vence was a disaster. The weather was terrible, Mrs. Barnes caught a bad cold, and Barnes spent most of his time in a frigid hotel room, warmed only by his profanity. His sole amusement was a short visit to Monte Carlo where he played roulette and won ten francs. Nonetheless, his dreams of the Greco consoled him.

When he was finally summoned to examine the picture, however, he was furious. It was, he felt, second rate at best. He accused Mayer of having touted an inferior work. The expert was equally angry at Barnes for questioning his judgment, but the collector, who knew better, held firmly to his position and refused to buy the painting. Before long, he had still another run-in with Mayer.

This time a dealer in Biarritz called his attention to four more Grecos for sale in Bilbao, Spain, all of them reproduced in Mayer's definitive work on the artist. Barnes traveled the long distance to see them and discovered that not one of them was an authentic Greco. That was the last time he would rely on Mayer's expertise. The German was, according to Barnes, "an extreme myopic and can't see the whole of any painting at once."

The doctor had even harsher words for Bernard Berenson, whom he characterized as "the king of experts, a multi-millionaire, a scout for Duveen, and the god of all collectors and dealers." He didn't approve of the American art historian's taste for what he himself considered weak and sentimental art, and he especially deplored his influence. "Mr. Berenson's work deals not with the objective facts that enter into an appreciation of art-values, but with a form of antiquarianism made up of historical, social and sentimental interests entirely adventitious to plastic art," he wrote in *The Art in Painting*. "It would be unworthy of serious attention except for the regrettable influence his writings have had in filling our universities with bad teaching on art and our public galleries with bad Italian paintings."

Furthermore, he had no faith in Berenson's judgments or attributions, often based on the examination of photographs rather than on a careful study of the works themselves. The doctor himself had evidence of one of Berenson's mistakes—a Giorgione which he had been able to buy at a low price because the "king of experts" had certified that it was the work of a lesser-known artist. (It might have been a Giorgione, and it might not. Following Barnes's death, two eminent art historians, Sidney Friedberg and Frederick Hartt, charged that twenty-six of Barnes's paintings, among them a Giorgione, were "misrepresentations" and of little value.)

Barnes was sure of his own judgments. He became his own expert. Disillusioned by false attributions too easily pronounced by those who wanted to earn money dishonestly, he felt certain that he himself could recognize the true value of a work of art through the application of his own scientific method of study. He needed no help from others.

In its issue of September 22, 1928, *The New Yorker* published a short profile of Dr. Barnes written by A. H. Shaw. Its title was "De Medici in Merion," and it included a short account of the doctor's daily activities apart from his duties at the Foundation. They were few. Taking note of Mrs. Barnes's interest in flowers and the fact that the couple was childless, Shaw wrote that they seldom entertained and rarely went out except to attend weekly concerts of the Philadelphia Orchestra. "Dr. Barnes usually spends his evenings reading and retires early," Shaw reported. "When he can't sleep he puts on his dressing gown and walks through a passageway that connects the house and the museum, and in the gallery he studies his pictures and sometimes spends hours arranging one to suit his taste. The doctor has many books and reads continuously in English, German, or French. When he finishes reading a book the margins are often black with notes, and when the author annoys him he writes in the margin a denunciatory epithet.

"Dr. Barnes is usually at breakfast before seven o'clock, visits his gallery each morning before going to business, and reaches his office by nine o'clock."

Less than a year after Shaw's profile was published, Barnes no longer had to go to his office. In July 1929 he sold his business and the factory to Zonite Products Corporation. The price was high—six million dollars' worth of Zonite stock—and the timing was excellent: only a few months before the collapse of the stock market. For years Argyrol had absorbed little of his time; management of the factory had been largely left in the competent hands of the Mullen sisters. But now he was free to devote all of his energies to the Foundation, and he had an enormous amount of additional capital with which to enrich it. The money was already in the bank, he wrote Edith Glackens jubilantly on July 19, and he could buy pictures and no longer had to work. He expected to get drunk every night, he added.

Barnes's high spirits and his hopes that he might finally give all of his attention to his Foundation were short-lived. At the end of 1929 he was again involved in a long, time-consuming battle with the authorities. This time the issue was neither art nor education, and his opponent was neither a museum nor a university but rather the Receiver of Taxes for the city of Philadelphia.

The issue was clear-cut and simple. To replace the office space at the Argyrol factory, which had been used as the Foundation's administrative headquarters, Barnes had purchased a three-story brick residence at 4525 Spruce Street in Philadelphia. Soon after converting the home into an office, he had been presented with a tax bill. The money—$756—was of no importance, but the principle was, and the doctor refused to pay, protesting that his newly acquired property was part of a tax-exempt educational institution. The city of Philadelphia disagreed and twice rejected Barnes's appeal. As a result, in an effort to restrain the city from making further efforts to collect taxes, Barnes brought the matter to court.

The tax collectors' case was a weak one. Its attorneys charged that the building didn't look like an office, that it contained a kitchen and a bathroom with an "electric cabinet" and was actually a residence. They tried to show that the Foundation was not a nonprofit organization because of its commercial book publication program, and that there was no reason for a Philadelphia-based annex since there was room for an additional building on the Foundation's property at Merion. They even questioned the validity of the Foundation's entire educational program. At one point, they offered an astounding hypothesis concerning the doctor's goal:

> He conceived, or had suggested to him, the idea of establishing something under the guise of its being a charity, that would enable him to pose as a general benefactor, and yet allow him to have absolute control of the property involved. . . . He had some paintings, he would place them in a gallery and he would claim to be an instructor in art. He would purchase a tract of land upon part of which were growing plants and trees and call it an arboretum. . . . The corporation was formed, the endowment made to it, the deed of donation containing a clause that would enable him to take back the property when he desired. He grows tired of his surroundings and desires a handsome dwelling house in Philadelphia. This he purchases with the endowment funds, has title taken in the name of the corporation and the house fitted to suit his comfort and convenience, even to electric baths for himself. He publishes books at a price too high to find enough purchasers to pay for their production and parades as a man of culture and erudition, a great public benefactor. . . . All through his testimony he speaks for the corporation in the first person singular. He wishes his project to have the status of a purely public charity and appeals from the levy of taxes against the dwelling house, which he calls an office. . . .

The tax board's rather desperate tactics were of no avail. The Court of Common Pleas, which first heard the case, ruled in favor of the Foundation, as did the Superior Court and the Supreme Court of Pennsylvania, to which the board appealed. The entire process lasted three years; in the end it was a decisive victory for Barnes.

It should have been a routine case—its conclusion was predictable—but from the very start Barnes refused to let it go at that. Instead, he used the courtroom as a forum for a summary of his ideas and the aims of his Foundation.

He mustered all of his forces to join in the battle: among them Dewey, Buermeyer, de Mazia, Geiger, Nelle Mullen (Mary Mullen was inexplicably absent), and Mrs. Barnes. Each attested to the educational value of the Foundation. He also summoned experts in the fields of botany, horticulture, and landscape architecture to endorse the work done at the arboretum. His most distinguished witness was Dewey, whom Barnes had urged to come from New York to offer testimony on the Foundation's behalf. After being requested to present his own credentials—which Dewey did at great length—the philosopher was asked to describe the work done at the Foundation and explain how it differed from educational work done elsewhere. His reply was, for Dewey, succinct; for the court it might have been confusing:

> If I may go back to the earlier conversations—first, the aim that he had in mind—it was to differ from an ordinary museum in having a definite educational purpose. It had a social as well as an individual value, in using art, through pictures, especially, and sculpture—plastic art, as a means of getting a more intelligent attitude of appreciation of life in general— that is, the ultimate desire was to break down the separation of fine art from other things, and show what it could contribute to ordinary lives—the enrichment of life. That is, as far as this method was concerned it was one that he had worked out through many years of personal study and contact with pictures and artists and also the qualities that make painting what it is, so that the ordinary person could be trained to see pictures, and in seeing them feel what there was in them that was of artistic value, and that would also enrich the life of the individual. It is that combination of his social or human ideal— purpose—and the carefully worked out technical method of the study and analysis and understanding of pictures, observing them and feeling them, that as far as my knowledge goes

differentiates the educational work of Doctor Barnes from anything that has been done elsewhere.

Laura Barnes proved to be an especially effective witness. She was calm, dignified, and articulate. To establish her credentials, she told the court that she had studied plants at several institutions in Germany and in England. She testified that as its trustee and vice president, she was thoroughly familiar with the Foundation's work and had for ten years devoted most of her time in Merion as director of its arboretum. She further testified that the Foundation was in touch with a number of universities and schools concerning the arboretum's program, which she described to the court in detail. She affirmed, unequivocally, that there were no buildings in Merion where the administrative and research work could be carried on without spoiling the art gallery, and that the construction of a new building on the Foundation's property would cause serious damage to the arboretum.

Barnes himself was, of course, the star witness. His testimony was long and discursive; he was, in effect, using a cannon to kill a mouse. He told of his background, his education, and his career as a chemist, gave an account of his early interest in art and of the growth of his collection. He described the early days at the Argyrol factory and his first attempts to educate illiterate workers, and he told of the genesis and development of the Foundation, quoting at length from its bylaws and outlining its educational program.

His answers to queries concerning the Foundation's book publishing program were informative. Books, he claimed, were the means by which other educational institutions became acquainted with the studies undertaken at the Foundation. As a result, he noted, these institutions sent their teachers to Merion for further training, which was given willingly and without charge. He read into the record a number of letters from prominent Philadelphians and various distinguished educators praising the activities of the Foundation and offered a partial list of universities and colleges which had ordered copies of its books. He scoffed at accusations that he or the Foundation had profited from the sale of these books and offered evidence that each one had lost money. (When asked if royalties from its publications went to him or to the Foundation, he replied, "The Foundation. My identity is lost here. I am non-existent for the rest of my life.")

As an example of the enormous amount of effort involved in the preparation of each book, he spoke of the Foundation's current publishing project, *The French Primitives and Their Forms*, the first of his collaborations with de Mazia, emphasizing the work done in Europe as well as at the Foundation's Spruce Street headquarters. As the only account of the Foundation's research methods, his testimony is valuable:

Q. Where was the material collected from to prepare that book?

A. Partly in our own gallery and partly in the galleries of Europe. We have had to make six separate trips to Europe in the last three years to get our material and verify our material for that work.

Q. Is more than one person working on that book?

A. Yes; this summer I had five assistants with me in Europe besides myself, and at present we have about eight or nine people indispensable to the conduct of the thing, because it is a research. It is like science. It is not something that you can write out of your head. It is something that you have to orientate. You have to get your data. You cannot go off at half-cock. You have to get your data. It has taken us three years to do that, and nobody but a trained staff of people could do that. We have been doing that for three years. I do not know what my trip to Europe cost this year. I had about five assistants with me.

Q. And was the trip devoted entirely to this work?

A. Absolutely. And I came back sixteen pounds underweight, and another came back twenty pounds underweight. We worked incessantly. We would merely get a suite of rooms for offices. No institution has money to start it and nobody but one who is interested in the fostering of education would do it. I am very able, and very glad that that will come out of Philadelphia.

Q. You said it will require a staff of eight or nine people to prepare a book of that kind—is that correct?

A. Yes. The way it is done is this. I take a couple of stenographers with me and I go to the Louvre, or the Prado. . . . I take the stenographer with me, and I get in front of a picture and I dictate, and when that stenographer falls over we get another one. She is right on top there to take it. And then we correlate that—in the afternoon we correlate that and we go back the next day to see if it is right. The next year we go back to the same path. We do that only in the summer. In that summer we work up that material and see how it lines up, and the next summer we go back. And in the meantime, on reflection, and observation, we work out our material. It is ramified and we have to go on a good many other tracks. And then the second time we try to corroborate it. We go back again to work over it—and this year I thought the book was all done, and in the third season we went over there and found a lot of new material, and I came back from Europe with five hundred typewritten pages of material which is germane to our new subject, and it has to be incorporated into the book, which I thought was already written. That is what we are doing now. And that is all we are doing now in that building. That is all we ever will do, until that work is done, and then we have a few more things to do.

Q. It is to that that the building 4525 Spruce Street is devoted?

A. Absolutely, exclusively, and for no other purpose.

Barnes had no difficulty in refuting charges that the Spruce Street building was too elegantly furnished to be an office. If he had the furniture in his own home, he stated, he would have a headache. It was all second-hand furniture that had been used for ten years, and when the company was sold, the Foundation bought it as junk for two hundred dollars. The kitchenette was there solely to provide lunch for his employees. As for the disputed electric cabinet in the bathroom adjoining his own office, Barnes explained that it had been installed so that he might take electric baths prescribed by his physician for "some internal disturbance."

Barnes had his long day in court, and he used his time effectively. Instead of regarding the many questions put to him as an invasion of privacy, he seemed to enjoy answering most of them. In the course of his testimony, he sometimes joked. When asked if any profitable business was carried on in the building, he replied, "Absolutely no—not unless our janitor runs a crap game or something like that, and I don't think that he does." At other times, he threatened. The bylaws of the Foundation, he noted at one point, stated "if at any time it is not a success that the assets of the Foundation will be turned back to whoever the Board of Trustees see fit, and I suspect they might give them back to me." At another point, when asked if it were true that the Foundation represented an investment in art valued at more than five million dollars plus an endowment of approximately ten million dollars, he reminded his questioner that there was a string attached to that. "If the people do not behave around here, I pull that string back and it all drops in my lap," he said. "I don't expect to pull it unless they hit me too hard," he added.

Once he slipped. Referring to his gallery and its admissions policy, he declared that it was "no place for the rabble." However, he recovered quickly, if only partially, adding: "I have nothing to say against the rabble, only that it is a rabble. I came from the ranks, as I think most of our people did—what was once the rabble. The only thing is, we have risen. I am making no social criticism at all. The only thing is that the great mass of people aren't so very much interested in pictures as they are in killing time or getting a diversion. . . ."

Once, too, he was genuinely moving. He had not contested the tax for the sake of the money, he assured the court. He had offered to donate the $756 to charity. "I do not want to fight any more. I am sick of crusading," he stated. "But I do know what I have given, I have given for the good of the cause, and I am not going to be diverted by the position which is representative of the general attitude of Philadelphia. I care nothing about the law; I care nothing about losing the suit. But if I did not come here and tell you how we hear that our work is being recognized all over the world, I would not be doing my duty. . . . And we won't stop fighting. If I did that, I would be disloyal. I think there is a misunderstanding, and I suggest that we get together, if it is possible, to avoid such things in the future. That is my sole object in coming down here. . . ."

In the fall of 1930 Barnes had some good news: Henri Matisse, in his opinion the most important of all living artists, was coming to Merion. The main purpose of the painter's trip to America was to serve as a member of the jury for the prestigious Carnegie International Exhibition in Pittsburgh, but following his stay there, Matisse and some of his fellow jurors were to be taken on a short tour by Homer Saint-Gaudens, director of the Carnegie Institute. Accompanied by Dr. John F. L. Raschen of the University of Pittsburgh, who was to act as interpreter, their program included two days in Washington and one day in Philadelphia. The brief Philadelphia visit was carefully planned. As part of it, Matisse had an appointment to see Dr. Barnes in Merion at ten in the morning, while the other jurors, not invited to the Foundation, were visiting the museum. The entire group was then to meet at a luncheon at the home of Mrs. John F. Braun—to which Barnes was not invited. Afterward, a visit to the Widener collection, then housed at Elkins Park, had been scheduled.

As far as the doctor was concerned, the only valid reason for Matisse's trip was his visit to the Foundation. He was proud to have the opportunity to show his collection to an artist he profoundly admired, one who shared his passion for Renoir and Cézanne as well as his enthusiasm for Soutine. Furthermore, in greeting the most celebrated visitor to set foot in the Foundation, he was welcoming one of the few artists whose company he genuinely enjoyed—in Barnes's words, a man "of vigorous intelligence and enormous erudition," the best-informed painter he had ever met. The two men had met many years before through Leo Stein and had since that time maintained a cordial personal relationship based on mutual respect if not camaraderie—warm, intense friendships were difficult for both of them. Both were reserved and, on the surface at least, uncommonly serious, though Barnes credited Matisse with "a wit and humor that is both subtle and penetrating," not unlike his own. Both scrupulously avoided any show of bohemianism, and each was singlemindedly absorbed in his own work— Matisse in his art and Barnes in his educational theories and his collection.

In addition to the pleasure and honor he would derive from receiving Matisse at the Foundation, Barnes had professional reasons for eagerly anticipating the artist's visit. For one, it would give him an opportunity to discuss with Matisse his and de Mazia's plans for what they expected to be a definitive study of the painter's work, which they had begun only a short time before—and to discuss them in front of paintings that Matisse himself had not seen for many years. Even more important, however, Barnes planned to take advantage of the artist's visit to Merion to make him an offer that would be of great significance to both men.

Matisse had no forewarning of any such offer; he had come to the Foundation to see the collection. When he arrived there, accompanied by Dr. Raschen, Barnes met them at the door and immediately informed the interpreter that his services were not needed—though Matisse knew no English, Barnes's own French was fluent. He suggested that Raschen take a walk and return at noon to take the painter to the scheduled luncheon. He made it clear that he wanted to be alone with his celebrated visitor.

Raschen followed the doctor's orders. He returned to the Foundation at noon and rang the doorbell several times. There was no answer. In desperation he walked around the Foundation's building in search of another entrance. Finally he came upon a door to the cellar, entered it, and found himself in front of a coal shute through which he was able to reach the inside of the building. Once there the enterprising scholar found his way to the gallery, located Matisse and, taking him by the arm, led him out of the Foundation and into a waiting taxi.

It is impossible to know whether or not Barnes heard the sound of the doorbell or whether he simply ignored it. Undoubtedly he did not want his conversation with Matisse to be interrupted, above all for an inconsequential social occasion. Had it not been for Raschen's persistence, Barnes would have happily continued his talk with Matisse, causing the artist to miss the luncheon. Nonetheless, in spite of the brevity of the visit, Barnes had used his time well. He had shown the artist his extraordinary collection and had managed to ask him the question that was uppermost in his mind: would Matisse accept a commission to execute a large mural to decorate the walls of the Foundation's large, two-stories-high central gallery? Matisse was stunned. When their meeting had ended, he could do no more than promise to give this extraordinary proposal his most serious consideration.

A few days later the painter returned to France. He had been stimulated by his trip to America and had been profoundly impressed by his short visit to Merion. "One of the most striking things in America is the Barnes collection, which is exhibited in a spirit very beneficial for the formation of American artists," he told an interviewer. "There the old master paintings are put beside the modern ones, a Douanier Rousseau next to a primitive, and this bringing together helps students understand a lot of things that the academies don't teach. . . . The Barnes Foundation will doubtless manage to destroy the artificial and disreputable presentation of the other collections, where the pictures are hard to see—displayed hypocritically in the mysterious light of a temple or cathedral." He respected Barnes, too. When asked by another interviewer if the collector were really a man with a "sensuous, sensitized eye," he replied without hesitation, "He must be or how else could he have made his collection?"

While at home Matisse carefully weighed his decision. There

were good reasons to agree to Barnes's proposal. It was an unprecedented opportunity—no major European artist before him had been asked to undertake a work of such importance in America—and the doctor had granted him complete freedom. "Paint whatever you like, just as if you were painting for yourself," he had told Matisse. Furthermore, the artist believed that the Foundation, which already contained so many masterpieces of modern art, including several of his own, would be a fitting site for a new major work.

There were also negative factors to be considered. The momentous undertaking—the decoration was to fill an empty space eleven feet high by forty-seven feet long—would occupy most of the painter's time for many months. He had already accepted another commission, to illustrate an edition of Mallarmé's poetry, and the two assignments would rule out conventional easel painting during the entire period. In addition, the Barnes commission would be greatly complicated by the unusual location of the mural—it was high on a wall, above three eighteen-foot-high windows facing the entrance to the central gallery, and the wall's surface was divided by three minor vaults into three lunettes, one above each window.

It took Matisse only a short time to reach a decision. The painter had, for more than a year, been restless. Rather than return to the routine of conventional painting, which he had already neglected over the past two years, devoting his time instead to sculpture and graphic art, he was prepared to accept the difficult challenge of the Barnes commission. By late December he was back in New York, met at the pier by John Dewey, who had been delegated by Barnes to welcome him. (A few days later, the philosopher came to Matisse's room at the Hotel Plaza to pose for a portrait. The result was a series of charcoal drawings, intended as preliminary studies for a lithograph.)

From New York Matisse traveled to Merion. Once again, he studied the site's possibilities and limitations. The problems were even greater than he had remembered. His mural would have to compete with some of the finest paintings in the Foundation—

major works by Cézanne, Renoir, and Seurat lined the walls of the central gallery, and between the enormous windows, directly under the space for his mural, hung two large, powerful masterworks—Picasso's 1906 *Composition* and his own *The Riffian*, an enormous painting of a seated Moroccan, completed in 1913. Because of this, he decided to paint one continuous flowing work rather than three separate units, one for each lunette, which would add an additional row of paintings to the gallery's wall.

The location of the proposed mural, too, would cause more complex problems—of lighting and perspective—than he had originally anticipated. Light—and it was often dazzlingly bright—reached the gallery through the three windows below the lunettes, making the mural difficult to see; furthermore the area to be painted remained in the shade much of the time. In addition the mural would be seen from two perspectives. From the floor of the gallery it would be viewed only with difficulty, at an awkward angle; it could be seen with ease and at eye level only from a mezzanine facing the windows. These difficulties, he felt, could also be overcome, and in January 1931, having been given the precise measurements of the space he was to fill, he returned to Nice, ready to begin work on the monumental task.

The painter's acceptance of the commission, which would add immeasurably to the prestige of the Foundation, had been a triumph for Barnes, yet it was one he could enjoy fully for only a short time. Only weeks after Matisse's return to France, the collector was at the center of still another controversy, this one involving Philadelphia's museum and, indirectly, Matisse himself.

In February 1931, little more than a year after Barnes had rejected the museum's request to borrow his El Greco, another museum official, R. Sturgis Ingersoll, tried subtly to enlist the collector's aid in building the museum's collection. On the face of it, Ingersoll seemed destined to succeed where Kimball and Marceau had failed. A tall, thin man with a bald head and a pointed mustache, Ingersoll, the youngest of the museum's trustees, had a passion for art, especially modern art, equal to that of Barnes. The two men had known and admired one another for years. Barnes had invited Ingersoll to see his collection before the construction of the gallery, and Ingersoll had attended the official inauguration of the Foundation. Their relationship had been an altogether cordial one, and because of this, the museum trustee felt free to send a telegram to Barnes, who was now more than ever a Matisse expert, asking his advice concerning the museum's intended purchase of the painter's 1917 triptych, *The Three Sisters*, which he and Kimball had seen at Valentine Dudensing's gallery in New York. Barnes immediately granted Ingersoll's request for a meeting, during which he recommended the acquisition. He went even farther in his effort to cooperate: when Ingersoll said it would take him several days to raise the $15,000 asked by Dudensing, the doctor generously agreed to take an option on the painting on behalf of the museum. He warned, however, that the option would be a short one, since the dealer needed the money urgently and could easily sell the painting elsewhere.

On the day before the deadline, Ingersoll regretfully notified Barnes that the trustees had been unable to raise the money; the deal was off. The next day, however, their luck unexpectedly changed and he, Kimball, and Carroll Tyson, a wealthy Philadelphia collector, managed to obtain a note from the Provident Trust Company which would enable them to buy the triptych for the museum. They acted quickly. As soon as they left the bank, Kimball and Ingersoll hurried to the latter's office to phone the news to the doctor. They had heard of another collector who, while crossing the Atlantic with Barnes, had mentioned his intention to buy a certain painting and had learned after his arrival that Barnes had radioed from the ship and bought that same painting ahead of him. They didn't want the same thing to happen to the museum and so they took every possible precaution. Ingersoll instructed his secretary to put in a call to Dudensing, hold the line, and then on another line, put in a call to Barnes. Kimball, eavesdropping on a third telephone, made careful note of the conversation which followed:

INGERSOLL: We take the picture.

BARNES (*after a silence*): You're just too late. Dudensing said he had to have cash at once and I have paid for it.

INGERSOLL: But Dr. Barnes . . .

BARNES: I have the picture.

INGERSOLL: You're going to let us have it?

BARNES: The hell I will.

INGERSOLL: I am very much disappointed.

BARNES: It is a peach of a picture. I told you I couldn't obligate myself. Yesterday you told me you couldn't get the money.

INGERSOLL: You say the door is closed?

BARNES: Yes.

INGERSOLL: I have the check for $15,000 to your order on my desk.

BARNES: There is nothing I can do about it.

After Barnes hung up, Ingersoll learned from his secretary that she had been disconnected from Dudensing. She tried the number again, but the line was busy; when Ingersoll finally reached the gallery, he learned that the picture had been sold to Barnes. Though he made every effort to do so, Kimball never managed to find out exactly when Barnes had purchased *The Three Sisters*, but he suspected he had done so while Ingersoll was trying to reach the dealer. He returned the check to the bank and sent the canceled note to Carroll Tyson, adding his own comment, "We always knew that Barnes was a son of a bitch, and now we can prove it." Tyson returned Kimball's letter, with his own notation, "Approved. Please return for signing."

For the museum's directors, it was one more proof of Barnes's unreasonable hostility; even worse, in depriving the institution of a painting which would have enriched its collection, he had once again demonstrated his insatiable greed. Barnes, on the other hand, maintained that he had kept his word and had bought *The Three Sisters* only when Ingersoll had notified him that the museum could not raise the money in time. As far as he was concerned, Ingersoll's request for advice had been only a deception; the trustee had really been trying to get him, Barnes, to buy the painting for the museum. In New York stories spread that Dudensing himself had been at fault and had played Barnes and the museum against one another. Whatever the truth, Philadelphians preferred to believe that their museum had been the victim of the irascible doctor's deception and immoral behavior. Threats of suits and countersuits followed, but nothing came of them. The charges hurt Barnes, however. He was unable to forget them, and almost four years later he made public a letter he had received from Dudensing as proof that the widely circulated rumor was a lie and that "the story could have originated only in the imagination of either an ignoramus or an ungrateful son-of-a-bitch." Dated November 22, 1934, the letter read:

Dear Dr. Barnes:

Permit me to confirm the following facts concerning the sale and ownership of the picture "Three Sisters" by Matisse:

On February 21, 1931, you offered me fifteen thousand ($15,000) dollars for the picture and I accepted on condition that you pay the money immediately because I needed it to make settlement on a property which I was buying. You asked me to allow you a couple of days delay so that you could talk to Mr. R. Sturgis Ingersoll and see if he could raise the $15,000 to buy the picture for the Pennsylvania Museum of Art. I agreed to the delay requested but again insisted that it might not consist of more than two or three days. On February 25, 1931, you telephoned me and stated that Mr. Ingersoll informed you that he could not raise the money immediately and asked for a delay of one week so that he could try to obtain the necessary $15,000. My reply to you at that time was that I sold the picture to you under certain conditions, that you had not complied with the conditions, and that if I did not receive your check on the following day your option would expire and I would sell the picture to another client.

On the morning of February 26, 1931, I received the check

of the Barnes Foundation for $15,000, with the clear under-
standing that the picture belonged to the Barnes Foundation
and that the transaction was completed.

Along with this letter, Barnes provided the press with copies
of a letter he had written to Ingersoll. Noting that he had not sued
the museum trustee because "in economic, intellectual, and aesthetic capital you are what is termed 'a poor fish' " (in the future
he referred to him as "sturgeon"), he continued:

> Before you sent me the telegram . . . asking for my help to
> keep up your bluff in public as an art connoisseur, I was
> already familiar with your reputation in Paris as a boob to
> whom the dealers could sell any worthless picture so long as
> it bore the name of a well-known artist—a reputation amply
> corroborated in Philadelphia by the junk you exhibit in public
> as your collection of modern art. I knew also of your activities
> among the groups of tea-tasters, morons and social parasites
> to whom you purvey piffle in the form of lectures on modern
> art. For the past three years I have known you as the alleged
> circulator of a libel; in short, as a person who has neither the
> basis of fact to face an issue in Court or the guts to settle a
> grudge with his fists. . . .

Barnes never forgave Ingersoll, who wrote of his last meeting
with the doctor, a chance encounter on a trolley car a year or so
before Barnes's death: "On my alighting from the car . . . he leaned
out and shouted: 'You are not only a liar but a son-of-a-bitch.' "

Probably oblivious of the controversy concerning the purchase
of *The Three Sisters*, Matisse had, upon his return to Nice, rented
an enormous abandoned movie studio in which to work on his
mural. As his inspiration, he drew on his earlier composition, *La
Danse*, a large canvas depicting six dancing figures commissioned
by the great Russian collector Sergei Shchukin and completed in
1910. In an interview with Gaston Diehl, Matisse described the

genesis of his idea, and the methods used in painting the Barnes mural:

> I had conceived *La Danse* long before, and had put it in
> *La Joie de Vivre*, then in my first big *La Danse* composition.
> But, this time, when I wanted to make sketches on three can-
> vases of one metre, I couldn't get it. Finally, I took three
> canvases of five metres, the very dimensions of the panels, and
> one day, armed with charcoal on the end of a bamboo stick,
> I set out to draw the whole thing at one go. It was already
> there, in me, like a rhythm which carried me along. I had the
> surface in mind. But once the drawing finished, when I came
> to colour it, I had to change all the pre-arranged forms. I had
> to fill the whole thing, and give a whole that would remain
> architectural. On the other hand, I had to be closely allied to
> the masonry, so that the lines should hold their own against
> the enormous, projecting blocks of the down-curving arches,
> and even more important, that the lines should follow across
> them with sufficient vitality to accord with each other. To
> compare all that and obtain something alive and singing, I
> could only proceed by groping my way, continually modifying
> my panels in colours and in black.

Then followed what the artist described as a giant game of checkers. He drew the forms of his dancers on large sheets of colored paper, cut them out, and directed his assistants to pin them on the canvas. Only by arranging them and rearranging them con-stantly could he finally achieve his aim.

It was an exhausting undertaking. Both at work and away from it, Matisse was obsessed with the mural. When the summer after he had begun his work, he joined Barnes and his students in their visits to many of Paris's museums and galleries and Barnes asked, jokingly, why he was spending time with them instead of working on his mural in Nice, Matisse could only reply wearily that he was really working on it all the time.

Matisse continued to work feverishly, without interruption,

until late February 1932, when he finally obtained a balance of form which completely satisfied him. Only when his gigantic task was near completion, and the design transferred in oil onto a huge canvas, did he realize that he had miscalculated the measurement of the mural space, which had been correctly given to him by Albert Nulty. The meticulous artist was distraught. It was his own mistake, not Nulty's as Barnes's critics later charged. He cabled his deepest regrets to Barnes and without hesitation made a decision that was to cost him several more months of arduous work. Instead of trying to adjust his nearly completed canvas to the correct measurements (the error was a small one), he would begin again on what would be known as the second version of *The Dance*. (The first version, different in many ways from the second, was presented to the Modern Art Museum of the City of Paris.)

Using the same method he had employed for the first version, Matisse spent several more months on the mural—a period marked by nervous tension, anxiety, and occasional bouts of despair. Finally, on March 7, 1933, he was able to write to a friend, Simon Bussy: "The end is near—won or lost." In May, his task completed, the painter accompanied his enormous canvas to Merion for the installation. According to Violette de Mazia, the installation did not go as smoothly as it might have—the artist rather insistently demanded the removal of the low-relief African frieze running below the mural as well as the removal of the large Picasso and his own *Riffian*, demands to which Barnes would not accede. Matisse, for his part, made no mention of any such disagreement. He told an interviewer, Dorothy Dudley, that he had been "*ravi*" by his experience at the Foundation. "I reached Merion on a Friday and all was installed by Monday," he reported. "As soon as I saw the decoration in place I felt it was detached absolutely from myself, and that it took on a meaning quite different from what it had had in my studio, where it was only a painted canvas. There in the Barnes Foundation it became a rigid thing, heavy as stone, and one that seemed to have been spontaneously created at the same time with the building. . . ."

In the same vein, he described his feelings in another letter to

Simon Bussy written from New York on May 17: "It is a splendid thing," he said, "which one can have no idea of without having seen it—since the whole arched ceiling radiates out—and this effect even extends down to the ground. I am extremely tired but very pleased. Having seen the picture in place—I now feel disconnected from it. I feel it has become part of the building—and I no longer think of the work that has gone into it, the past; it has acquired its own personality. . . . Seeing the picture again was a real *birth*, relieving me of the labor and pain that led up to it."

Matisse returned to Europe in a state of physical and nervous exhaustion—he immediately traveled to Italy for a treatment of restorative baths—but the experience had been a rewarding one. "When I'm on the point of sinking into a depression," he wrote Bussy on June 18, "I pull myself together by reminding myself of the complete success of that famous panel. I could have exhausted myself without the consolation of having brought it off success-fully."

While Matisse was expressing his satisfaction with the mural, Barnes had surprisingly little to say about the dynamic composition of leaping, spinning faceless figures which adorns the space above the windows of the Foundation's main gallery. It was rumored that he didn't like it. He told the artist, according to Matisse himself, "One would call the place a cathedral now. Your painting is like a rose window of a cathedral"; but he made no public pronounce-ments. Nor did he mention the mural in his enormous book on Matisse, though he had written Dewey that he would not deliver the manuscript to the publisher, Charles Scribner's Sons, until he had had a chance to study it.

Instead, *The Art of Henri-Matisse* was published in early 1933, before the mural had been installed. The book had consumed a tremendous amount of the doctor's energy as well as that of his collaborator, Miss de Mazia. During June and July of 1931 alone, they accumulated more than one thousand pages of typewritten notes of analysis, based on their daily visits to a Matisse retro-spective held at the Georges Petit Galleries in Paris. Since then they had spent as many as twelve hours a day—from nine in the morning until nine at night—working on the book. In September 1932, after three and a half more months of intensive study in Europe, the manuscript was delivered to the publisher.

The result of their efforts, unusual in that it devoted much space to the artist's limitations, was not very well received by the press. Anthony Blunt, writing for *The Spectator*, summed up the opinion of most reviewers by finding the 464-page volume heavy going. "This is not a book to be put in the hands of a generally intelligent person wishing to be converted to Matisse," he wrote. "Its massiveness, its gloomy binding which makes it look like a nineteenth-century treatise on birth-control, its pretentious chapter headings would all repel any but the most serious-minded devotee of modern painting. Any reader, therefore, who is prepared to surmount these minor, superficial difficulties will hope to find in the book a permanent contribution to our knowledge of painting, a sound evaluation of the achievement of Matisse, a systematic analysis of his methods. But he will be disappointed. If he succeeds in toiling through the 300 pages of text [there were 135 pages of illustrations], he will probably be left at exactly the same point as at the beginning."

For once, Barnes, already absorbed in his work with de Mazia on their more exhaustive and more enthusiastic study of Renoir, didn't bother to answer his critics. Surprisingly, he even ignored the mildly negative comments of his old friend, Leo Stein. Relations between the two men had been unfriendly since their bitter quarrel over *The Art in Painting*—they had been, in Stein's words, "on unspeaking terms." They had reconciled during a brief meeting in a Parisian gallery in the early thirties, but following that they had again lost touch. For this reason Stein was shocked to learn, through a letter from a friend a year later, that the dedication of Barnes's recently published book on Matisse—which he had never received—read: "To Leo Stein, who was the first to recognize the genius of Matisse, and who, more than twenty years ago, inspired the study which has culminated in this book."

Stein was amused. "Otherwise I have heard nothing of the book or from Barnes," he wrote his friend Mabel Weeks. "Who could have done this except Barnes?"

Several months later a copy of the book finally arrived, accompanied by an apologetic note from its author explaining that the delay had been caused by his inability to find Stein's address. Stein replied as soon as he had read the book. His letter of October 20, 1934, began with words of praise. "It seems to me much better than your first book—the style is more elastic and agreeable," he wrote, and he concluded on a similar note, stating that he was "quite content to stand as godfather to its remote beginnings." In between, however, Stein complained of the lack of colored plates— a complaint the doctor chose to ignore.

The publication of *The Art of Henri-Matisse* marked a renewal of the friendship between Barnes and Stein. "Barnes and me has become the greatest chums that ever was," Stein wrote Weeks in November 1934. Curiously, however, the book—and the completion of the mural—signaled an end to the relationship between the collector and Matisse. Following the installation, they spent time together at Mallorca, but the weather was bad and their visit was not too pleasant. At another time Matisse greeted Barnes on his arrival at Villefranche. Barnes's first words were, "Could you lend me money for a tip?" The artist did and never again saw Barnes. According to Pierre Matisse, the artist's son, his father had become irrelevant to the doctor.

16

Dr. Barnes wasn't always angry. For a period, during the mid-1930s, he seemed to mellow, to be uncharacteristically—if not quite comfortably—at peace with the world. The devil, who some believed had frequently taken possession of his soul, had apparently been exorcised. He was willing to forgive and forget his past quarrels with his two most hated enemies—the university and the art museum—and to share his achievements with the public and the press.

In this spirit of reconciliation, he replied graciously and helpfully in 1934 to a request from George Simpson Koyl, the new dean of Penn's School of Fine Arts, for suggestions concerning a reorganization of the school's program. But when Koyl ignored his advice and instead sent Barnes a series of fulsome, flattering letters implying that a permanent alliance between the university and the Foundation might still be realized, the doctor responded predictably. He again fired the university and added that steps had already been taken to "make sure that, after my death, the University will have no finger in our pie." Yet inexplicably he took no such steps at the time. The Foundation's bylaws were not changed, and the university remained empowered, after his death and that of his wife, to play a role in the choice of its trustees. Whether to gain respectability through an alliance with the establishment he claimed to hate or merely to find a home for his collection, he still hoped to work out an arrangement between his alma mater and his Foundation.

Evidently he had not yet abandoned all hopes of working with the Philadelphia Museum either, and this time the doctor himself took the initiative. In 1936 a series of tapestries based on designs by France's leading contemporary artists—Picasso, Matisse, Rouault, Raoul Dufy, and Fernand Léger among them—and woven in the world-famous factories of Aubusson and Beauvais, had been exhibited in New York. They proved to be of considerable commercial as well as artistic value, and Barnes, who saw himself as France's unofficial cultural ambassador to the United States, took special pride in their success, proclaiming it to the nation via the facilities of the National Broadcasting Company. These tapestries represented "an epoch in art history," he told his listeners, while at the same time explaining at considerable length the educational methods and achievements of his Foundation, which he announced had acquired some of the tapestries for its own collection.

When, only a few months later, he learned that a new series of tapestries had been completed, he decided to share his discovery with the Philadelphia public. In November 1936, putting aside his long-standing differences, he wrote to John S. Jenks, a vice president of the Philadelphia Museum. Enclosing a copy of his earlier radio address, he offered to arrange for an exhibition of these new tapestries at the museum. Museum officials, stunned by their old enemy's unexpected show of good will and his apparent desire to ingratiate himself with his fellow Philadelphians, responded immediately. Within a week Jenks was able to report that the museum's committee had approved the plan. There was only one problem: the museum could contribute no more than one hundred dollars toward the costs of the exhibition. Barnes remained undaunted. As a civic-minded Philadelphian, he agreed to help solve this problem. "It's a big event for Philadelphia," he wrote Jenks, "so we'll have to put our heads together and get the money somehow."

He remained undaunted, too, when only a few weeks later he

received a cable from Paris informing him, without explanation, that the exhibition would have to be postponed. Immediately relaying the news to Jenks, he assured him that he would continue to pursue the matter and still hoped that the museum would be able to show the tapestries. As a consolation he invited Jenks and Henry McIlhenny, who was to be in charge of the exhibition, to "come to our gallery on Sunday, December 13th, at which time we shall have some good singing of Negro spirituals, and if I'm not too lazy I'll have something to say about the relation between what Negroes sing and what our painters put in their pictures." (It had become the doctor's favorite lecture, and he was never too lazy to deliver it.)

Shortly after that Sunday afternoon, the doctor traveled to Paris. There he learned the reason for the postponement—the French government had bought some of the finest tapestries from the new series for its own museums. Still undiscouraged, he wrote McIlhenny that this would only add to the prestige of the exhibition, which he assured him could be held in Philadelphia in the fall of 1937. Making it clear that he was working for the good of his native city, he offered to take care of each and every detail while acting as liaison between French officials and the museum. There were, he was certain, no obstacles that could not be overcome. His idyllic relationship with the museum continued.

During these relatively trouble-free years, too, Barnes's collection grew in quality as well as quantity, and he seemed to find increased satisfaction in it. Once again, because of the Foundation's refusal to allow outsiders—and this included even the most serious of scholars—to examine its records, it is impossible to learn exactly what he bought and when. Nonetheless, through a study of contemporary newspapers and magazines, memoirs of the doctor's associates, and statements by Barnes himself, it is clear that his aim during the thirties was to deepen rather than to broaden the scope of his collection. Modern art had come of age in America. New York's Museum of Modern Art had opened in 1929, and the Whitney Museum was created in 1931. Americans were talking about

Kandinsky and other abstract artists and about members of the German school: Klee, Kokoschka, and Beckmann. They debated the merits of the Surrealists Ernst and Dali, and discovered Rivera and other Mexican painters and muralists. But Barnes ignored these and went his own way. His acquisitions reflected his desire to fill in the gaps in his collection and to make it a more useful educational tool rather than to extend it to new territories. To achieve his goal he continued to buy from any and all sources.

He made many purchases from New York's Anderson Galleries, among them a portrait of a Dutch burgher by Franz Hals for which he paid $47,500. He frequently lunched with the galleries' director, Major Parke, who after watching his client's dramatic gestures and listening to his rambling diatribes, unfailingly returned to his job exasperated. In 1931 he acquired a Matisse and what he considered an extraordinary Rouault from a New York gallery—and, even more important, he wrote Dewey, two dozen bottles of a twenty-five-year-old Scotch, which was said to be the favorite of the King of England. That same year he purchased a major El Greco and returned two Georgia O'Keeffe paintings— among his very few acquisitions from Stieglitz, for which he had paid $2,400—because of a disagreement over a damaged frame. (His interest in American art had diminished—he wanted another O'Keeffe but refused to pay Stieglitz's price—though in the thirties he bought his first and only Milton Avery, *Nursemaid*, from Valentine Dudensing's gallery.)

In 1932 Barnes bought two paintings from Knoedler's, one of New York's most distinguished galleries. One was a small Renoir, *Femme Tricotant*, for which he paid $6,000; the other was a Cézanne landscape, *Les Terres Rouges*, which cost him $30,000. Through Knoedler's and Berlin's Matthiessen Gallery, he also tried to acquire major works from a private Russian collection which had been expropriated by the Soviet government and were being offered for sale in Western Europe. Complicated negotiations lasted for several months—understandably Barnes was excited by the prospect of purchasing many of the Matisses, Gauguins, Cézannes, Picassos, Van Goghs, and other masterpieces which might be available—but the political and legal situation was confused and the rights of ownership unclear, and by January 1933 he lost interest.

In 1934 alone, he managed to acquire three paintings by Seurat, two Cézanne landscapes, and five Renoirs. One Renoir was, in his opinion, a work of rare artistic importance. Another—and this continued to delight him—was a genuine bargain; a collector who had paid $74,000 for it a few years before had sold it to him for $27,000. The worldwide Depression and unsettled conditions in Europe had deflated the art market. Big spenders, he explained to Dewey, no longer had money, and as a consequence he had for some time been able to buy the cream for less than the price of skim milk in more prosperous times.

In April of the following year the doctor caused a stir in New York art circles by acquiring (not at bargain prices, it can be assumed) two undisputed masterpieces of Renoir's classical period— a portrait of Mademoiselle Jeanne Durand-Ruel and *La Famille Henriot*. He not only purchased them, but he announced his acquisitions to the press. Reporters made much of the fact that the astute collector had bought both paintings within a period of less than twenty-four hours, and that it took him only minutes to make up his mind on each, but the truth is less dramatic. Barnes, fully aware of their importance, had been after the two canvases for a number of years, and the news was that he was finally, through long and patient negotiation, able to add them to his collection.

Barnes was now an acknowledged Renoir expert. The book on the Impressionist master on which he and de Mazia had worked so hard was published in 1935, and he derived special satisfaction from it. An homage to his favorite painter, it contained a foreword by Dewey, praising the work of the Foundation, as well as his own lengthy introduction restating and clarifying his educational principles and his method of art appreciation. Reviews of the 515-page volume (including 158 illustrations) were once again mixed—most critics agreed with Edward Alden Jewell of the *New York Times*, who noted that "the going is very heavy, due in part to the stiff, dry, stodgy style, in which the whole book is written"—but the doctor could find solace in the words of James Johnson Sweeney, a respected critic and art historian he esteemed and had befriended, who hailed the work as "an achievement in America as well as the milestone in the appreciation of Renoir it represents."

Barnes could find even more consolation in his own collection. The number of Renoirs at Merion had now reached more than 175, but the collection was distinguished not just for its size, but for the wide range of the artist's work it represented. There were selections from each period of his career, canvases of tremendous beauty and fundamental importance as well as minor, apparently insignificant, and sometimes second-rate examples of the art of an acknowledged master. Whatever Barnes bought, he bought for a reason, and he wanted his Renoirs to include every aspect and stage of the painter's development. One French dealer, Marcelle Berr de Turique, who feared that her selection of Renoirs would be of little interest to the world-famous collector, was surprised when Barnes, without hesitation, chose to buy an early, immature head of an Italian woman, a painting influenced by Courbet and not at all a reflection of Renoir's own genius. Only later, after talking with the doctor, did she understand that he purchased not only what he liked but also what he felt was of significance in the artist's progress. (She was even more surprised to find the notoriously cantankerous Philadelphian to be a charming and affable companion, as she drove him through the streets of Paris while he taught her English by naming the parts of an automobile.)

Though Barnes's taste remained unchanged during the 1930s— he bought paintings which would have interested him twenty years before—he seemed more relaxed and comfortable as he went about enlarging his collection. If this was indeed the case, his new mood might be attributed to a change in dealers, for in his acquisitions during that period he was, for the most part, represented not by his old friend and colleague Guillaume, but by another Parisian, Étienne Bignou.

Not long after Guillaume's memorable visit to Merion, he and the doctor had begun to grow apart. Though Guillaume continued to act effectively for several more years as Barnes's man in Paris, he did so with diminishing dedication. Under the influence of his wealthy and glamorous wife, who liked Barnes as little as she liked American cooking, he devoted less of his time to his principal client and became, himself, primarily a curator and a collector, often unwilling to part with the masterpieces he had bought over the years. (Guillaume's collection and that of his wife is now housed in Paris's Orangerie des Tuileries. When the collection was first shown in 1984, many critics were disappointed, one of them, Pierre Schneider of *L'Express*, noting that "to discover the boldness and soundness of Paul Guillaume's taste, one must go to Merion, Pennsylvania, to the Barnes Foundation.")

Guillaume died in 1934 at the age of forty-two. Before his death, he and Barnes had quarreled, and their relationship had come to an end. According to one New York dealer, Guillaume had slipped on a banana peel, placed there by a rival who resented Guillaume's role—and profits—as the Philadelphian's exclusive representative, and who had quite probably let the collector know, correctly or incorrectly, that his old friend was taking double commissions on his sales. Barnes never aired his differences with Guillaume in public; obviously he was hurt by the manner in which their long and warm relationship had come to an end. He preferred to remember the man he had come to know in "The Temple," and an "interview" which he presumably granted to *The Art News* in October 1934, lauding the recently deceased dealer, was nothing but an abbreviated version of the article he had written about Guillaume for *Opportunity* ten years earlier.

Following Barnes's break with Guillaume, Bignou became the doctor's principal dealer. A small, trim man, with an enormous knowledge of European art, artists, and dealers, Bignou had been born in Paris in 1891 and had spent much of his youth in London. At the age of eighteen, he was called back to the French capital by his stepfather, an art dealer on the rue Lafitte. There he learned the business. His tastes progressed steadily. Until 1914 he sold old masters of the Italian and Flemish schools; after the war his interests turned to Boudin and Fantin-Latour; following that, he championed the cause of the Impressionists, above all in England; and by

1923 he was deeply involved with painters of the modern school. In 1927 he opened his own small gallery—not far from Guillaume's—on the rue La Boétie.

Restless and energetic, more excited by discovering and acquiring fine paintings than by selling them, Bignou maintained that he was neither a poet nor a philosopher. Unburdened by theories of aesthetics, he was, in his own words, "a merchant of beautiful things . . . the right man in the right place." As such he was immensely successful, especially as agent in France for the distinguished American collector Chester Dale and as a discerning, knowledgeable guide for Barnes. Bignou's drive and his instincts impressed even the master dealer Vollard, who wrote in his memoirs: "In the morning he is in London; in the evening he opens an exhibition in Paris; the next day he takes a ship to New York. . . . If he is always traveling around the world, it is because wherever there is a painting to see, he is attracted as if by a magnet."

Because of this feverish activity, which prevented him from giving any one client his undivided attention, Bignou in time ceded his role in Barnes's life to his partner, Georges Keller, who had originally introduced him to the Philadelphian. Keller, born in Paris of Swiss parents, had served his apprenticeship under a legendary dealer, Hodebert, at the Barbazanges gallery—it was there that he first met Barnes and sold to him. Following Hodebert's death in the late 1920s, the young man set up his own gallery, and in 1932 he entered into a partnership with Bignou. Together they ran the original Étienne Bignou gallery in Paris and, later, the Bignou gallery in New York, which was established in 1935.

Diplomatic and taciturn—he once reported that during a heated discussion with an opponent he looked him "blank in the face"— Keller was ideally suited for his position as Barnes's man, both in Paris and in New York. He was not only a dealer of taste and intelligence and a skilled negotiator; he was also—and this was essential—willing and able to meet the collector's considerable demands and conditions for employment. He was unfailingly loyal to his client, and he made certain that the doctor knew it. When another dealer, Pierre Matisse, complained to Keller that he came away hungry from a Sunday-night dinner at Merion, Keller dutifully passed along the word to Barnes—who mentioned it to Matisse but was completely unaffected and kept offering Sunday guests the same spartan meals, usually consisting of ham and lettuce.

He also, at times, played another role in the doctor's life, which was described by a rival dealer, Julien Levy, after he met the two men during an ocean voyage to Europe. "Keller's major responsibility," Levy wrote in his memoirs, "was to nurse the doctor, to suggest his menu, recommend wines, plan his itinerary, see to his amusements, and possibly, in fact quite probably, even brush his teeth." There was far more to it than that, however, and in spite of Levy's derisory comment, Keller, while subservient, was far more than a nursemaid-secretary to Barnes. He and Bignou both proved to be of immeasurable help to the doctor in his quest for significant additions to his collection during the 1930s and later, until, according to one report, Keller finally tired of his principal client's demands and retired to an island in the Caribbean.

The new Barnes—an enthusiastic collector, proud of his achievements and eager to let the world know of them—was very much in evidence during the fall of 1936. It was the peak of his period of good will, and he wasn't angry at anyone. When, accompanied by de Mazia, he returned from Europe in early September, he was positively exuberant. Apparently willing to forgive still another enemy—the press this time—he granted an interview on board the *Normandie* shortly before its arrival in New York. It was the first time he had done so following a buying trip since his triumphant Parisian visit of 1922. Unusually excited by what he had seen and done and acquired, he was unable to keep the news to himself. Chief among his satisfactions were the many hours spent at l'Orangerie, at the enormous Cézanne retrospective—he and de Mazia were already at work on a study of the painter, who was to be the subject of their third and final monograph. On the occasion of the exhibition (the Foundation owned seventy-five Cézannes), he was again honored by the French government, promoted to the rank of Officer of the Légion d'Honneur at a private dinner held in the French capital.

He had added significantly to his collection as well. His new acquisitions—he had spent more than a half million dollars, he reported—included nine paintings: Manet's well-known masterpiece, *Le Linge*; two Cézannes, *The Drinker* and *The Woodchopper*; four Matisse interior scenes; and two canvases by Raoul Dufy. In addition, he had purchased two rare pieces of Classical Greek sculpture and an Egyptian sculpture of 1800 B.C. He was particularly pleased with the latter. "I was thunderstruck when I saw it," he told the reporter. "The chap who had it had been over to London with it, but the British Museum couldn't raise the money."

The doctor was equally exuberant in his treatment of two distinguished visitors from abroad. The first of these was Giorgio de Chirico, who had come to América in the summer of 1935. Barnes did more than welcome him; he tried to appropriate him during his entire extended stay in the States. As one of the first Americans to collect the artist's work—the Foundation owned twenty-five of his paintings—and as his sponsor (it was reported that Barnes had paid for the Italian's passage), Barnes felt he had every right to control the artist's career in America.

De Chirico apparently disagreed. At first he observed the overbearing collector's behavior with a combination of amusement and mild irritation, but by the fall of 1936—the time of the painter's first large New York exhibition, at Julien Levy's gallery—he was tired of it. From the outset, Barnes made it known that he was in charge by demanding that he himself write a long preface to the catalogue. Levy hesitated—he thought Barnes was a pompous writer—but when the doctor agreed to subsidize the catalogue, he had no choice—the gallery didn't have sufficient funds to pay for the lavish catalogue it would have liked to issue. "One shouldn't look a gift Barnes in the mouth," the dealer noted in his memoirs.

Barnes insisted, too, that the pictures be hung exactly the way he wanted them to be hung—this, after the painter and his dealer had spent the entire evening hanging them to their own satisfaction.

After reluctantly agreeing to Barnes's demands, Levy and the painter worked for hours, moving the pictures from place to place at the doctor's command. Finally they were hung in the manner dictated by the collector. "To my intense amusement," Levy wrote, "they now hung in precisely the same order that Giorgio and I had originally placed them."

Barnes wanted his way when it came to pricing the paintings as well. When the two men told him what they had decided would be fair prices to ask, he became furious. Insisting that their low prices would undercut the value of his own paintings, he demanded that the gallery's prices be raised tenfold. Afraid to do otherwise, de Chirico and Levy agreed; but they also agreed secretly that the doctor would be shown one price list, his own revised one, and the other clients another, their original one. At the opening Barnes carefully selected five paintings that he wanted to reserve. When he asked the prices, Levy dutifully showed him the special Barnes price list. The doctor was horrified—the prices were far too high, he claimed, and he insisted on a fifty percent discount. Levy quickly agreed to his terms, to the satisfaction of all concerned.

Following the exhibition the relationship between Barnes and de Chirico came to an end. The doctor, apparently agreeing with most critics that de Chirico's creative gifts had started to wane at the time, stopped buying his paintings after 1936. For his part, the artist, upon his return to Europe in 1938, paid what can only be considered a surrealistic tribute to his former patron. It appeared in the magazine, *L'Ambrosiano*, and in it he wrote:

> When Dr. Barnes started his museum, many years ago, he raised a wave of indignation and protest from right-minded society. He was mocked and thought of as a madman, and because of that today he is a kind of Captain Nemo, the Jules Verne character: a lonely man who, because of a highly developed feeling for justice, cannot forget and therefore punishes those who have risen up against him. Dr. Barnes has been offered, many times, enormous sums of money to yield his museum to the government so that it could be transformed

into a public museum. Dr. Barnes doesn't even answer these offers. He lives there, alone, with his Patagonian mastiffs, among the paintings he loves so much. He knows that those paintings will disappear with him. Indeed, the basement of the museum is mined. It is written in Dr. Barnes's will that when he dies he is to be laid in the main room of the museum; then, after everybody has been led far away, an old, loyal servant—positioned at a safe distance—will push a lever and the magnificent collection, together with the mortal remains of its creator, will float up in the air.

Later de Chirico turned decisively against his Captain Nemo, and in his memoirs he wrote bitterly of his collection. "In reality," he wrote, "his museum includes merely the paintings that everyone can see in Paris by taking a walk along the rue La Boétie or the rue de Seine. The usual ridiculous Cézannes, the usual badly painted and formless Matisses. . . . In addition, on the walls of the museum can be seen paintings which look like frescoes by Matisse and seem to be frescoes when you first look at them, but I believe that they are canvases stuck on to the walls, and they are the most insipid, silly, vacuous and grotesque paintings that I have ever seen."

In the fall of 1936 Barnes welcomed to America another visitor, and a far more appreciative one—Ambroise Vollard. Though he sometimes referred to him jokingly as Vollard-*voleur* (Vollard-thief), the collector had long revered the legendary dealer who had defied popular taste and had gone his own way in championing the works of Cézanne, Renoir, Van Gogh, and many others long before it was fashionable to do so. Admiring his courage and his taste, Barnes saw in him a kindred spirit as well as a shrewd and perceptive dealer, "a leader in molding intelligent, well-informed public opinion," entitled to "high esteem as an educator."

Vollard, who had often sold to the Philadelphian, returned the compliment. "Mr. Barnes comes to see you," he wrote. "He gets you to show him twenty or thirty pictures. Unhesitatingly, as they pass before him, he picks out this one or that one. Then he goes away. In this expeditious fashion, which only a taste as sure as his made possible, Mr. Barnes has brought together the incomparable collection which is the pride of Philadelphia."

The seventy-one-year-old dealer, a bearish figure with a short-cropped, scruffy beard, arrived in New York on October 27, 1936. It was his first visit to the United States. Though he hated traveling and avoided it whenever possible, he had accepted Barnes's invitation and had given in to Bignou's and Keller's pleas to attend the opening at their gallery of an important Cézanne exhibition, which included the artist's well-known portrait of Vollard. From the very beginning of this visit, too, it was clear that Barnes was in charge—but this time nobody complained. The opening of the exhibition was serious and dignified, as the doctor wanted it to be. The main gallery, to the surprise of those who had come merely to look at paintings, was filled with chairs. There were speeches to be heard as well as pictures to be enjoyed. The speakers had been chosen by Barnes. The first was Dewey, and the second was the doctor himself, who, after addressing the audience, introduced the guest of honor.

On November 8, Vollard traveled to Merion—to see the collection, which included many works he himself had discovered, treasured, and sold many years before, and to deliver a lecture before an audience made up of the Foundation's students and a small number of specially invited guests. Barnes had taken the opportunity of the dealer's visit to ingratiate himself with many of his old enemies, among them some of New York's leading art critics, most of whom had previously been refused permission to come to the gallery.

It was an unprecedented gesture of reconciliation, and Barnes, the perfect host, made the day a memorable one for all concerned. The guests were permitted to wander through the gallery unescorted, enjoying the rare privilege of seeing the collection's many masterpieces. They were also permitted to sample their host's extraordinary Scotch, and they were treated to an uncommonly sumptuous dinner. "If there had been the faintest touch of eccentricity anywhere in this entertainment," Henry McBride of the New York

Sun, among those staggered by the collection and stunned by their host's gracious behavior, commented, "I failed to notice it."

Vollard was as enthusiastic about his day at the Foundation as were the other guests. In his memoirs he recounted an amusing anecdote concerning his visit. "While I was at Dr. Barnes's, I fell from the top of a flight of stairs," he wrote, "and it's a miracle that I didn't break a bone. 'Ah, Vollard,' cried my host, when I was back on my feet. 'If you had been killed, I would have buried you in the middle of the Foundation.' " More seriously, on the eve of his departure for France, the dealer expressed his gratitude to America and Americans via a radio broadcast on station WINS— he was introduced by Barnes, whose introduction was considerably longer than Vollard's own speech. "The great experience of this very short trip," the Frenchman told his listeners, "has been my visit to the Barnes Foundation. . . . I assure you that there does not exist and will never exist in the world another collection of masterpieces of the two greatest painters of the nineteenth century, Cézanne and Renoir, comparable to the one assembled there by Dr. Barnes."

The afterglow of Vollard's visit was short-lived, as was Barnes's truce with a whole world of enemies, real and imagined. The devil repossessed his soul, and the Philadelphia Museum was the first to feel the force of the blows delivered by the man the press had sometimes disrespectfully characterized as the "Fighting Philadelphian." The truce with the museum was still in effect in March 1937, when John Jenks wrote Barnes that he was delighted with the arrangements for the tapestry exhibition (for which he gave the doctor full credit). But it came to an end only two months later, when Barnes informed Henry McIlhenny that the exhibition was to be canceled "because of factual corroboration of my previous statement that the Pennsylvania Museum of Art is a house of artistic and intellectual prostitution."

Though it might have seemed abrupt, the end of the warm relationship was inevitable. Barnes, no gentleman, and the museum's gentlemanly officials, in their temperaments and methods, were fundamentally incompatible. Even while cooperating with the museum, the doctor had found fault with its employees, but he had overlooked these relatively minor grievances. By the spring of 1937, however, he had had enough.

The provocation this time was serious: the museum's sponsorship of an exhibition, "Forms of Art," created and organized by the chief of its Division of Education, E. M. Benson. It led to what Barnes looked upon as an irrevocable break with the museum.

The exhibition, in the words of its creator, was "based on the belief that it is more important to understand what an artist is trying to say and how he says it, than to know when and where it was said. Historical facts may explain many things, but they seldom tell us very much about the one thing in a work of art that is essential to appreciation—and that is why and how it functions as a work of art; and why artists of all ages . . . have been moved to express themselves in much the same way." The works shown were arranged by "unanimity of purpose," rather than by period or medium of expression.

"Forms of Art" opened on April 24, 1937. After Barnes saw it, a few days later, he exploded. The whole concept, he believed, was nonsense. Even worse, he saw in it a clumsy attempt to plagiarize his own ideas. The result was an insensitive distortion of those same ideas. He wrote immediately, and with indignation, to J. Stogdell Stokes, the museum's president. Citing no fewer than thirty-four examples of plagiarism, he demanded that the exhibition be closed at once. Stokes, undoubtedly anxious to avoid an open battle with the man who was responsible for the museum's eagerly anticipated tapestry exhibition, turned the matter over to Benson (whom he identified as a former student of John Dewey's).

Benson was polite but firm in his reply. He wrote that while he had read and admired Barnes's book, he had also read the work of others, who had arrived at analogous conclusions, each through his own experience. "These writers, including yourself, have undoubtedly left their mark on the development of my ideas, but nothing could have or would have come of it, if fresh personal experience with art and life over a period of many years had not confirmed a point of view. We may be walking towards a similar goal, but we are traveling different roads. Mine is one I have painfully blazed for myself," he wrote.

Barnes was not pacified. Benson's audacity, he commented, was equivalent to that of "a citizen of another city who came to Philadelphia and tried to sell to the local residents the right, titles and interests in and to the City Hall. . . ." Nor was he satisfied: he was out to get the museum and not merely Benson. Its officials continued to maintain a discreet silence. Frustrated in his attempts to rouse them himself, he enlisted the aid of allies, among them the local Artists Union, which issued an angry denunciation of the exhibition and of the museum. Even the union's rousing words of support were not enough, however, and in the end Barnes turned once again to Dewey. The battle he was waging, he wrote the philosopher dramatically in early May, was an important one. It would determine whether or not Dewey's own ideas were valid and whether or not they should be allowed to be perverted as "instruments of educational chaos." In conclusion he urged his friend to come to Philadelphia to see the exhibition for himself.

Dewey, as always, gave proof of his loyalty. He arrived in Philadelphia on May 14 and visited the exhibition. Shortly afterward, he issued his own public statement. It read, in part:

> I found the "Forms of Art Exhibition" even more confused, both intellectually and esthetically, than the correspondence about it had led me to anticipate.
>
> It was bad enough to call it, in the accompanying circular, a "fresh approach" when the leading idea of the circular is obviously borrowed from *The Art in Painting* without referring to that book. The exhibition itself not only fails to carry out the borrowed idea, as expressed in the circular, but so completely contradicts it as to show that Mr. Benson never got the idea, but only some verbal expressions of it. . . .
>
> . . . That Mr. Benson should be thus confused personally is not a matter of great importance. That a great public institution should lend itself to propagating the confusion is serious. Such exhibits ought to direct the efforts of students, both beginners and those more advanced. The present exhibit prevents this education, because of institutional prestige and its virtual endorsement of meaningless language.

This time, though the museum had still issued no reply, Barnes was satisfied. Dewey had been a forceful spokesman for his cause, and Benson's exhibition had, he felt, been thoroughly discredited. The Foundation's relationship with the museum, however, was another matter. In refusing to admit its guilt in having given space to the exhibition, and in ignoring Barnes's pleas to cancel it, the museum had precluded any possibility of collaboration with Barnes or his Foundation, and that, of course, included the tapestry show.

Though the battle over "Forms of Art" had ended, Barnes's war with the museum was resumed only six months later. He was back in fighting form, and he seemed eager to prove it. The call to arms this time was the museum's announcement, on November 11, 1937, that it had purchased Cézanne's *Les Grandes Baigneuses* from France's Pellerin collection, for a sum of $110,000. The acquisition had been made by Joseph E. Widener, on behalf of the Wilstach Fund, of which he was administrator. The purchase came as a surprise. Widener, a distinguished collector of old masters, had made no secret of his contempt for modern art. (His interests had, in fact, turned to horseracing.) Nonetheless, at the urging of Kimball and other museum authorities, the sixty-four-year-old collector, whose father had worked alongside Barnes's as a butcher many years before, had agreed to make the purchase in order to strengthen the museum's collection of modern art.

It was a major acquisition for the museum. The huge painting— six-feet-ten by eight-feet-three—had been named "The Large Bathers" to differentiate it from other smaller paintings in the series. "No person informed in the field of modern art will be able to miss the opportunity of seeing and studying a picture which has been described as 'the master invention of Cézanne's architectural imagination,' " the official announcement noted, adding, "The acquisition of the Pellerin 'Bathers' gives to Philadelphia and its neighborhood the distinction of owning the two best-known versions of the painter's famous subject. The second version, and a slightly smaller picture, is in the collection of the Barnes Foundation at

Merion and was purchased by Dr. Albert Barnes from the Vollard collection in 1933."

The apparently inoffensive wording was unfortunate—even Kimball soon realized that it would have been wiser to have said merely that "the other chief version, and a slightly smaller picture, is in the Barnes collection"—for Barnes saw the announcement as an attempt to minimize the importance of his own painting.

"The reference to me in this morning's newspapers," he wrote to Stokes, "had the reporters on my track before noon with a request for a statement. I dictated something, but instead of giving it to the reporters at this time, I am sending it to you, with the suggestion that you use the matter to correct, in a public statement, the stupid assertions of the Museum officials in reference to our picture, and to tell them never again to use my name as a stalking horse in their circus."

Stokes ignored this demand for a correction, and a few days later Barnes issued his long statement to the press under the heading, "Ballyhoo at the Pennsylvania Museum of Art." It was an attack on the museum and the man who had made the purchase on behalf of the museum, and it read, in part:

> The opinion of discriminating collectors and dealers generally, that the unfinished Museum "Bathers" is of about fifth-rate quality for a Cézanne—in contrast to the newspaper statement that it is his "greatest masterpiece"—explains why the picture went begging for a buyer for more than five years. . . . Its former owner, in the presence of witnesses, offered to sell the picture to me for eighty thousand dollars; shortly after that, a Paris dealer asked me to offer fifty thousand dollars for it, and he assured me it would be accepted. My reason for rejecting the painting was that it was too sketchy and poor in quality to be even feebly representative of Cézanne's fully-arrived expression—an opinion which coincided with that of the other well-informed buyers to whom the painting had been proposed. . . . [Barnes concluded that] the city

has been "stung" with an inferior painting, and that the officials have propagated rather transparent ballyhoo and misrepresentation. That situation, of course, reflects upon the city's reputation, but there exists this significant extenuating circumstance: the painting's presence in Philadelphia represents not the intelligence and cultural levels of the general population, but the evil of having an absentee dictator of the local official art situation, who functions principally at the race-tracks of Miami, Saratoga, and Deauville.

To Barnes's dismay, the Philadelphia press refused to take his charges seriously, and its members ridiculed what became known as the Battle of the Bathers. "Both paintings doubtless have their place in the fine arts," a reporter for the *Inquirer* wrote. "However, to plain citizens, to whom art appraisal is caviar, $110,000 or even $50,000 will seem plenty to pay for a picture of a group of undressed fat women." The *Record,* commenting that the amount of money paid for the painting would buy bathtubs for a large number of Philadelphia homes, made its calculations and concluded: "We can figure that the city paid at the rate of $7,857 per bather, which may or may not seem excessive, depending on whether you prefer Cézanne's bathers to those you can see on the beach at Atlantic City for nothing." The writer for the *Bulletin* sided with the museum, noting that since there were more bathers in its version, the city got more for its money on a per-capita basis.

While the newspapers enjoyed themselves, most serious art lovers were saddened by the meaningless dispute. "Art is too beautiful to argue about," was the opinion of the collector Sam A. Lewisohn. Nonetheless, Barnes, again frustrated by the museum's refusal to respond to his taunts, continued his attack, even after the press and public had lost interest. "It came down to someone's screaming 'My baby is prettier than your baby,' " Kimball later noted, "something one obviously does not answer."

Throughout the controversy, Widener made no comment. The man who had bought the painting for the museum and Barnes, his adversary, both remained silent the following spring when they were assigned adjoining deck chairs on the *Normandie,* which was taking them to Europe. Too proud to request different chairs, each was also too proud to exchange a single word during the whole crossing."We just sat there, a couple of millionaires on the luxury liner *Normandie,*" Barnes noted, "just as his old man and my old man had once worked, side by side, in a slaughter house."

In the winter of 1937–38, at the same time he was engaged in his futile attempt to draw the museum into the Battle of the Bathers, Barnes was bringing to a close another battle, which he had waged over a number of years. In this case the enemy was the state director of the WPA's Federal Arts Project, Mary Curran, the owner of a small art gallery, who had, not insignificantly, been expelled from the Foundation's classes in 1926. But the museum was involved because two of its officials, Kimball and Marceau, had recommended Curran for the job and had continued to praise and support her actions.

Barnes had nothing against the WPA; unlike most millionaires, he was an enthusiastic supporter of Franklin Roosevelt and the New Deal. He was also—above all—in sympathy with the plight of the arts and artists during the Depression. Nonetheless, certain rules of the Arts Project irked him, and he held Curran responsible for enforcing them.

Chief among these was the regulation that required participating artists to work in their studios from nine to twelve and from one to four each weekday. Obviously, this schedule was an impossible one for artists accustomed to a flexible workday, as it was for those who took courses at the Barnes Foundation. When in 1934 one of those students wrote Barnes that he would be unable to attend his Monday afternoon class because of these rules, the doctor exploded.

He advised the student to continue to come to the class, "thereby defying the dictator," and suggested that he call a mass meeting of protest. He also wrote a letter to Robert L. Johnson, Executive Director of the Emergency Relief Board at Harrisburg, furiously attacking Curran as well as Kimball, and asking for a public inquiry into her administration. The charges leveled at her were many. Artists had already been picketing the Arts Project's Philadelphia office, he noted, and he was doing his best to prevent them from throwing bricks. "I want to help you solve the problem, not add to its difficulty," he concluded.

Johnson turned Barnes's letter over to his assistant, Frank Schmitt, who wrote a calm, conciliatory letter, but the doctor was not mollified. He answered that Schmitt's letter was, among other things, "a farrago of nonsense, irrelevancies, hot air, and issue-dodging . . ." and gave Schmitt his choice of a public debate or a court inquiry. He also offered to bet him five-to-one "that the first effect of a disinterested investigation would be to crystallize the organized public indignation which manifested itself in the picketing of your local office . . . with a social force that would sweep into the discard the politicians who are now trifling with basic human needs."

Schmitt was stunned. He turned to Kimball for advice on how "to stop this constant flow of abuse from such an irresponsible individual." Kimball's answer was based on his own experience. "Barnes," he wrote, "has been trying to get under my skin for years, and is now trying to get under yours. Personally, I don't do anything about it, because he seems to hope that I will do something about it, and because it seems to annoy him more that I don't. The chief objections to going after him are that he would like nothing better, and that he would devote himself twenty-four hours a day to the fight, whereas you and I have something else and something better to do."

Barnes kept up his attacks on Mary Curran over a period of four years, often joined by local artists and educators who agreed that she should be dismissed from her influential post. The charges against her included inefficiency, dictatorial methods (she told artists how to paint), anti-unionism (her hostility to the Artists Union was undisguised), and favoritism. The work of artists who had shown at her own gallery, it was charged, dominated the occasional group exhibitions of the works of WPA artists, and union members as well as students of the Barnes Foundation were discriminated against. "Miss Curran is not only profoundly ignorant of what constitutes a work of art," Barnes stated at one point, "but is so handicapped mentally that she is incapable of obtaining the experience that would enable her either to form an intelligent opinion of art values, or to direct any project participated in by normal human beings."

The doctor's fury reached its peak in January 1938. The cause was an exhibition, at the museum, of what was called a representative selection of the work of WPA artists. Arranged by Curran and Kimball, the show was greeted with cheers by several critics, including another of Barnes's enemies, Dorothy Grafly, who reported that "the general level is higher than that displayed in many a non-relief exhibition." Barnes dissented vigorously. Words were not enough, however; it was time to take action. On the day of the exhibition's public opening, sixty pickets assembled at the entrance to the museum, loudly denouncing Kimball, Curran, and the administration of the Arts Project. Not surprisingly most of them were members of the Artists Union, always friendly to Barnes, and students of the Barnes Foundation.

That evening Barnes personally joined the battle, challenging reporters to picket "in protest against the Fascistic way" in which the museum was being operated. The challenge, issued at the opening of an anti-Fascist mural in Philadelphia's New Theatre, made it clear that the enemy was now the museum and not merely Curran, and, a few days later, at a meeting of the city's People's Forum, Barnes issued his formal call to arms: "If you are really interested in painting, go out and raise hell at the museum. . . . If the time ever comes when we can lead a mob, maybe we can take it away from them."

Barnes was unable to incite the mob to attack the museum. Nonetheless, he found another way of making his displeasure known—it was to become his favorite means of protest: he published or had published three pamphlets summarizing all of his differences with the museum. In the first, "A Disgrace to Philadelphia," which was dated January 3, 1938, and which he himself signed, he alleged that "Philadelphia now stands as a symbol of ignorance and gullibility in matters of art." He cited as evidence the "Forms of Art" exhibition, the museum's cooperation with Mary Curran, and the Cézanne incident. "The present disgrace brought upon the city is due largely to the fact that a main function of the Museum has been to serve as a pedestal upon which a clique of socialites pose as patrons of art and culture," he concluded.

The second pamphlet, issued a short time later, was called "Philadelphia's Shame: An Analysis of the Un-American Administration of the Federal Arts Project in Philadelphia." In a prefatory note its author, Barnes's friend Henry Hart, a journalist, defined its scope: to show that the Arts Project "has been inhumanly, inefficiently and illegally administered by the Regional Director for Pennsylvania, Miss Mary Curran, and that she should be dismissed immediately." It was notable as the first publication of the Friends of Art and Education. The organization, defined as "an association formed by citizens of Philadelphia to develop, protect and advance the educational and cultural interests of the community," was a new one, but its officers were familiar to the cause: Dewey was its honorary president and Barnes its president.

A more comprehensive document, "The Progressive Decay of the Pennsylvania Museum of Art," was published by the Friends of Art and Education two months later. The author this time was Harry Fuiman, a lawyer who had been trained as a sculptor and had studied at the Foundation. Fuiman had been personally offended by the "Forms of Art" exhibition and had voiced his complaints to Barnes, who in turn suggested that the young lawyer put his objections into writing, using the research facilities at Spruce Street. Though the voice seems to be that of Barnes, Fuiman vigorously denies charges that the doctor actually wrote the brochure. While admitting that it was Barnes's idea, he maintains today that all the work was his own. Whatever the case, it was an eloquent summary of the doctor's ideas. A broad attack on the museum— its administration and financial structure—it presented evidence of the so-called deterioration of the institution, which Fuiman called "a private club supported by taxpayers' money." Examples of this deterioration were the familiar ones: "Forms of Art," termed "perhaps the most outrageous fraud perpetrated upon the public since Dr. Cook's claim to discovery of the North Pole"; the museum's support of Curran; the Cézanne incident, as well as the museum's entire educational program. Among the remedies suggested were the end of "the anomaly of having as virtual dictator of city art matters an absentee, Joseph E. Widener, whose principal occupation is the promotion of race-track activities," and the dismissal of both Kimball and Marceau. In other words, nothing short of a thorough housecleaning could save the museum.

Shortly after the publication of Fuiman's pamphlet, the Friends of Art and Education disbanded. It had published its broadsides, and it had held a few meetings. It had also—and Barnes's foes never gave him credit for his victory—achieved one of its main goals, for Holger Cahill, national director of the Federal Arts Project, had found enough truth in the charges against Mary Curran to relieve her of her position. In Cahill's words, "She was very opinionated and some of her opinions weren't too good."

In 1939 Barnes and de Mazia's *The Art of Cézanne,* the third and last of their comprehensive studies, was published by Harcourt, Brace and Company. In view of his quarrel with the museum over *The Bathers,* the doctor must have been particularly pleased by the warm reception accorded the book by most critics, for it established him in the eyes of many as an unrivaled expert in the field of Cézanne studies.

Surely most satisfying, if surprising, were the comments of *Time* magazine (frequently the target of his wrath), which made specific note of the doctor's impressive credentials in his dispute with the museum and began its review with an unequivocal endorsement of the book. "Liberal lawyers hold that the law flourishes by truing up ever more wisely with new and unblinkable social conditions," it read. "Liberal artists conceive the tradition of the fine arts as involving a like growth and adaptation. Occasionally, in each field, progress in interpretation is marked by a commentary so learned as to become a classic. Published last week was a serious book which may well become a sort of *Blackstone on Coke* to future art students. The subject: *The Art of Cézanne.* The commentators: Albert C. Barnes and Violette de Mazia."

The Art of Cézanne was Barnes's last book. With the exception of a few articles, it was also his last piece of published writing. The doctor, in his late sixties, had apparently said all he wanted to say. There are indications, too, that he had bought all, or almost all, that he wanted to buy, for the number of important additions to his collection began to diminish significantly. (Among the few exceptions were Renoir's enormous *Mussel Fishers at Berneval,* which he purchased in 1942, and Titian's *Endymion,* which entered the collection in 1951.) The outbreak of World War Two had made collecting difficult; travel to Europe was impossible, and the art market in America was unstable and depressed. Nonetheless, these were not insurmountable obstacles for a man of Barnes's tenacity, and it seems likely that he sensed instead that his extraordinary collection, within its scope as an educational tool, was reaching its completion.

Perhaps this explains why, during what was to be the last decade of his life, Barnes's anger intensified. He swung wildly, and often irresponsibly, at his enemies. His tireless energy was wasted on useless, petty controversies, and he became known increasingly for these rather than for his genuine, positive contributions to the world of art.

CHAPTER

18

In late February 1940 it was announced that Bertrand Russell, then teaching at the University of California, had been appointed professor of philosophy at the College of the City of New York—a city-run institution known for its liberal policies—for a period of eighteen months, beginning the following February. The outspoken British philosopher, whose unconventional views often scandalized the public, was accustomed to controversy, but even he could not have predicted the uproar that greeted this seemingly innocent announcement. The reaction was immediate and violent. It was set off by an open letter, published in a number of New York newspapers on March 1, written by Bishop William T. Manning of the Protestant Episcopal Church, an expatriate Englishman and long an opponent of Russell and his ideas. In the letter denouncing the philosopher as well as the Board of Higher Education which had offered him the new position, Manning portrayed Russell as a corrupter of public morals and called his appointment a threat to religious life. "What is to be said of colleges and universities which hold up before our youth as a responsible teacher of philosophy and as an example of leading, a man who is a recognized propagandist against both religion and morality, and who specifically defends adultery?" he asked.

Manning's was only the first of many protests. He was soon

joined in the fight against Russell's appointment by equally enraged conservative members of the clergy, journalists, and politicians, many of whom quoted, out of context, from the philosopher's writings on premarital and extramarital sex, nudity, and masturbation to support their objectives. Russell had his impassioned supporters—students, members of the academic community, and distinguished intellectuals (among them Einstein, Thomas Mann, Alfred North Whitehead, and Aldous Huxley)—but the vehemence of the anti-Russell faction was such that the Board of Higher Education announced on March 7 that the whole matter would be reviewed at its next meeting on March 18. As expected, the announcement served to intensify pressure from conservatives and liberals alike, but the former were disappointed when, after a long and stormy debate which lasted into the night, the board refused to annul the controversial appointment.

The victory of the pro-Russell forces was, however, short-lived. On the following day Mrs. Jean Kay—a resident of Brooklyn, with no academic connections, who was identified merely as a taxpayer—petitioned the New York State Supreme Court to order the Board of Higher Education to "rescind and revoke" Russell's appointment, principally on the grounds that the philosopher's teachings were immoral and constituted "a menace to the health, morals, and welfare of the students who attend the College of the City of New York." Arguments were heard before Justice John E. McGeehan of the Supreme Court on March 27. On March 30, the judge ruled in favor of Mrs. Kay. "The appointment of Dr. Russell," he declared, "is an insult to the people of the City of New York," and the Board of Higher Education in making it is "in effect establishing a chair of indecency" at the college. A subsequent appeal was denied, and by mid-April Russell's appointment was officially canceled.

Russell, in effect stranded in the United States because of the war, was desperate. Though attempts to curtail his appointment at the University of California and to annul his engagement to lecture at Harvard for a few months starting the following September failed, the prospects for 1941 were bleak. He had his supporters, and they were both vociferous and articulate, but they could do nothing to stem the witch-hunt that was instituted against him. "I became taboo throughout the whole of the United States," he wrote in his autobiography. "I was to have been engaged in a lecture tour, but I had only one engagement before the witch-hunt had developed. The rabbi who had made this engagement broke his contract, but I cannot blame him. Owners of halls refused to let them if I was to lecture. . . . No newspaper or magazine would publish anything that I wrote, and I was suddenly deprived of all means of earning a living. As it was legally impossible to get money out of England, this produced a very difficult situation, especially as I had my three children dependent upon me. Many liberal-minded professors protested, but they all supposed that as I was an earl I must have ancestral estates and be very well off. Only one man did anything practical, and that was Dr. Barnes. . . . He gave me a five-year appointment to lecture at his Foundation."

Barnes's appointment of Russell to the staff of the Foundation was well-timed—for both men. It was most probably made at the suggestion of Dewey, who, though he disliked Russell personally, had been outspoken in his defense of the British philosopher and had undoubtedly influenced Barnes in his own publicly expressed support for him as well as in his decision to subsidize the publication of a series of essays on the entire case. Nonetheless, the offer, which saved the philosopher from what he termed "a bleak prospect," also served Barnes's purposes well. The addition to his staff of a philosopher of Russell's prominence could only add to the prestige of his Foundation, and the course that Russell was to teach—an account of the ideas and cultural values that developed from the period of the early Greeks up to the present time—would be useful as a background for the Foundation's own courses in the traditions of painting. In addition, Barnes hoped to find in Russell, whose writings and opinions he had long admired, a new friend as well as a loyal ally.

Whether or not he was instrumental in convincing Barnes to make the offer, it was Dewey who relayed the doctor's proposal to Russell in May. The British philosopher was both grateful and interested. In early June Barnes himself sent him further details, and on June 18 Russell replied from California:

> Thank you for sending me an account of the Barnes Foundation. I am deeply grateful to you for the suggestion that I should join it. It seems extremely unlikely that the Courts will reverse the New York decision against me; unless they do so, I should be free to perform whatever duties you desire, and I am capable of, at the beginning of February 1941. I am in some doubt as to what you would consider that I could contribute that would be not too remote from your object; if you have any views on this point, I should be glad to know them sooner or later. Could you also let me know whether my appointment, assuming that I am free to accept it, would be for a definite or indefinite period? I cannot tell you what an immense boon your offer is to me. One is almost ashamed at such a moment, to think of personal things, but when one has young children it is unavoidable.

It was the beginning of a warm correspondence, during which the doctor offered his own opinions and recounted his own experiences while Russell concentrated on his own plans for the future. On June 24 Barnes wrote, in answer to Russell's query concerning his contribution to the Foundation:

> If I am not mistaken in your attitude toward life—from "A Free Man's Worship" to *Marriage and Morals*—the hope for a better social order lies in the development of intelligence as a guide to living . . . that general idea is the main root of our enterprise even though we happen to use the material of art to put it over. In doing it, I've had many doses of the same bitter medicine you've been forced to swallow recently; for example, in 1923 the principal Philadelphia newspaper printed an editorial denouncing me as a "perverter of public morals" because I exhibited, wrote and talked about such painters as Cézanne and Renoir. . . .

I think you'll see in this incident an illustration of how you could function here, granting that life has many phases not many of which have been frankly, honestly and fully presented to people because institutionalized ignorance and prejudice have ganged up on them—as you know, to your sorrow. In short, if you want to say what you damn please, even to giving your adversaries a dose of their own medicine, we'll back you up. We can do it because we are on a par with universities as a chartered institution and we ask no financial support from the politically controlled public treasury. . . .

Obviously Russell was heartened by the tone of the doctor's correspondence, and in response to a subsequent letter, which he received at his summer home at Lake Tahoe, he wrote:

Thank you very much for your letter of July 13. Your suggestions are entirely agreeable to me. . . .

All that you say about the work sounds most attractive, but it certainly needs conversation. I do not know whether you want me to lecture on philosophy or on social questions. I should be very reluctant to lecture on sexual ethics, which have quite wrongly been supposed to be my special field. Actually the subject interests me much less than many others and I should be sorry to be diverted from philosophy and history to sociology. I could, if it suited you, lecture on different philosophies of the past, and their influence on culture and social questions: for example, Platonism and its influence, or the Romantic movement of the nineteenth century.

Details we could discuss later, but I should be very glad if you could give me some idea now of the sort of subject you are thinking of.

We should be delighted to see you here at any time before the end of August, though I am afraid we could not offer you hospitality, as we are living in a tiny log cabin. There are however hotels all around.

In early August Barnes flew to Lake Tahoe, where Russell was living with his third wife, Patricia (Peter) Spence Russell and their four-year-old son, Conrad Sebastian Robert Russell. By August 8 the two men had reached a verbal agreement concerning Russell's duties at the Foundation, which were to commence in January 1941 and to extend for a period of five years. It was Russell who suggested the five-year term. "I was warned that he always tired of people before long," he wrote in his autobiography.

Barnes was jubilant upon his return to Merion, and shortly thereafter he wrote Russell, asking which books were to be used for his course and offering to help him find a house near the Foundation. Russell replied on August 17. "As regards books," he wrote, "I know no book dealing in general with my subject; I propose that my lectures for you should become such a book. In any case, a very little of original sources is better than a great deal of textbook." Among the sources, he recommended works of Plato, Plutarch, and Jean-Jacques Rousseau. He was more specific concerning the house. He required several bedrooms, a living-and-dining room, and a large study, and he insisted that the house be in the country, at least fifty miles from Philadelphia, so that he and his wife might work in peace.

As always, Barnes answered at once. He had gone about the job of finding a home for the Russells energetically, and in his letter of August 21 he made it clear that his plans for that home were grandiose. He also made it known that he would be responsible for the Russells while they were in Merion and that he would personally see to it that the philosopher and his family lived in a manner that he, Barnes, considered suitable. Russell's reply of August 24 was polite; he nonetheless did his best to restrain the doctor's enthusiasm and assert his own right to choose suitable living quarters:

> ... There are ... some points that I should like to put to you, as I am a little afraid that your enthusiasm for lovely places may lead to your not quite realizing my circumstances.

In the first place, it is impossible for us to buy: I cannot get money from England, and have here only what I have saved during the last twenty months. In the second place, I shall, out of $6000 a year, have to keep my two older children at the university, and perhaps spend money on refugee children; I must therefore have a house which not only has a low rental, but is cheap to run and requires little service. I should not know what to do with 60 or 70 acres of farmland. . . .

Choosing a house is a very personal matter, like choosing a wife. I know that in China the latter is done by proxy, but although people make mistakes, we are apt to prefer our own folly to the wisdom of others. We should neither of us wish to decide on a house until we have seen a considerable selection. I am deeply touched at your even contemplating spending $35,000 on the matter, but I am sure we can be happy at very much lower cost, and we could not possibly pay a rent corresponding to such a price, so that, in effect, you would be paying me a bigger salary than was agreed upon. . . .

I am very much afraid all this may sound ungracious, but it is not so intended. You have given to both my wife and me the opportunity for the sort of life we want, in which, without undue financial worry, we can devote ourselves to serious work, and to writing long-contemplated books. But in order to achieve this we must organize our living on such a scale that I shall not have to do a lot of hack-work to avoid debt. This wants care and thought, and I am made somewhat nervous by the very generosity of your suggestions. I doubt whether it is ever possible for one person to know another person's needs and tastes. So I think it is impossible to come to a decision until we are in the East, and one or both of us has had a little time to look around. What you have already done in giving me the post is so much that no more is needed to secure my life-long gratitude . . .

P.S. . . . When my wife first gets to Philadelphia, she will be staying with some very old friends of ours.

If Barnes was in any way offended by Russell's tactful but firm refusal to be dominated, or by his wife's refusal of what must have been an invitation to stay at the Barnes home, he gave no indication of it. On the contrary, he eagerly looked forward to the philosopher's arrival at the Foundation. "Bertrand can put us on the intellectual-educational map in a manner I have long wished for," he wrote Patricia Russell on August 28; "we can give him an opportunity to fulfill his heart's desire; and woe be to those who attempt to pull off another stunt like that of recent times in New York." For his part Russell was equally delighted. "My personal problems have been solved by a rich patron (in the eighteenth century style) who has given me a teaching post with little work and sufficient salary," he wrote his friend, Gilbert Murray, on September 6.

On October 15, the *Evening Bulletin* reported Barnes's announcement of Russell's appointment to the staff of the Foundation. Noting that the philosopher's ouster from his post at City College was "a wanton act inspired and fostered by bigoted authoritarians," Barnes declared that "there will be no restrictions on Mr. Russell at the Barnes Foundation. The sky is the limit. I wouldn't think of telling any of our staff what they should or should not say." He added, "Mr. Russell will be a permanent figure at the Barnes Foundation. . . ."

Response to the announcement was tremendous; more than five hundred students wanted to attend the lecture. "I'm in a quandary about your classes—we're swamped with applications from outsiders, some of them of the right sort," Barnes wrote on November 1. "What I'd like you to tell me is—how many students do you prefer to have? We limit our classes to 20, but prefer 15. I'll leave the decision entirely in your hands." (A far larger number, sixty-five, was decided upon.) It was a friendly letter, and only a postscript sounded an ominous note, though no one suspected it at the time. "I had to fight with Peter," the doctor added, referring to his efforts to help the Russells set up their home, a two-hundred-year-old farmhouse at Malvern, thirty miles from Philadelphia, which was owned by Barnes and rented to the philosopher. "Kiss her for me and tell her I hope to make amends for all the crimes I've committed."

Russell's first class was held on the afternoon of January 2, 1941, in the Foundation's main gallery—subsequent classes were held in a small gallery, since the philosopher found the paintings distracting. Barnes, seated in an armchair at the side of the room, looked on proudly. The occasion is remembered by Barrows Dunham, a member of the faculty of Temple University in Philadelphia and the only "professional" philosopher among the listeners who had been invited to join the class by the doctor himself:

> Russell talked for about an hour, and then again asked if there were any questions or remarks. Silence. He asked again. Again silence. We were all in awe of the great man—I perhaps more than any of the others. Nobody wanted to risk saying something silly. So then Dr. Barnes proclaimed an end to the proceedings. Russell was taken into an office to be interviewed and photographed by the press. Meanwhile, Dr. Barnes came over to me, took me by the lapels, hammered on my chest, and said: "Why didn't you fight him?" This was meant as banter in Barnes's heavy style (he was no wit). I suppose he could hardly have guessed what a youngish professor would do in the presence of fame.

The "press" referred to by Dunham consisted of only one reporter, from the *Evening Bulletin;* the other reporter, representing the *Inquirer,* was ushered out of the Foundation before the lecture on the grounds that her paper had been unsympathetic editorially to Russell. In the course of what was an exclusive interview, the small, wiry, white-haired philosopher briefly outlined his views on pacifism, politics, and academic freedom, again noting that he was glad to be at the Foundation and "to know that I am not under any censorship."

Barnes thoroughly enjoyed his role as Russell's patron. Soon after the philosopher's first class, the doctor, through his friend

Henry Hart, found a publisher—The Viking Press—for the series of essays dealing with Russell's dismissal from CCNY, which he had agreed to subsidize. The volume, *The Bertrand Russell Case,* edited by Dewey and Horace M. Kallen, a professor at the New School, included contributions by a number of distinguished members of the academic world. In his introduction Dewey wrote that Barnes felt hiring Russell was not enough—"he felt that the social importance of the case demanded there be a public record of the issues." Dewey also noted that Barnes neither selected the contributors nor told them what they should or should not write. The volume also contained a brief foreword by Barnes himself. This was included at Dewey's suggestion, which Kallen accepted on the condition that Dewey—whose prose was no more readable than Barnes's—do the actual writing. (The book, which was published the following June, cost Barnes close to two thousand dollars. Though its sales were small, the doctor expressed no dissatisfaction with the project.)

Barnes was also enthusiastic about Russell's lectures, which were a great success. On March 13 he wrote Russell a glowing letter, expressing his appreciation and that of the members of the class:

> My associate Angelo Pinto told me of his conversation with you and asked if I had anything to suggest to facilitate your wish to get a "closer contact with the students" in your class. I know of nothing better than what you are doing but if you would like to try any other plan, you have only to do it without consulting anybody here.
>
> One thing I can say in all sincerity is that your lectures are doing more for those students than you think, or what I thought anybody could do—it's no easy job to jump into a group of mixed and very different backgrounds and create in all of them a genuine interest that makes them go into a subject further and on their own in an effort to link up what you give with what the other teachers put over in their own classes. Moreover, you've endeared yourself to all of them and if I were a

Frenchman I'd kiss you on both cheeks for the benefit you've brought to our efforts to do something worthwhile.

Don't you worry about your work here: take it in your stride of living a peaceful, carefree life. And if I can further that wish in any way, you may count on me to do it.

He was not nearly so pleased, however, with the way his personal relationship with the philosopher was developing. Russell liked to keep to himself, and it soon became apparent that he would never become as close to the doctor as Dewey had. Resenting what he considered his aloofness, he wrote Dewey that Russell, though in theory democratic, was an aristocrat at heart.

Barnes's real quarrel, however, was with Russell's wife—a strikingly attractive woman, half her husband's age—who he felt was responsible for Russell's unsocial behavior. Since they (or he) had kissed and made up following their disagreement in November, he had grown to dislike her intensely. For one thing, he found her unpardonably pretentious. Though the philosopher preferred to be addressed as "mister," she continued to refer to herself as "Lady" Russell. "She seems to have difficulty in swallowing the impressive title of Lady Russell," Barnes was quoted as saying. "It evidently gets stuck just below her larynx, for she regurgitates it automatically." Barnes also complained—in a letter to Dewey written two months after her arrival—of her insulting behavior toward the Foundation's staff, including Laura Barnes, and of her attempts to run the Foundation's affairs. "When she came to the Foundation," he told a journalist, "the simplicity and democratic spirit there struck her as the ideal place to do her stuff. She high-hatted the officials. She acted as if she had the right to abolish the Foundation's rules. She indulged in grandstand stunts. After she had exhausted her repertory, we changed her name from Patricia to Plebeia. . . ." Even worse, Barnes came to believe that Russell was totally dominated by his wife, and he saw in this a major problem: how could he put Lady Russell in her place without destroying his own relationship with her husband?

Barnes went about his task of solving the problem with little grace. Patricia Russell had offended him by, in his words, "bursting" into the gallery (on February 27, 1941) and, as a consequence, interrupting one of Russell's interviews. She continued to offend him by attending some of her husband's classes (she drove him to work each Thursday) and causing a disturbance by knitting while he delivered his lecture. (According to Dunham, Barnes might have been distracted by her beauty, but not by her knitting.) For months Barnes's rage simmered, but in late October it reached the boiling point. On October 31, Nelle Mullen wrote to Patricia Russell, informing her that the board of trustees had discussed her behavior of the previous February and had also examined complaints of her knitting. "The Foundation has never been a place where people may drop in occasionally, at their own volition, nor is any person whosoever allowed to do things that interfere with the rights of others or are harmful to the Foundation's interests," the letter read. "Admission to the gallery is restricted to persons enrolled in the class. . . ." In conclusion Mullen informed her that in the future she would be prohibited from entering the Foundation's premises.

Patricia Russell responded swiftly. On November 1 she addressed a letter to the trustees of the Barnes Foundation. It read:

> The first sentence of your letter of October 31st has seemed to me incomprehensible. My husband has, however, recalled to me an occasion when Miss Mullen appeared to him to have been annoyed by me; and so, fantastic as the charge appears, I must suppose that you are referring to the following incident: On a particular day last winter my husband asked me to be not a moment later than 3:45 in calling for him, as he had an important engagement elsewhere. When, therefore, I called at 3:45, and was told indirectly that my husband was busy talking to a reporter and did not wish to be disturbed, I knew that someone had presumed to interpret my husband's wishes, and that in fact he could not have been told of my arrival. I therefore went into the building and spoke to a white-haired lady who approached me, and whose name I did not know, saying in a normal voice, "Where is Mr. Russell? Will you

please let him know that I am here?" I then left the building. If this seems to the Trustees of the Barnes Foundation a disturbance of the peace, may they long continue to enjoy the unreal paradise where such trifles may be so accounted, for I cannot suppose that they would have the fortitude to endure a true disturbance of the peace: for example bombs tearing through the roof.

As for my occasional attendance at my husband's lectures: I have always acted as his assistant in research for and preparation of his lectures, and when, as is usually the case, I am familiar with the subject he is to speak about, he does not desire my attendance. On other occasions, when the subject is not one that I have studied, he has wished me to be present, not for my own sake, but for the sake of his lectures, since I cannot assist him adequately with the preparation of any one lecture without a thorough grasp of the whole course. In every other institution in which my husband has taught since I was his assistant, it has only been necessary for him to mention that he would like to have me present at some of his lectures, and the permission has been most readily and courteously granted. I had understood that my husband had arranged this with the Barnes Foundation, but if he forgot to do so, or understood that permission was granted when in fact it was not so, we can only apologize for my unintentional trespass.

It is in any case necessary for me to drive my husband to his lectures, as he cannot drive himself, and he had not supposed that the Trustees could wish me to wait outside.

I cannot imagine anyone regarding the Foundation as "a place where they may drop in occasionally."

As for my knitting: it was with some hesitation that I took it with me—on two or perhaps three occasions—to the Barnes Foundation; but when I consulted my husband he remarked that I had disturbed no one by knitting at far more difficult and technical lectures at the Universities of Oxford, Chicago, California, and Harvard, and that therefore, I might assume that I would be giving no offense. I am distressed that in fact

I did disturb someone, and would be glad if you would convey to all the students my sincere apologies.

It would only have been necessary for you to say to me, "Mrs. Russell, would you mind not knitting," just as you only need have told my husband, "If you want your wife to come to your lectures it will be necessary for her to obtain permission of the Trustees."

My knitting is in no sense an "indulgence" and I would not have run the risk of annoying anyone by it, however slightly, but for a purpose that seems to me serious, the wish to diminish the number of those who suffer from cold.

If I am sometimes a little cold myself in future, when, having no errands, I wait for my husband outside the Barnes Foundation (outside the grounds of course), I will knit with more zest from a nearer realization of what it must mean to be cold and really without shelter; and I will marvel that in such a world anyone should be willing, deliberately, to make one fellow-human cold even for one hour. And I will marvel, too, as I do now, that anyone should wish, in a world so full of mountains of hostility, to magnify so grandiloquently so petty a molehill.

On the same day Russell himself came to his wife's defense. In a letter addressed to the trustees, he wrote: "The letter written on your behalf to my wife is astonishing by its incivility. I fail to see why what you wished to convey could not have been said orally without formality and completely unnecessary rudeness. I had not before understood that my wife was not allowed at my lectures; I do not know why I was not informed of this. I regret that by asking her to be present I infringed, by ignorance or by oversight, the rules of the Foundation."

Nelle Mullen, representing the trustees, replied to Russell's wife on November 5. The letter read, in part: "It was sweet of you to tell us how low-class the Foundation is compared to Oxford, Harvard, etc.—in short, that a superior, well-bred, learned, charitable soul should not be informed by barbarians that her presence in their midst is undesirable. How to bear up under the disgrace is our most serious problem at the moment."

At his next lecture, Russell apologized to his students for his wife's knitting and her presence at his class. He explained that there had been no objection when his wife attended his lectures at Oxford, Harvard, Chicago, and California. Barnes was present—he attended most of the classes; usually, to Russell's dismay, summarizing the philosopher's lectures at their conclusion. This time, following Russell's apology, he arose from his armchair and asked, "Mr. Russell, in saying that Oxford, Harvard and Chicago did not object to your wife's presence at your lectures, do you mean to imply that there is anything wrong with the way the Foundation conducts its affairs?" Russell answered, politely, "No."

The battle was nearing its end, but there was one more minor skirmish, managed by Barnes, who had obviously been encouraged by Russell's civilized, if seemingly mild, behavior. On November 11 Angelo Pinto, an instructor at the Foundation, wrote the doctor to ask permission to take photos during Russell's lectures; Barnes generally granted such permission if the individual instructor agreed. Accordingly, shortly afterward Pinto put the question in a letter to Russell himself. The letter was answered not by the philosopher but by his wife, who wrote that her husband had no objections, but that since members of his class had reputedly been disturbed by the sound of knitting needles, he would have to consult with them first. The following day, Salvatore Pinto, writing on behalf of his brother, sent a letter to Russell's wife, informing her that his brother had shown her letter to the board of trustees, who, as a consequence, had withdrawn permission to take photographs during the philosopher's lectures.

In December Barnes was somewhat conciliatory. He did not want to lose Russell, and he wrote to tell him how much everyone at the Foundation liked him and profited from his classes. He did, however, find it necessary to add that "when we engaged you to teach we did not obligate ourselves to endure forever the trouble-making propensities of your wife." The philosopher quickly came to his wife's defense. He wrote, "I shall continue to do all in my power (including utilization of my wife's valuable help in research) to make my lectures as good as I am able to make them; but, so far as any personal relationship is concerned, you are mistaken in supposing that there is no quarrel with me, since whoever quarrels with my wife quarrels with me."

The exchange of letters was ending, but Barnes insisted upon having the final word—and he had it. "Your statement 'including utilization of my wife's valuable help in research' is a pure gratuity in the present controversy, unless you mean by that, that your wife will, if you so wish, perform that service on our premises," he wrote. "If that is what you mean, I feel that you should be informed beforehand that if your wife ever enters the door of our gallery, the 'whitehaired lady' [Nelle Mullen] whom she tried to bully on February 27 has been informed officially how to deal with the situation."

With these words the quarrel came to an end. There was no need for Mullen "to deal with the situation." Patricia Russell— the alleged cause of Barnes's displeasure—stayed away from the Foundation, and her husband continued to teach there each Thursday throughout 1942. Meanwhile, the doctor took on another formidable adversary—the press.

19

"**M**any years ago I began to suffer from statements in the public print about my personal life and my work at the Foundation," Barnes had written Russell in the fall of 1940, when the two men were still friends. "At first I corrected these statements, but when the same newspapers and magazines—and the weekly *Time* has been the worst offender in this respect—again dealt with me in print, they published the same false statements that I had already denied. How to deal with a situation of this kind is beyond me. . . ."

This was a complicated problem for Barnes, and his attitude toward the press was an ambiguous one. On the one hand he depended on journalists to spread the word of his anger at the museum, at Penn—at any of his enemies. He saw to it that copies of his vituperous letters were delivered to each and every newspaper, and he took delight in their publication. On the other hand he complained bitterly of inaccurate reporting and regretted that stories of his various battles were given far more space than were reports of the Foundation's serious educational endeavors. Surely, though, he must have realized that a rude letter to a celebrity would make for more interesting copy than would an explanation of William James's influence on the Foundation's educational program.

In any case Barnes had for several years turned down requests for interviews. He had even turned down as reputable a scholar as Archibald MacLeish (whom he admired) when MacLeish, as an editor at *Fortune* in 1935, asked him to write an article (to be illustrated with color reproductions) about the Foundation. His response to the request then was polite and reasonable. "Your plea ranks in quality with the way you write it, and your admission 'that there is no valid reason why you should let us do such an article' really answers your letter; since, however, it leaves my reasons for refusal unsaid, I'll state them briefly," he began. He continued:

> What we are trying to do at the Foundation has never been attempted before—that is, to link an objective study of pictures to the powers possessed by every normal human being and to do it with the aid of respectable educational methods. We've been doing just that for twelve years and the rumor has circulated that we have succeeded to some extent; as a result, we have classes in the gallery every day, every class is filled and we have a waiting list of about four hundred. That's a big job to carry on, one that makes students and staff work seriously. Now, every time that flip bird on *Time* pipes one of his romantic tunes about me, or another journalist publishes something nearer the facts, letters, telegrams and calls pile up by the hundred, nearly every damned one of them from a diversion seeker pleading for admission. The fact that we never answer the requests does not alter the more significant fact that all such things do butt in on an already overfilled program and an overworked staff. What would happen if a really first-rate intelligence like yours let itself go, God only knows. I imagine we'd need the state militia to protect us. And don't let anybody tell you that a colored reproduction by even the best specialist has any real relation to what the painting contains; its analogue is a hearsay version of a honeymoon narrated by an octogenarian.

In 1942 Barnes changed his mind. In a privately published pamphlet, expressing his regrets for having done so, he elaborated on the same reasons for the long-standing policy and explained why he had decided to open the doors—and the files—of the Foundation to at least one journalist:

> Much has also been written about us in newspapers and magazines that deals with topics of interest to the general reader. Almost without exception these articles were the outcome of the disturbing impact of our work upon institutions and individuals that have not kept pace with the educational and cultural progress of our age. Pioneers have always encountered this obstruction and have had to fight against it in order to survive. Our methods of fighting it, often strenuous and not always free from the use of invective, have brought many inquirers to our doors, sometimes reporters looking for sensational bits of news, at other times gifted, honest writers pleading for a first-hand, human-interest account of our work.
>
> Our uniform practice has been to refuse all such appeals; we have preferred to let what we are doing speak for itself to those qualified to understand the basic principles involved. That speaking is done best by our books and by our former and present students.
>
> However, since we had utilized so many other existing social factors as experimental matter for educational purposes, it was decided to see what could be done with one or more of the many writers who were constantly knocking at our door for a story about our work.

The first writer chosen by the doctor to tell the Foundation's story was Carl W. McCardle, of the *Evening Bulletin,* the same reporter who had been allowed to interview Russell on the philosopher's first day at the Foundation. (Barnes had been so pleased with an earlier story of McCardle's that he even allowed the journalist to bring along a photographer, who was permitted to take a photo of the doctor and Russell in front of Cézanne's *The Card Players* on that occasion.)

Barnes liked the results of that interview and, after several meetings with the young reporter, agreed to let him write what he hoped would be a definitive article on the Foundation. For his part Barnes agreed to answer questions, allow McCardle access to all relevant files, and, surprisingly, even to furnish him with color photos of the collection which had been taken by the Pinto brothers. In return McCardle promised to concentrate on the educational aspects of the Foundation in his article and submit whatever he wrote for approval by Barnes before it was given to a magazine for publication.

It didn't take Barnes long to realize that he had made a mistake. The copy McCardle showed him sporadically contained countless distortions and misstatements. Furthermore Barnes later noted that "the whole spirit of his treatment of the subject was a flagrant violation of the agreement according to which I granted him the privilege of writing the article and gave him access to my files." According to the doctor, McCardle assured him that he would make the necessary corrections and show him the revised copy, but when no such revisions were shown to him, in early February, Barnes started legal action to force the journalist to submit a copy of everything he had written.

McCardle's response came on February 10. It came in the form of four sets of galleys (there was no longer any question of seeing the manuscript) sent to Barnes by *The Saturday Evening Post,* which had bought the long article and planned to run it in four installments. The galleys, Barnes was told, were to be returned the same afternoon. He read them with dismay: the many errors could, with time, be corrected, but the whole tone of the article was offensive and could not possibly be changed in one day. In preparation for a legal battle to prevent publication of the articles, he had photostatic copies made of the proofs and on the first sheet pasted a label which read: "Every one of these twenty-eight (28) sheets of these galleys contains statements which are false and misleading and some of which I saw for the first time in this copy."

After consultation with his lawyers, however, he was convinced that there was no legal means of stopping publication. His own agreement was not with the magazine, which could therefore not be forced to suppress the article, and which apparently had not been aware of the doctor's agreement with the author. The most Barnes could do would be to sue the magazine for libel following publication.

Thwarted legally, Barnes tried to convince the *Post*'s editor that it would be morally wrong to go ahead, but this proved futile. Under the circumstances the only remedy was to call together his colleagues and correct the most obvious errors and distortions.

The first installment appeared in the magazine's issue of March 21, 1942. The series was entitled "The Terrible-Tempered Dr. Barnes"—which gave a fair indication of its point of view and its contents. In that first installment McCardle, while expressing admiration for Barnes's courage and independence as well as his collection, characterized Barnes as a "frustrated artist" as well as a "combination of Peck's Bad Boy and Donald Duck." He called him a man who "has made capital out of rudeness" and "gets his greatest personal satisfaction out of writing poison pen letters." Though McCardle did briefly discuss Barnes's views on art and education, the emphasis in the first installment, as in the three that followed, was on the subject's colorful eccentricities and irascibility. McCardle had given the magazine what its readers must have wanted: a large number of lively anecdotes—some true, some half-true, and many completely false.

In his fashion Barnes too gave the *Post* what it wanted—free publicity for the series. Instead of ignoring the article, he spent a good part of March 21—the day the magazine was placed on sale— riding up and down the Main Line, stopping at newsstands and invading drugstores to rip down the three-foot-high posters advertising the series on "Philadelphia's Millionaire Pepperpot." Confiscation of the posters was not enough. Inside each available copy of the magazine, he inserted his answer, a seven-page pamphlet, "How It Happened," which he had written to explain the events that led to the publication of the series. The *Post* took full advantage of the doctor's prolonged tantrum; at hand to meet him at a number of his stops was the magazine's publicity and promotion representative, who saw to it that Barnes's antics were fully reported in the local press.

Though prepared to carry on the battle, Barnes in the end listened to his friend Dewey, who suggested that any further action would merely sell more copies of the magazine. He would, he said, "charge it up to Profit and Louse." Apart from a sober defense of his position, presented on a local radio station, he let the matter drop. This incident had confirmed his opinion of the press, which he felt had once again deceived and misrepresented him. His outrage was, in this case, justified. Even a cursory checking of many of the journalist's sources confirms that the series was an irresponsible mixture of fact and fiction. The question remains, however, as to just how much fiction was supplied by Barnes himself—he often enjoyed startling the public by dramatizing and inventing episodes of his own life.

Barnes made one final attempt to have the story of the Foundation told to the general public through a popular magazine. Shortly after the *Post* debacle, he was approached by the editor of *House & Garden,* who expressed interest in running an article about Barnes's recently acquired country house, Ker-Feal, and about the Foundation itself. Hoping that such an article, published in a magazine he considered somewhat more serious than the *Post,* might serve as an antidote to McCardle's series, he agreed—this time on the condition, which he insisted be put in writing, that nothing be printed without his consent.

Once again he provided a reporter with the necessary information and background material, and once again the material submitted to him was unsatisfactory, in many ways an imitation of what the *Post* had done. This time, however, Barnes had the legal right to stop publication, and he threatened to exercise it. Realizing that it would be impossible to please the doctor, the magazine proposed that the article be written by the one person with whom he could not quarrel: Barnes himself. The proposal was accepted, but, pleading lack of time, the doctor turned most of the job over to his alter ego, Miss de Mazia. He himself undertook to write only a short piece about Ker-Feal.

De Mazia's article was, of course, just what the doctor wanted. Based on material already available in the Foundation's official publications, it dealt solely with the Foundation's methods, aims, and educational program. There were no anecdotes. Illustrated with many reproductions of paintings from the collection, of Ker-Feal and of Barnes teaching at the Foundation, it appeared in the year-end Christmas issue of *House & Garden*. The magazine's cover was appropriate: it showed Barnes (looking remarkably young for his seventy years), his wife, and, at his master's feet, the doctor's dog Fidèle-de-Port-Manech, in front of the entrance to Ker-Feal, apparently welcoming the magazine's readers to join them for a holiday look at the family's country home.

This time Barnes had no complaints. He had learned the never again forgotten lesson that only he or one of his loyal colleagues could accurately tell the story of the Foundation. His dealings with *House & Garden*—no matter how satisfactory the result—had convinced him that, he wrote Henry Hart, "there is an intrinsic, ineradicable, putrid core to journalistic methods as practiced." He vowed he would never again tell his story to the press.

Not long after the festive issue of *House & Garden* appeared on the newsstands, Bertrand Russell received a letter from the Barnes Foundation which was clearly a violation of the spirit of Christmas. Dated December 28, 1942, it read in part:

> For a long time past, our Board of Trustees has had under consideration certain events which have occurred since your contract with us was executed, and which seem to bear directly upon its validity. One of these events concerns the conditions which determined the modification of the terms of the original contract with you.
>
> The details of the matters referred to have been carefully studied in their legal and ethical aspects by properly qualified,

disinterested persons. The legal factor in the situation—breach
of contract—is the basis upon which our Board decided that
the existing contract with you be terminated as of December
31, 1942. . . .

Russell was stunned—by the contents of the letter and the fact
that he had been given only three days' notice. (The letter also
contained an offer that would allow Russell to continue teaching
at a reduced salary, subject to thirty days' notice, but he considered
it derisory.) He was, in his words, "reduced once again from af-
fluence to destitution." For a year he had worried about losing his
job and had done his best to get along with Barnes, under terms
dictated by the doctor himself. Patricia Russell stayed away from
the Foundation. At first she dropped her husband off at the Foundation's gate. Later he took a local train to and from Merion and
walked to and from the Foundation. Aware of Barnes's insistence
upon punctuality, he was frightened of being late for work. "I
remember one day when," Barrows Dunham wrote, "the Paoli local
having been late, Russell arrived at the Foundation also late by
perhaps ten minutes. He was red in the face, out of breath, and
showing anxiety, having run or walked fast from the Merion station
(about half a mile). I was pained to see the leading British philosopher in such a plight."

Socially, too, Russell tried to remain on good terms with the
doctor. "I accepted his invitations and invited him in return. The
amount of social contact was regulated by his wishes," he wrote
William Schack. "At first, I was sorry for Barnes because he suffered
tortures from an inferiority complex. I thought I should be able to
reassure him and get on good terms with him, but he made this
quite impossible."

Barnes found it equally impossible to get along with Russell,
for a number of reasons. In refusing to befriend the doctor and
give in to all of his wishes, he felt Russell showed a lack of gratitude
to the man who had come to his rescue when he needed him. Even
more serious, perhaps, Russell was far too popular with the students at the Foundation. This certainly irritated Barnes, who was

accustomed to being the center of attention. In a letter to Dewey, to whom he sent all copies of their correspondence, Barnes accused Russell of preciosity, of talking down to his students, and of unjustly criticizing America, where he enjoyed "the generosity and advantages he couldn't get in his native country." For many months he had sought an opportunity to fire the philosopher, and that opportunity had arisen when, according to Barnes, the philosopher had broken his contract with the Foundation by accepting outside speaking engagements—at Temple University and at the Rand School of Social Science.

It was a complicated issue. According to their original agreement, Russell was to be paid six thousand dollars a year by the Foundation. When, not long afterward, the philosopher complained that he needed more money and would have to deliver popular lectures to supplement his income from the Foundation, Barnes raised his salary to eight thousand dollars. The only existing contract between the two men, dated August 16, 1940 (though the new terms were actually agreed upon in October), gave the figure of eight thousand dollars and made no mention of outside speaking engagements.

Only a few days after Russell received his letter of dismissal, he turned the matter over to his attorney, Thomas Raeburn White, who decided that it was Russell who could sue for breach of contract. The philosopher issued a statement to the press, making public his contract with Barnes. He also added for the record an article from the *New York Times* of October 23, 1940, which noted that "Mr. Russell is to give one lecture a week for five years at Merion, and is free to teach elsewhere," a statement which Barnes never contradicted.

Barnes did, however, answer Russell's statement to the press:

> Mr. Russell, in his statement to the press, runs true to his familiar form of presenting himself to the public as a martyr— just as he did when the British government put him in jail during the First World War. In the present case he tells the public that he is a poor man deprived of his bread and butter

by an arbitrary act; the facts are that he was dismissed for reasons which he really knows—for they are part of the record—but does not disclose. The letter of 28 December 1942, which discharged him, shows that both the legal and ethical phases of the matter were considered and approved by persons other than ourselves; it shows also that his alleged financial predicament is purely of his own making. . . .

Barnes also commented that Russell's departure had come as a welcome relief to the best of them, but the philosopher's students at the Foundation were confused and upset. They had been told, upon returning to the Foundation after the holidays, that their teacher, finding them dull, inert, and unresponsive, had abandoned them. In response Russell furnished one member of the class, Caroline Lewis Lovett, with copies of his letter of dismissal, asking her to see that his case was presented to as many members of the class as possible, and expressing his regret and indignation at having been parted from his students. At the same time others did their best to spread the truth, though, with one exception, they stopped short of public statements, which certainly would have resulted in their own dismissal from the Foundation. The one exception was Barrows Dunham.

Following Barnes's statement to the press, the *Bulletin* had printed a letter sent to the doctor by one of Russell's students, R. D. Bulley. "Most everything Mr. Russell read to us I found dull and could not remember it without referring to notes," Bulley wrote. "He has not the slightest notion of how to be a good teacher."

Dunham, not interested in returning to the Foundation, replied. His own letter was published in the *Inquirer*. "In my judgment, Mr. Russell's lectures at the Barnes Foundation deserve the highest praise," he wrote. "They were wonderfully clear expositions of a difficult subject, they were full of wit, and they were set forth with that literary grace which has characterized all his writings. Many people have found Mr. Russell to be 'dangerous,' but R. D. Bulley is certainly the first to find him dull." (Dunham later commented: "My own position in the affair was a little awkward. Barnes had been extremely kind to me. I was in his debt. But it was of course quite impossible to think that such an indebtedness could outweigh the defense of a great philosopher.")

When the matter reached the court, it was immediately made clear that Russell, legally, needed no defense. After each side had presented its case, the philosopher's attorney asked for a summary judgment on his client's behalf. It was granted by the judge, who dismissed as immaterial Barnes's contention that Russell had violated an oral agreement reached prior to the execution of the written contract and ruled that the oral agreement, because its provisions were not specified in the subsequent written contract, was of no legal importance.

Barnes was, of course, furious. He blamed his defeat on his friend and lawyer, Robert T. McCracken, who had predicted the verdict and had presented his brief with little hope. McCracken countered by charging that the doctor was at fault for not having consulted him about either the original agreement or the revised one. McCracken was fired—he never saw his client again—and was replaced by Gerald A. Gleeson, who was retained to take charge of the doctor's appeal to the U.S. Circuit Court. In spite of Barnes's claim that Russell had not only broken a promise but that the quality of his lectures had deteriorated since he had started accepting outside engagements, and that he did not live up to the professional and personal standards of conduct required by the Foundation, the appeal was dismissed. There was only one question to be settled by the court: the exact amount of damages to be awarded to Russell as a result of his dismissal from the Foundation.

The trial was held on August 12, 1943. Those who expected fireworks between the two angry, articulate opponents were disappointed. Because they dealt solely with monetary matters, the proceedings were dull. Russell—"at times testy, sometimes laughing nervously, often prim," according to a reporter for the *Inquirer*—testified for two and a half hours; Barnes—"portly, his lower lip protruding bulldog fashion," according to the same reporter—for little more than an hour. Neither added anything of significance to their well-reported statements. Russell noted that because of his dismissal, he would be forced to return to England or starve. His age, seventy, was against him, as was the fact that colleges were curtailing cultural subjects. "And," he added, "there may be lots of people who think I am no good as a philosopher." Barnes claimed that Russell's lectures were perfunctory, that he arrived only two minutes before they began and left after allowing no more than fifteen minutes for questions. In the course of his testimony, he read a list of lectures given by Russell containing the names of eminent early thinkers. "His pronunciation," the philosopher told reporters later, "was very peculiar. In fact he didn't pronounce one of those names correctly." (To which Barnes answered: "I'll tell you what's wrong with that guy—no, I won't, either. You might print it.")

In mid-November Russell was awarded twenty thousand dollars' damages. This represented three years' salary minus four thousand dollars which the court determined he would have been able to earn through outside work during the period remaining in the contract. Barnes promised to appeal—"it's only the first inning and we have not yet gone to bat," he said—but the Supreme Court, a year later, unanimously refused to hear the case.

Unable in his view to obtain justice from the courts, Barnes appealed to the public, and in December 1944 he published another pamphlet, *The Case of Bertrand Russell vs. Democracy and Education*. The purpose of the publication was "to put on record publicly the facts responsible for a serious break in the most vital strands in the fabric of American life." It was, however, nothing more than a summary of the Foundation's relationship with Russell, from the time Barnes hired him—"though I knew of Mr. Russell's propensity for getting himself embroiled with established law and order, and was aware that after brief engagements at Harvard, Chicago, and the University of California, he had been permanently retained nowhere"—until "we decided that the farce could go on no longer, and he was dismissed." There were no new charges in the pamphlet—sent to, among others, the master of each of the fellows of Trinity College, Cambridge—and it ended on an indignant note:

If education is designed to enrich the experience of the student by making him an active participant in the widest and deepest experiences which art, science, and civilization have developed, then Bertrand Russell contributed little or nothing to the education of his class. The reason for his failure was that he himself had no conception of democracy as a sharing in significant experience. The history of ideas about which he lectured was a history of abstractions torn from their human context, with not the slightest recognition of the concretefulness of experience throughout all its history. In the religious and moral history of the past, Mr. Russell could see mainly an occasion for derision and contempt. Above all, he felt so little share in the desire of his students to relate the things he was talking about to their own experience, that the fear of his ridicule froze on their lips the questions that they would have liked to ask. If they learned anything whatever of democracy in education from him, it was because he presented them with the perfect example of its antithesis.

Presumably this was Barnes's last salvo in the Russell case. On February 20, 1945, Lucy Donnelly, the philosopher's friend, wrote him from Bryn Mawr that the doctor had been "quiet as a mouse these last years," and the following year, on November 29, Barrows Dunham wrote Russell, back in England, that "Dr. Barnes has been singularly quiet since his defeat at your hands." Dunham, however, added a note of caution: "I don't know whether this portends a new eruption or whether the volcano is at last extinct. The latter hypothesis seems, however, improbable."

As Dunham predicted, the volcano was not extinct. Barnes was not about to forgive an enemy, and this time the victim of his wrath was Dunham himself, who had become an enemy by praising Russell's lectures publicly in his 1943 letter to the *Inquirer*. The letter, which had in no way attacked Barnes or the Foundation, had infuriated the doctor, according to Claude Bowman, a professor of sociology at Temple and a friend of both Dunham and Barnes, who warned Dunham that Barnes might try to have him fired from his position at Temple as a consequence. Apparently nothing came of this latter threat, but if Dunham believed that his "betrayal" had been forgotten, he was wrong. Barnes was merely waiting for the opportune moment to seek his revenge.

That moment came in 1947 with the publication of Dunham's first book, *Man Against Myth,* a witty and devastating radical exposure of many of the beliefs, slogans, superstitions, and myths commonly held in contemporary society. It was a great success, selling seventy-five thousand copies in its first hardcover edition. Among its admirers, whose endorsements appeared on the jacket, were Albert Einstein ("it is an instructive, amusing and courageous book") and John Dewey. Dewey's praise was unequivocal: "Professor Dunham has written a remarkable book . . . one does not know which to admire most, the pertinence of the book to the present situation or the extraordinary clarity and deft wit with which the book is written. For me, it is most decidedly the book of the year (and in the interest of good sense and intelligent, clear-headed action, one can hope the book of the year for many years to come)."

Barnes was, of course, shocked by Dewey's endorsement. Once again he had been betrayed, but this time the traitor was his best friend, whose loyalty he never doubted. He thought Dunham's book was superficial, one-sided, often silly, and very sophomoric, and he told Dewey so. Apparently Dewey replied by offering to write a letter to Little, Brown, the publisher, withdrawing his endorsement, for Barnes wrote him another letter, stating that Dewey's "stop-notice" to the publisher was too late, and that Dunham was still exploiting the statement. He reminded Dewey that as soon as he had heard of Dunham's book he had offered to bet him that it would be a phony. Worse than that, he continued, it fit smoothly into the Communist Party line. It contained nothing original, and was "a full meal of fellow-traveler nourishment." He concluded angrily: "Your endorsement of the book purports to be 'the sound judgment' of a philosopher recognized as the most distinguished in America. If that judgment is sound, you repudiate the ideas which for twenty-five years we have drilled constantly into students from the day they enter our place until they leave. . . .

"It's a hell of a mess, and I am going to do my damndest to get us, and you, out of it, and help the Federal Government show up these fellow-travelers so they cannot interfere with the foreign policy of the Government."

One week later Dewey answered Barnes, justifying his endorsement of Dunham's book on the grounds that Dunham was hitting at things he felt needed to be exposed. While admitting that there was nothing original in the book, he refused to dismiss it as a mere rehash and reiterated his belief in its usefulness. He had offered to withdraw the endorsement not because he had changed his opinion but out of consideration for Barnes, his friend.

In spite of this reasonable defense of his position, Dewey was obviously stung by Barnes's anger. In the end he wrote to Little, Brown, asking that his endorsement be withdrawn on the grounds that the author was pro-Russian and anti-American and that the book was being used to aid fellow-traveler organizations. At the same time he informed Dunham of his letter to the publisher, explaining that when he endorsed the book he had no idea that Dunham's economic views agreed with those of pro-Soviet partisans.

Dunham was puzzled by Dewey's change of heart, little suspecting that Barnes was responsible for it. Nor was it possible for him to suspect that his mild defiance of the doctor a few years before would have a far-reaching effect on his academic career. At the end of July 1953 he was called before the House Un-American Activities Committee in Washington. When he refused to answer the committee's questions, he was suspended from his professorship at Temple, subject to the university's further examination of the case. In spite of the vigorous intervention of his friend, Bertrand Russell, Dunham was, the following September, dismissed as the chairman of the university's department of philosophy—for displaying "intellectual arrogance" in refusing to cooperate with the committee.

Years later Dunham discovered that Barnes was at least partially responsible for that dismissal. He learned, from the files of the Federal Bureau of Investigation, that the doctor had furnished the bureau with copies of his 1947 letters to Dewey and had, in addition, written personally to the FBI stating, in part: "My interest in counteracting these subversive elements, besides a wish to support the Government's program, is a desire to rid honest, scientific educational methods of the obstructions carried on in underground movements in various institutions. I am particularly incensed at DUNHAM because he duped DEWEY into endorsement of his book by the smooth, slick methods of cheap journalism. . . ."

Ironically though Dunham suffered from his encounter with Barnes, Russell, in the end, profited from his experience with the doctor. His *History of Western Philosophy,* two thirds of which was based on his lectures at the Foundation, is one of his most successful works and was the main source of his income for many years. In the preface of the book he wrote: "This book owes its existence to Dr. Albert C. Barnes, having been originally designed and partly delivered as lectures at the Barnes Foundation in Pennsylvania." He added, "As in most of my work during the years since 1932, I have been greatly assisted in research and in many other ways by my wife, Patricia Russell."

20

With Russell's departure, life returned to normal at Merion. Though the British philosopher's lectures and the publicity that accompanied his dismissal had overshadowed its regular activities, there had been no significant changes in the Foundation's educational program since the early days. Its overall enrollment remained small—limited to about two hundred students—and its admissions policy continued to be eccentric.

Typically the first step in gaining acceptance was a letter to Barnes, with a careful explanation of the applicant's reasons for wanting to study at the Foundation. If the letter was meticulously written on engraved stationery or if mention was made of membership in a prestigious club or of affiliation with a prestigious university, there was little chance of a positive response. If, on the other hand, the preliminary letter was sloppily written (misspellings helped) on cheap paper and signed by an Italian- or Jewish-sounding name (blacks, who were treated similarly, were impossible to identify from their names but not from their Philadelphia addresses), the odds in favor of the applicant rose sharply. Evidence in the letter of a knowledge of the doctor's books was also useful.

A positive response meant a summons to the Foundation's Spruce Street office for an interview with Mary Mullen. If this went well, an invitation to visit the gallery was issued within a few weeks.

Once there, applicants were formally ushered into the main hall. There were no examinations, only a lecture by Barnes, to which the candidates were expected to pay close attention. Apparently the group was carefully observed during this lecture, for after it, only certain members were approached by Mullen and invited to study at the Foundation. No explanations were given to those not accepted.

Once admitted to the tuition-free classes, the students followed a carefully planned schedule. Each attended one session per week. Though classes began promptly at two o'clock, class members were asked to arrive at the Foundation an hour or two earlier so that they might study the collection on their own. The five or six members of the faculty who delivered the lectures and led the discussions that followed were all Barnes-trained; Russell, an outsider, had proven to be an intrusive and even threatening element. Generally the doctor himself conducted one class, on Thursdays. He was, indisputably, the star professor, a vital and commanding, if intimidating, presence. Refusing to rhapsodize poetically over the merits of a work of art and scorning the use of typical art jargon, he spoke in colorful, down-to-earth terms easily understood by his listeners. Frequently he underscored his points by means of unconventional illustrations—sometimes even a piece of music, whether a Beethoven sonata or a Negro spiritual, interpreted in a number of ways to demonstrate the possibility of different approaches to a single theme. By all accounts his lectures were fascinating—far easier to understand than were his books—and those fortunate enough to attend them never forgot them.

Those not so fortunate, whose courses were conducted by lesser members of the faculty, were also given a chance to talk to (or rather listen to) the doctor following their own classes. Permitted to examine the collection at leisure until five o'clock, they would often find Barnes in the main gallery, seated in his favorite armchair, under the Matisse mural, a dog at his side. It was there—a good vantage point from which to watch the behavior of his students as they studied the paintings—that he told anecdotes and dispensed opinions. One former student remembers today:

He had stories to tell about Matisse (his favorite modern), Picasso (his least favorite), Soutine, Pascin, Leo Stein, and others. He especially relished accounts of fights he had with people, how he called Thomas Craven a literary streetwalker, how he and the Foundation's students picketed the Philadelphia Museum, etc. One thing that annoyed many students was Barnes's smoking in the gallery when no one else could. Sure, he owned the paintings, we felt, but if smoke damaged them then his behavior implied that he was more important than they. Most shocking was his delight in setting his ashtray on fire. The first time he did it I thought it was accidental. Then I decided it was a perfect symbol of Barnes's compulsion to shock others and to show the world that he was bound to no law except his own.

When students asked why he let no one in the Foundation except his students and hand-picked visitors he had two answers. One was that Philadelphia had spurned him and called him a degenerate because he liked modern art in the 1920s and '30s. The other was that he only wanted those who could profit from seeing his pictures, those whose minds had not been "debauched" by university art departments (i.e., those who had never questioned his ideas as set forth in *The Art in Painting*).

Few students had the courage to question Barnes during these sessions or at other times. Occasionally he came in at the end of one of the classes and held forth. Once a student named Millstein posed a question, expressing mild disagreement with what the doctor had said. The next week Millstein was missing. He was, Barnes explained, "emotionally unstable." According to a member of that class, "Very few students from then on made anything but very safe comments, which is ironic because Barnes always bragged about the democratic atmosphere at the Foundation."

Disagreement with the doctor was not the only grounds for expulsion. The Foundation's rules were rigid. Two absences, for whatever reason, meant automatic dismissal, as did late arrivals or early departures from a class. Everyone was on trial at all times. "The students have to be in earnest," Barnes once told an interviewer. "Prestige doesn't count. Ph.D. or Harvard are zero to us. If the student doesn't have the interest or the ability, he is dead as far as we are concerned, and gets the gate."

Inflexible rules also governed members of the Foundation's faculty and staff, though these were of a somewhat more complex nature. Barnes saw the Foundation as a patriarchy, over which he ruled, stern but protective. He nurtured and took care of his employees, and he generously provided for their futures. In return he demanded unfailing loyalty and subservience from his staff, whatever their capacity within the Foundation's walls, much as he had from his workers years before at the Argyrol plant. Childless, with no family member other than his wife to look after and with few close friends, he engulfed these employees, many of whom he adopted as he would children. He was a possessive and demanding parent. The slightest sign of independence or disobedience meant immediate expulsion from the family, and few of those cast out were ever allowed to return to the Foundation, even for an informal visit to look at the paintings.

There were some whose loyalty could never be questioned: among them were the Mullen sisters, de Mazia, and Angelo Pinto, a painter, whose career was encouraged by the doctor (Barnes arranged for exhibitions of his work in America and in Europe), who was several times sent to Europe at the Foundation's expense, and who, at this writing, still teaches at Merion and refuses to discuss his work there with anyone not connected with the Foundation. Included among this small group of loyalists, too, was one of his first employees, Fire Chief Nulty, who started working at the Foundation before the beginning of the First World War and continued to work there for the rest of his life. Hired by Mrs. Barnes as a chauffeur, he was soon promoted to the job of general handyman, after which Barnes, recognizing his manual skills, turned over to him the physical care of the paintings in the collection. It was a tremendous responsibility for which he was totally unprepared, but Barnes tried to make up for Nulty's lack of education by sending him to school to learn the art of restoration. By the early 1920s, Nulty was not only the gallery's official restorer, but also a Foundation trustee and curator of the collection. As a restorer, he sometimes showed more enthusiasm than skill. When a piece of paint fell off Manet's *Le Linge,* he knew how to paste it back on; he was also said to have retouched a Tintoretto. However, when he cleaned some of the Foundation's antique ironwork, he did so in an acid bath which made it bright and shiny.

Barnes remembered Nulty in his will, leaving his faithful employee the sum of $5,600 a year for life, stipulating, too, that his wife was to receive the same amount if she survived her husband and did not remarry.

Nulty was an ideal worker, appropriately rewarded by the doctor, as were all these loyal employees, who were also provided for after his death. (Among them was Dewey, who was given a stipend of $5,000 a year until his death.) Cynthia Flannery, who became Barnes's secretary in 1936, enjoyed a less successful stay at the Foundation. She was not remembered in the doctor's will; instead, she was unceremoniously fired after five years of service. Few former Barnes employees wrote of their experiences, but Miss Flannery (later Mrs. Stine) did, in an article published after the doctor's death in the August 1956 issue of *Harper's* magazine—she wouldn't, she said, have dared to have it published while Barnes was still alive. Her portrait of Barnes is not a flattering one.

The young woman's qualifications for her job were impeccable: a graduate of both Vassar and a business school, she also had a working knowledge of French, Italian, and German. In addition, she was more than eager to please her employer—jobs were hard to find. Nonetheless, from her first day, when she took dictation from Barnes in his bathroom at the Spruce Street office (he was composing letters from his steam cabinet), to her last, she suffered, and usually in silence.

Her first morning—she was in tears at the end of it—was no different from the mornings that followed. "As perspiration began to roll from his forehead and vituperative words from his tongue," she wrote, "apoplexy would stalk, and every phrase would be

libelous. Half an hour later, showered, rested, relaxed, he would
nod at the invective I read back to him, but never once did he
mitigate his abuse or hesitate to add still more defamatory words."

During her time at the Foundation, she learned many lessons
for which her education had not prepared her. For one, she was
taught the art of forgery. During her first week at work, the doctor
spent twenty minutes a day teaching her how to sign his name. In
this way no matter how skillful the forgery, he could deny having
written the letter if the defamed recipient brought the matter to
court. He also taught her to sign the name of his imaginary secretary, Peter Kelly, and that of his small mongrel dog, Fidèle-de-
Port-Manech, both of whom took responsibility for some of his
vituperous letters. She also learned the importance of thrift. The
doctor was livid one day when he noted that she had put a three-
cent stamp on a letter that only required two cents postage, and
he demanded that she steam it off the envelope and replace it with
the less valuable stamp. Above all, however, she learned that when
the doctor summoned, the whole world (at the Foundation, in any
case) ran to him.

Once, and only once, did Flannery defy her employer, and the
result was more amusing than devastating. Each day, at noon, the
entire office staff, led by the doctor, would assemble for lunch.
Prepared by the Foundation's chef, Paul, it invariably consisted of
a bowl of chopped lettuce and tomatoes, without dressing, accompanied by a glass of freshly squeezed orange juice. It was Barnes's
choice, and he assured his employees that it was good for them.
Flannery, understandably, never dissented. After more than a year
and a half at her job, however, she decided to assert herself. It was
her twenty-fifth birthday, and to celebrate she summoned up her
courage and announced to Paul, who habitually and uselessly took
luncheon orders, that she wanted a dish of peas, and only peas.
The chef was stunned, but when Flannery reached the luncheon
table she found her plate filled with peas, as she had wanted. "I
waited for Dr. Barnes, seated at the head of the table, to plunge
into his own salad, but his eyes were on my plate," she remembered. " 'What have you there?' he demanded and reaching out,

put a fork loaded with my peas into his own mouth. Wordlessly he rolled them around, savoring what I so happily anticipated. Then his arm shot out, and he exchanged my plate for his. 'They're absolutely delicious,' he announced. 'Let's change.' ''

The same performance was repeated for two more days. Finally, on the morning of the fourth day, Flannery asked if the doctor would like Paul to prepare peas for him, too. Absolutely not, Barnes stated. They were fattening and starchy, and he preferred salad. Nonetheless, when lunch was served, Barnes again ate Flannery's peas. With that, her defiance came to an end. For the next three and a half years, the young woman dutifully ate her salad for lunch.

During her fifth year at the Foundation, Flannery's office was moved to a newly acquired building in Merion—only a short distance from the gallery. As a consequence her contact with the doctor became more frequent, and their relationship steadily deteriorated. Irritated because the war prevented his annual summer trips to France, the doctor's disposition had worsened. "His temper," the young woman noted, "was five years older, five times as unmanageable, and I was at least twenty-five years older."

The end, though not unexpected, came abruptly. Flannery had omitted quotation marks from an important letter, and she was fired—without notice. The news was conveyed to her by Mullen, who asked that she leave the building before the doctor's arrival. Her presence might embarrass him. She stayed too long, however, and as she was gathering her possessions she heard Barnes enter his private office. On an impulse she joined him there. "I just wanted to say good-bye," she told him. "Then," she wrote in her article, "I stared at him. Tears, yes, tears, were streaming down his cheeks. I dug into my bag for a handkerchief. Tears were dripping from my eyes, too."

Apparently farewells were difficult for the doctor, even when they involved saying good-bye to a lesser member of the family. Miss Flannery was never considered more than a distant relative, but his separations from three others, gifted members of his faculty, were considerably more painful.

The first of them, Fred Geasland, was summarily dismissed after several years of faithful service. An earnest, sensitive young man, Geasland had first heard of the Foundation from his friend Ralston Crawford, while both were studying at the Pennsylvania Academy. Crawford told him that he had learned more from Barnes than from all of his teachers at the Academy, and Geasland, impressed, applied for admission to the Foundation's classes in 1931. His application was answered with an invitation to come to Merion on a Sunday. After examining the collection, he was accepted. In 1934, after three years of study, he was given a Barnes Foundation fellowship to travel in Europe, and on his return he was asked by Barnes to join the faculty. Though he had planned to leave the Foundation and go to Mexico with the painter Diego Rivera, Barnes's offer seemed too good to refuse. He was aware of the drawbacks—above all, that he would have to be totally subservient to the doctor's wishes—but he also realized that an association with Barnes, with his intense enthusiasm and passionate interest in art, as well as exposure to the extraordinary collection, would be a unique experience he could not pass up.

Geasland's time at the Foundation was as rewarding and stimulating as he had anticipated. He learned to see in Barnes's way and found the experience enriching. Furthermore, unlike many other members of the faculty, he was rarely aware of tension at the Foundation. His classes were not interfered with by the doctor, who rarely attended them, relying instead on another instructor, Edward T. Dreibelbies, a commercial artist whose loyalty to the Foundation was never questioned, to let him know if Geasland ever strayed from the Barnes doctrine. On the whole Geasland, even today, remembers his work at the Foundation as a joy rather than a job.

In the spring of 1938, however, his tenure at the Foundation came to an end—and the cause, apparently, was a minor incident. It occurred during one of de Mazia's lectures to the faculty—attended by both Geasland and Barnes. In the course of it, the lecturer repeatedly asserted that Picasso "took" this from Cézanne, that from El Greco, something else from Toulouse-Lautrec, etc. At the end of the talk Barnes asked if there were any questions—there seldom were, since few instructors ever dared question the doctor or his trusted assistant. Geasland, however, did have a question this time, though he realized the possible consequences of asking it. Interested in an artist's growth and the sources of his originality, he wanted to know just what de Mazia meant by the word "took." It was a valid question, which could have led to a stimulating discussion, but Barnes was furious. He angrily demanded that Geasland put his question in writing so that it might be properly discussed at the next staff seminar—these meetings, held each Thursday morning, were generally presided over by either de Mazia or Drei-belbies.

Geasland dutifully and carefully wrote out his question, but it was never discussed. Instead Barnes called a special meeting of his faculty—minus Geasland. He wanted to know their honest opinions of the heretical instructor. When they proved unwilling to speak out against a colleague they all liked, he asked them to sign a statement condemning the question as a foolish one. Risking their own jobs, most of the faculty declined, and Barnes took matters into his own hands.

At his next class Geasland was informed that the doctor wanted to discuss an important matter with him in his office. Present, in addition to Barnes, were the Mullen sisters and de Mazia. (The doctor liked to have witnesses, especially silent ones, which the three women inevitably were.) There was nothing to discuss, however. The instructor—to whom Barnes had personally inscribed a copy of *The Art in Painting* with the words "To Fred Geasland, who not only learned but helps others to learn"—was handed a letter of resignation, which he was asked to sign. This time Geasland refused—he saw no reason to put his signature to a meaningless document. As he left Barnes followed him down the stairs, more enraged than ever, this time because his victim had failed to say good-bye.

The second instructor, John Condax, managed to leave undramatically, though his departure must have hurt the doctor, who considered every leave-taking a betrayal. Condax, who had also studied at the Pennsylvania Academy, was associated with the Foundation for ten years, from 1933 to 1943. After he had studied there for a year, Barnes asked him to teach a class of first-year students. Condax accepted the position on two conditions: that his work would be limited to one day a week and that Barnes— known to harass members of the teaching staff—would promise not to interfere with his classes. The doctor agreed, and he kept his word. He came to Condax's classes only when invited, and when he did he spoke well of the novice instructor. Outside of the classroom, too, he showed a similar respect for the young man. He allowed him the rare privilege of photographing many works from the collection—including, most surprisingly, a few in color, and he included him among those given trips to Europe at the Foundation's expense. He also gave him personal letters of introduction to Leo Stein and to Matisse.

Most of Barnes's efforts to become more than a mere employer to Condax failed, however. Though he admired Barnes and was grateful for his generosity, Condax felt no filial responsibility toward his employer, and when he neglected to tell him that he had moved to New York, the doctor was hurt. He could have helped him there, he said, but Condax neither needed nor wanted help. By keeping his distance and by refusing to get involved in the Foundation's controversies, the independent young man kept his job. When, however, he finally left the Foundation for commercial work (he is today a successful photographer), his days at the Foundation and his relationship with Barnes—officially and unofficially—came to an end. Though he left while still on good terms with the doctor, his subsequent requests to visit the gallery were answered by the standard printed rejection forms.

Jack Bookbinder, the third instructor, was for Barnes perhaps the most promising of all the young members of the Foundation's faculty, and for that reason Barnes felt his "act of treason" most deeply. Bookbinder, another graduate of the Pennsylvania Academy, was also a graduate of Penn's School of Social Work. In 1935, while on a government fellowship to study psychology, he became a student at the Foundation. During the three years he attended classes there—among his teachers were Geasland and Dreibelbies—Bookbinder had no personal contact with Barnes. Though he would see the doctor holding court in the main gallery, he was never able to summon the courage to engage him in conversation. Because of this he was more than surprised when one day the doctor singled him out—the timid young man had unobtrusively joined a group of his fellow students in the gallery following the end of the classes—by informing him that he knew he was studying psychology and suggesting that he read a most interesting book, the name of which he had forgotten. Based on the doctor's vague recollections, Bookbinder took a guess and was right—it was Bernard Hart's *The Psychology of Insanity*. Barnes was impressed. Within a few weeks the young man was invited to the home of the doctor's emissary, Dreibelbies, who asked him if he would be interested in teaching at the Foundation. Bookbinder, honored, replied that he would accept any proposal that Barnes might make. Out of curiosity, however, he wanted to know why he had been chosen for the position. He learned that the doctor's method of selecting his staff was not always scientifically valid. He had been chosen, he was informed, because by sitting on the edge of his chair throughout the lectures he had shown himself to be an unusually attentive student. Actually, according to Bookbinder, he sat uncomfortably on the edge of his chair merely to keep himself awake—not because the lectures bored him, but because of the poor ventilation in the classroom.

If Barnes's scientific method was faulty in this case, his instincts proved to be correct. Bookbinder became a highly valued member of the Foundation's faculty. He was an excellent teacher, with a knowledge of psychology and education as well as art, who could, in the doctor's own words, "recite the pattern of our principles in an entertaining, histrionic fashion." Barnes also liked him personally: he sent him to Europe twice at the Foundation's expense and often visited him in his apartment. During these social visits, he usually managed to sell the young man, at cost, American antiques that he himself had collected. (During this period Barnes, unable to buy paintings in Europe, was buying antiques in Pennsylvania.) Bookbinder never knew whether the doctor was trying to do him a favor or was merely getting rid of pieces he no longer wanted—though he suspected the latter.

Bookbinder taught at the Foundation for seven years and was eventually promoted to the rank of senior instructor. During this time, his excellence as a teacher and the esteem in which his students held him even convinced Barnes to forgive him his few transgressions. Barnes was furious that, when discussing Venetian painters, the instructor dared to refer to the historical background that had contributed to their development—a clear violation of the Barnes doctrine—but he overlooked it. He was disappointed when Bookbinder refused to denounce Geasland and even more disappointed when the instructor failed to put potentially embarrassing questions supplied by Barnes to Bertrand Russell following a lecture on India which the philosopher had given at Temple University—but these were not sufficient causes for dismissal. In 1944, however, Bookbinder's tenure at the Foundation came to an end—ironically as a result of the doctor's having given him permission to work for the Philadelphia Board of Education.

Bookbinder had, for several years, given courses in art at Philadelphia's evening schools. He had also served as instructor in painting in three Board of Education–sponsored summer workshops, which encouraged teachers to develop their own skills in the arts. In the summer of 1943 Bookbinder was asked by the board to write an extended essay summarizing his experiences. The result, a seventy-four-page pamphlet, was published in 1944 and given to every member of the professional personnel of the Philadelphia Public School system—principals, supervisors, superintendents, and all teachers. Entitled *An Invitation to the Arts,* it is an enthusiastic, well-written statement of the author's belief in the importance of education in the arts within the regular school curriculum, as well as a plea for greater efforts at creative self-expression on the part of all adults. Its message is as valid today as it was then.

Several advance copies of the brochure were sent out, and one of them reached Barnes's desk. After reading it, he summoned its author to his office. When Bookbinder arrived, he found the doctor seated with his usual star witnesses, Mary Mullen and de Mazia, ready to take notes. It was a stormy meeting, during which Barnes—who had carefully analyzed the essay—angrily enumerated his complaints. For one, C. Leslie Cushman, associate superintendent of schools, had, in his introduction to the essay, identified Bookbinder as a lecturer at the Barnes Foundation; in stating this simple, irrefutable fact, he had associated the Foundation with the Board of Education, an organization Barnes looked upon as the enemy. (The doctor was, he later wrote a friend, "sick and tired of these fakers and their charlatanry in exploiting our name in their publications.") Equally important, the pamphlet misrepresented the ideas Bookbinder had learned and had later taught at the Foundation.

Bookbinder remained calm during most of the session. At one point he commented that he couldn't have been a total failure as a teacher, since his students liked him and Barnes himself had promoted him and often raised his salary. (The doctor replied that he must have hypnotized the students.) He kept his sharpest ammunition for the end, however. As the doctor concluded his tirade, Bookbinder noted that at least one educator, whom they both held in esteem, had expressed admiration for the brochure—and the educator was John Dewey. Barnes was flabbergasted. Bookbinder offered to go home to get a copy of the letter—in it Dewey had written that he enjoyed Bookbinder's "excellent account"—but the offer was rejected. Instead the doctor issued an ultimatum: either Bookbinder request that the Board of Education withdraw the pamphlet from circulation, or he must resign from his position at the Foundation.

Bookbinder needed no time to come to a decision. He turned to de Mazia and Mullen, shook their hands, and left the room. Barnes, shocked, ran after him. "You son of a bitch!" he shouted. "Somewhere in your pamphlet you mention a warm handshake. You shook their hands, but you wouldn't shake mine." Bookbinder was determined to make this a memorable farewell. "Doctor, read the pamphlet again," he replied. "Nowhere does it say to shake the hand of a Hitler."

The handshake incident did not bring the matter to a close as far as Barnes was concerned. Days after it he wrote the first of a long series of angry letters to Bookbinder, his lawyer, Robert D. Abrahams (whom the teacher had hired to protect him legally from the doctor's wrath), and to the Board of Education. It soon became obvious that Barnes wanted to pick a fight with the board and not with Bookbinder, who, though guilty of collaborating with the enemy, was merely the excuse for the fight. The board survived the doctor's attacks, as did Bookbinder, whose career flourished after his resignation from the Foundation, both as a painter and as the Director of Art Education of the Philadelphia Public Schools, a position he held until his retirement in 1977.

In spite of these setbacks Barnes persisted in his search for additions to the Foundation's faculty—the defectors had to be replaced—and in the fall of 1945 he discovered another young man, Roderick M. Chisholm, who seemed a likely candidate. Chisholm, then an army lieutenant, had written to Barnes, requesting a copy of *The Case of Bertrand Russell vs. Democracy and Education* and enclosing a two-dollar check as payment. Barnes sent the pamphlet and returned the check, good-naturedly suggesting that the soldier use the money for a couple of drinks of good Scotch.

A correspondence between the two men followed. Chisholm, a graduate of Brown and of Harvard (where, as a philosophy major, he received his doctorate), was an intelligent and articulate scholar, and Barnes was impressed by his letters. Before long he invited him to Merion. The young man was, in his own words, "quite overwhelmed, though in somewhat different ways, by Barnes and his collection of paintings." He found the doctor to be extraordinarily opinionated, but he thoroughly enjoyed talking to him about art—though he admitted that he himself knew next to nothing about the subject. To his surprise this confession seemed to please his host, who vaguely suggested that Chisholm might teach a course in the philosophy of art at the Foundation following his discharge from the army.

It seemed to Chisholm an unlikely possibility. He knew no more about the philosophy of art than he did about painting, and he had done no teaching of any kind. He had no reason to suspect that for exactly those reasons he might be just the man Barnes wanted—a gifted student of philosophy, not yet "debauched" by conventional art education, who could serve as a Foundation-indoctrinated replacement for Russell. Barnes was, however, not quite ready to make a proposal—first, he wanted Dewey's approval. A meeting was arranged. Chisholm went to the older philosopher's Fifth Avenue apartment in New York City, and following a long talk, Dewey concluded that the young man's keen mind, sense of humanity, and open-mindedness made him ideally qualified for the position.

Barnes took Dewey's advice, and a few weeks later he made his offer. Chisholm accepted it. Since Chisholm was to be discharged from the army in March, Barnes suggested that he take up his official duties at the Foundation the following fall. Before then, in the late spring, he would be given his own office at Merion— so that he could spend the summer studying the collection and acquiring a sound understanding of the philosophy of art and the Barnes-Dewey method of teaching it.

Barnes had ambitious plans for Chisholm, and they included not only the Foundation but also the University of Pennsylvania. He was once again considering the possibility of an alliance between the Foundation and his alma mater. All, apparently, had been forgiven. Time had passed since the earlier debacles, and the doctor had reasons to believe that an arrangement might now be feasible. This time he would be dealing with people he knew and trusted. He was working out the details of a new plan with a lifelong friend, Horace Stern, an attorney and scholar well acquainted with the goals of the Foundation and also a trustee of the university; and the intermediary between the two institutions was a man Barnes had grown to admire and respect, Dr. John Fogg, the university's vice provost, who, as professor of botany, had been working with the Foundation's arboretum for six years.

Barnes outlined his and Stern's plan to Fogg on the morning of April 19, 1946. In most respects it was similar to the one proposed in the past, but there was one difference: the university was to appoint Chisholm as a full professor in its department of philosophy. His appointment would be designated as the "Barnes Foundation Professorship in Philosophy," and he was to teach one class a week for Penn students in the Foundation's gallery. This time university officials acted without delay. Barnes's offer was gratefully accepted, and a joint announcement of the alliance was issued on May 10 by Barnes and George W. McClelland, Penn's president.

Chisholm arrived at the Foundation on June 1. He was warmly received: Barnes had tirelessly searched for a home for his new professor and his family, certain that their stay in Merion would be a long and successful one.

From the very beginning it was obvious that he was wrong. Chisholm thoroughly enjoyed his summer at the Foundation, learning to appreciate the magnificent collection and studying reading material supplied to him by his employer. Barnes, however, was not having a good time. After only a few weeks his enthusiasm for his new employee began to wane. His observations of and conversations with Chisholm led him to believe that he had made a terrible mistake in hiring him. Though he was careful to make no mention of his misgivings to Chisholm himself, he became alarmed that another attempt to collaborate with Penn might collapse—this time because of his own professor's inadequacies. In desperation he appealed for help to Laurence Buermeyer, the Foundation's former assistant director of education, who had remained Barnes's faithful friend.

Buermeyer, then in retirement, responded to Barnes's frantic plea to come to the rescue. He agreed to rejoin the Foundation's staff. His entrance on the scene, in midsummer, signaled the end of Chisholm's tenure as well as the end of Barnes's latest effort to join forces with the university.

Buermeyer's principal duty at the Foundation, it became clear, was to make certain that Chisholm's lectures adhered strictly to the Barnes doctrine. In early August the totally inexperienced professor submitted, at Barnes's request, a written outline of the topics he proposed to cover in his course. The doctor was dismayed, and Buermeyer carefully explained to Chisholm how his outline differed from the "objectively verified facts" as stated in the Foundation's publications. But neither felt that the young man had understood the problem. The lectures were to serve as a demonstration of the validity of the Foundation's views rather than as an independent examination of the basic philosophical questions with which Barnes's program was involved, which is what Chisholm had in mind.

Their fears were realized on October 1, two days before the start of classes, when they read a detailed summary of the contents of Chisholm's first Thursday lecture. They didn't like it, and—only one day before his first class—they ordered Chisholm to come up with something more in keeping with the Barnes doctrine. The result was equally disappointing. Chisholm's first lecture was, from their point of view, a total failure.

As a consequence a more drastic plan was put into effect. Each Tuesday Chisholm was to submit, in triplicate, a full outline of the lecture to be given two days later—one copy was for Barnes, one for Buermeyer, and one for de Mazia. That same evening Chisholm was to discuss it with Buermeyer and incorporate his corrections. The following morning, the results of the Tuesday evening session would be submitted to de Mazia, who would make her own corrections.

Chisholm's lectures, subject as they had been to constant revision, were, predictably, disastrous; he was often forced to mouth words that had been no part of his original scheme. To make matters worse, de Mazia was present during all of the lectures, and Barnes was present at most of them. They both took copious notes, a practice which unnerved the inexperienced teacher.

The situation deteriorated rapidly, and Chisholm realized that his days at the Foundation were numbered. The climax was reached in the middle of November. On November 8 Chisholm received a letter from Barnes with specific suggestions for the lecture to be given six days later. The occasion was to be a special one. The doctor had invited several university officials—among them, McClelland and Glenn Morrow, a professor of philosophy as well as dean of the college—to attend and form their own opinion of Chisholm's lecture.

The officials had been invited to witness the carefully planned humiliation of a gifted young teacher. Chisholm, understandably nervous, spoke for thirty minutes. When he finished, Barnes took the podium. For two hours he confidently expounded the Barnes doctrine, doing his best to counteract what he felt to be the baneful effects of Chisholm's earlier lectures and demonstrating that the young professor and not the Foundation had been responsible for the shortcomings of those lectures.

A week later, after one more lecture, the doctor demanded Chisholm's immediate resignation. Once again he found it awkward to say good-bye: he wanted the leave-taking to be amicable. He bore no ill will, he explained, toward a personable and decent young man, and, with consideration for his future, he told his students that Chisholm, who was to be replaced by a regular member of the Foundation's faculty, had been forced to leave because of other and more important duties at Penn.

Chisholm's dismissal did not mean the end of his academic career. He remained at Penn until the summer of 1947—Dean Morrow felt that he had not been given a fair chance by Barnes and asked him to teach at the university as a regular member of its faculty—after which he returned to Brown, where he later became chairman of the department of philosophy.

Nor was his dismissal the solution to all of Barnes's problems with Penn. These problems were, by this time, familiar ones, no different from those the doctor had faced years before in his dealings with the university: Penn's alleged lack of enthusiasm for the program, its unwillingness to share responsibility with the Foundation, and its inability to find adequately prepared students to attend the course. Only a few months after Chisholm's departure, Barnes, weary of the incessant bickering, gave up. He again fired the University of Pennsylvania, and he made no effort to disguise his anger. In a long report issued on April 10, 1947, he summarized this latest experiment with these words: "Thus ends a melancholy record of inertia, lethargy, disorder, blindness and futility on the part of Penn officials. . . . By their torpor, the authorities have forfeited for the second, and last, time one of the most valuable gifts, educational and material, ever offered to a university. . . ." In his statement Barnes made two errors: it was the third, and not the second, time he had ended his relationship with Penn; and it was not—yet—the last.

Throughout the years policy regarding admission to the gallery of the Barnes Foundation remained as unpredictable as that which governed selection of its faculty and admission to its classes. The large majority of those who asked to see the fabulous collection received the usual printed rejection form. Occasionally, when in the mood for a fight, the doctor himself would write a letter of explanation. The recipient of one such letter was Ben Wolf, of the *Philadelphia Art News*. Wolf had written, politely, in January 1938, praising the collection and asking that the doors of the Foundation be opened to the public at least one day a week. Barnes's response was insulting; it also contained an unequivocal restatement of the reasons for the Foundation's policy:

> Your letter of January 25 confirms the opinion I formed of
> you by reading the stupid, ignorant, gossipy, sensation-hunting
> "tripe" published in your paper; in other words, you hope to
> climb out of the intellectual and commercial slums by pan-
> dering to the ignorant, uninformed tribe that infests the fringe
> of art. If, in that adventure, you think you can make use of
> me or the institution which I founded, "go to it" and do your
> damndest. . . .
> Your statement that you write "on behalf of all those paint-

ers who are sincerely trying to create works of art, and of those laymen who are endeavoring to enrich their appreciation of art"—all that, viewed in the light of actual facts, makes it pretty clear that you are either a colossal ignoramus or a demonstrable liar.

Your plea that our gallery be opened even once a week to your hypothetical group, displays gross ignorance of the purposes of our project, of the decisions of the Courts that it is not a public gallery but an educational institution, that every day from sunrise to sunset the gallery is occupied in carrying out a systematic educational program, that every class is filled to capacity, and that we have a waiting list of several hundred desirable students who cannot be accommodated because every available place is occupied by earnest, intelligent persons. . . .

Among those not permitted to visit the gallery were some of the most illustrious figures of the time—names alone did not impress the doctor. When T. S. Eliot, lecturing at nearby Bryn Mawr, asked to see the collection, the answer, given to his hostess's chauffeur, was a straightforward "Nuts." No reason was given. The eminent art historian Meyer Schapiro was refused admission without an official explanation, presumably because he had briefly noted in an article his regret that works from the Barnes collection were not included in a major Matisse retrospective held at the Museum of Modern Art in 1931. Not even the intervention of Dewey, his colleague at Columbia, helped. A request by Jacques Lipchitz, eager to see his own sculptures displayed at the Foundation, was turned down; Barnes had never forgotten the artist's "betrayal" many years earlier.

Le Corbusier, too, while on a lecture tour in America, was a victim of the doctor's bad manners, though he almost had a chance to see the collection. His application for admission, he was informed at first, was approved—for a date and time specified by Barnes. When the architect replied that the time was not suitable because of a previously scheduled lecture, however, Barnes was offended. He wanted a fight. In a letter accusing Corbusier of being drunk during his stay in Philadelphia, he informed him that he was no longer welcome at the Foundation. The architect's reply was conciliatory. He was not interested in quarreling with Barnes, he wrote; he preferred to fight with those who disagreed with him on artistic matters, and he knew that the doctor, instead, shared his own enthusiasms. He was certain that he would never meet Barnes, but he wanted the senseless state of war that existed between them to come to an end. Barnes never answered the letter; he returned it, with the word *"merde,"* written in large letters on the envelope.

Though Le Corbusier refused to join battle with Barnes, Alexander Woollcott, the popular drama critic, journalist, and radio commentator, whose insults could be even more penetrating than those of the doctor himself, was delighted at the opportunity to do so. The result was a well-publicized feud which benefited Woollcott professionally and provided Barnes with a welcome, entertaining distraction from his more serious struggles.

Woollcott, the model for Sheridan Whiteside, the witty, egotistical protagonist of Kaufman and Hart's enormously successful comedy *The Man Who Came to Dinner*, came to Philadelphia in March 1941. Though not a professional actor, he played the role of Whiteside in the comedy's touring company, and shortly after the play opened either Woollcott or his press agent decided that an exchange between the two feisty Philadelphians (Woollcott was also a graduate of Central High) would be just the thing to stimulate business. Barnes, intentionally or not, proved to be the perfect foil.

Woollcott began the quarrel by sending off a collect telegram to Barnes, asking that he be allowed to see "an assorted dozen of pictures in your collection on Thursday or Friday of next week." The doctor responded immediately with a letter signed by his dog, Fidèle-de-Port-Manech, which read:

> I was alone in the house this morning when a telegraph office employee telephoned that she had a telegram for Dr. Barnes, charges collect. I explained to her that our financial condition made it impossible for us to assume additional responsibility and I declined to accept the telegram. She said

that it was from such an important man that I should call Dr. Barnes to the 'phone to take the message and accept the delivery charge. My reply was that Dr. Barnes was out on the lawn singing to the birds and that it would cost me my job if I should disturb him at his regular Sunday morning nature worship.

The telegraph office girl is evidently a person either very sympathetic to my lowly position or an individual who knows that to thwart a man of your eminence would be flagrant lèse majesté, for she read the telegram to me. . . .

A copy of this letter—not accidentally—reached the *Evening Bulletin*, to whom Barnes explained his refusal to even consider Woollcott's request. "I haven't seen Mr. Woollcott's play, and wouldn't dream of doing so," he said, "but I understand that he portrays someone who comes somewhere for dinner and stays for weeks. I would be afraid if I let him come to see a dozen of my paintings he might stay to see the more than 1,000 in the collection."

The following day, it was Woollcott's turn. "Of course, I never was foolish enough to send you that telegram collect," he wrote, "but I certainly did not have my wits about me when I asked to see twelve of your pictures. I could not possibly look at more than six in any one day with pleasure and profit."

Elsewhere in his letter, he said he hoped Barnes would not mind if he discussed the matter in a radio interview. "In that interview I shall have to explain that I have not enough leisure during this week in Philadelphia to see half the things I would like to see," he wrote. "In that connection, I shall make it clear that whereas I quite understand the pardonable pride in your collection which had led you to besiege me with invitations to examine it, my engagement at the theatre and my preoccupation with more important matters simply will not leave me time to see your pictures."

Barnes was fighting with a professional, and he warmed to the battle. While furnishing Philadelphia newspapers with copies of the correspondence, he sent an open letter to his adversary:

You entered the ring with a high-hat telegram which, public opinion says, was knocked into a cocked hat by Fidèle's letter of March 22.

Naturally you're sore that any person would have the effrontery to enter your own alley and swap punches with you. Your statement that you propose to use in your radio interview today the falsehood quoted above [the statement made by Woollcott that time would not permit him to see the Barnes collection] as a defense weapon is practically a declaration that you intend to use a blow below the belt in order to maintain your assumed position of world champion in a particular field.

I hope, entirely for your own sake, that you won't spread the threatened falsehood without, at the same time, quoting my refutation and the offer to back it up.

The refutation was this: "I have never spoken or written to you in my life about any matter whatsoever. Tell them, too, that if you will furnish incontrovertible evidence that I ever invited you to 'examine' our pictures, or even to visit our gallery, we shall give you, free of charge, the most important painting in our collection."

At this point Woollcott apparently grew tired of the correspondence—his play was ending its Philadelphia run.

"I am afraid it will be impossible for me to continue this correspondence after I have left Philadelphia," he wrote. "Perhaps that is just as well because inevitably you would grow more wary and not fall so readily into such a trap as my bogus threat to do a broadcast about you. . . . I am sorry my Philadelphia visit must be so crowded, but I promise to come out and see the pictures the next time I pass this way."

Barnes would not let the matter rest. He wanted the final word, and he wrote Woollcott that "tears dimmed my sight" when he read that there would be no more letters. He added: "My sorrow was like that of the prepared boxer who is told that the bout has been called off because his adversary has been inflicted with an acute attack of cold feet. To switch the metaphor, Philadelphia enjoyed the trimming of the fringe of your intellectual trousers carried so high that your mental bottom was exposed to the public at large."

In conclusion, in response to Woollcott's promise to come to the Foundation during his next visit to Philadelphia, Barnes wrote, "I must warn you that thousands of birds inhabit our park and they swoop down on every visible lump of suet and peck it to pieces."

Not every request to visit the gallery was met with hostility. Some applicants had no difficulty in gaining admission—and most of these were graciously treated by their host. Einstein came, as did Thomas Mann. Barnes seemed to have a predilection for actors: among his admiring guests were Katharine Cornell, Eva Le Gallienne, Edward G. Robinson, Edgar Bergen, and Charles Laughton. Carl Van Vechten, the writer and photographer, was not only asked to come to the Foundation, he was besieged with invitations to attend the Sunday concerts given by the Bordentown singers and to bring with him some of his celebrated friends, among them Marian Anderson and Ethel Waters (neither of whom ever accepted the invitations). Van Vechten often visited the Foundation, but under one condition, set by Barnes—that he "be unaccompanied by art critics or newspaper writers: these, after our dogs are finished with them, we bury in the manure pit."

There were exceptions, however, even to this seemingly inflexible rule. Barnes was rarely consistent, and some journalists and art critics were permitted to view the collection. Paul Bird, editor of *The Art Digest*, was astounded at his reception and, following Barnes's death, wrote, "It was with misgivings that we met him one afternoon years ago at the door of the Barnes Foundation at Merion. Yet, no one could have been a more gracious host that afternoon, and no experience more memorable than viewing the collection with Barnes as our guide, giving us the history of many of the works, and chuckling frequently over the bargains he had wrangled from Paris dealers."

Equally surprising was Barnes's treatment of the art historian

Kenneth Clark, who remembered his first visit to the Foundation in his autobiography:

> After careful scrutiny by a man who could properly be described as a roughneck (one could have struck a match on his neck) we were admitted, and found our host alone in his fabulous Gallery sitting on a kitchen chair, listening to a tape recording of his own speech of welcome to Vollard. We did not disturb him but ran rapidly round the other rooms, expecting at any moment to be chucked out by the roughneck. After about twenty minutes he confronted us, with beetling brows. He was dressed in St. Tropez style, and Jane was inspired to say, "What a beautiful shirt you have on, Dr. Barnes." "Yes," he said, "it's a good one. And I wear red pants on Sundays." This was the foundation for a friendship which became, in the next five years, almost embarrassingly warm.

Barnes's behavior surprised Bird and Clark. His quarrels and feuds were widely publicized (with the doctor's full cooperation), but his acts of kindness and generosity and his moments of relaxation—however brief—were not. On occasion the scowl which blanketed his dour face was replaced by a smile, and his customary hostility by an almost childlike playfulness.

When he wanted to, he could be charming and affable. He wrote Vitale Bloch, an art dealer from Germany, that the Foundation could allow casual visitors only "once in a blue moon," but "the moon takes on that hue on Thursday afternoon of this week, between the hours of one and four." In the same letter he suggested that Bloch contact Lady Christabel Aberconway, who had frequently applied for admission, to see if she might join him. "I don't know her from Adam's wife," he wrote, "but she might be young, attractive, and interesting." Apparently she was, for the visit was a great success. Upon her return to London, Aberconway wrote to express her thanks, and Barnes replied that his enjoyment in having her at the Foundation was equal to her own. He added, in answer to her letter, "You made a serious mistake when you were here in not telling me that I had the voice of an opera singer; if you had, I should have had the greatest pleasure, and you probably a great shock, in singing the largest repertoire of Methodist hymns of any person I know."

Barnes was equally gracious and friendly in his treatment of Dorothy Brett, a painter, daughter of an English lord, and a worshipping admirer and friend of D. H. Lawrence. Barnes met her during a visit to Taos, New Mexico, and had invited her to come to Merion to see the collection. In early February 1930 Brett wrote to accept his invitation. Barnes took obvious, good-natured pleasure in responding. Labeling her letter "sheer vituperation and boasting," he asserted that only extra-ordinary courage or ignorance of his reputation as an assassin could have permitted her to call his Foundation an "art school." If the Foundation was an art school, he claimed, she herself was a fat scrubwoman. He continued in the same vein. Recognizing that she was at an impasse in her own painting, he boasted that he was already more advanced than she when, many years ago, he had given up painting. Nonetheless, he concluded, though her letter indicated her lack of intelligence to appreciate them, he renewed his invitation to come to look at his paintings. All he needed was a few days' notice. When Brett arrived at Merion a few weeks later, she was enthusiastically greeted by her host, who had a car meet her at the station and who lunched with her at the Foundation. He shared her sorrow at the recent death of Lawrence, a writer he had placed "with the gods," and he became her friend, never in the future refusing her requests to see the collection.

Barnes's few friendships remained intact throughout his later years. Dewey never disappointed him. In 1939 Barnes spoke at a dinner in honor of the philosopher's eightieth birthday, and in December 1946 he and Laura Barnes were the only nonfamily members invited to the eighty-seven-year-old philosopher's wedding to the forty-two-year-old Roberta Grant.

His frequently stormy relationship with Leo Stein mellowed. He gave his old friend money when he needed it, and he was generous in his praise of Stein's book *Appreciations*, when it was published in 1947. He wrote Stein that it was a "knockout" and added that "I have never read any other exposition so clear, sensible and accurately descriptive as is the theme of your book." In conclusion, he noted, "What I have said above is but a feeble expression of my enthusiasm for the book and the deep admiration for its creator."

Barnes's friendship with Charles Laughton, an art collector as well as an actor, who often visited Merion, was untroubled and informal. The two enjoyed talking together as much as they did drinking together. One morning a Philadelphia dealer, Robert Carlen, responding to the doctor's urgent early call, arrived at the Foundation to find the two friends in the throes of a hangover. Carlen had been summoned to show the actor the paintings of Horace Pippin, a black, unschooled, and very gifted artist Barnes had discovered at the dealer's gallery and had subsequently promoted. (The doctor was later somewhat dismayed when, after showing Pippin through the gallery in Merion, the unassuming artist's only reaction to the Renoirs was "My, what big tits!") In spite of Laughton's shaky condition, the dealer managed, at Barnes's insistence, to sell the actor a Pippin.

On one occasion, in 1940, Barnes and Laughton granted a joint interview to Laura Lee of the Philadelphia *Bulletin*. During it, the doctor allowed a photographer to take pictures of his actor friend, curled up on a bench in the main gallery, gazing at a wall full of Renoirs, with Seurat's *Models* and Cézanne's *Card Players* behind him.

According to the reporter, the two men "cut up and joked just like kids." They had first met, they told her, five or ten years before—they were vague about that. "You asked to meet me," said Laughton, to which his friend replied, "You're a liar. I never asked to meet anyone in my life." They exchanged extravagant compliments. According to Barnes, the actor was "both a great artist and a great guy." In return Laughton called Barnes a genius. "Dr. Barnes is a national possession," he told the reporter. "In a hundred years the country will realize that. There have only been half a dozen such men in the world." As proof of his friendship the doctor lent Laughton twenty paintings and drawings to brighten up his new home in California and often advised him on his collection.

Toward the end of his life, Barnes made new friends, too. Among them was Dorothy Norman, who in 1948, many years after she had studied at the Foundation, joined with the doctor in an effort to promote the work of a little-known anti-Nazi German painter, Alo Altripp, a number of whose works were included in the Foundation's collection. In 1949 they both contributed articles on Altripp to *Vogue* magazine; and that same year Barnes arranged for an exhibition of the painter's work at New York's Van Dieman-Lilienfeld gallery—he also wrote the foreword to the catalogue. However, neither the articles nor the exhibition stimulated much interest in the artist's work. This time Barnes had bet on the wrong man, for neither the critics nor the public agreed with his assessment of Altripp.

Though their efforts to further Altripp's career failed, their interest in the artist marked the beginning of a warm friendship between Barnes and Mrs. Norman. They saw each other and corresponded frequently. Though she recognized his faults—his need to dominate and his paranoid fear of being used—Mrs. Norman today remembers none of the devil in Dr. Barnes. On the contrary, once he abandoned that familiar role—which she believed he felt he was expected to play—she found him to be a relaxed, affable companion, more at ease, perhaps, with women than with men. A woman of remarkable sensitivity and charm, she enjoyed the intelligence and range of his conversation. More important, she was profoundly impressed by his graciousness on at least one occasion. In 1947, even before their friendship had developed, Mrs. Norman had asked several prominent figures in the world of art to contribute to a memorial portfolio in honor of Alfred Stieglitz, her closest friend. Barnes was the first to respond, and his tribute was a generous one. "From my long and firsthand knowledge of Stieglitz's personality and pioneer work," he wrote, "I can say that I believe that the present status of good contemporary painting probably owes more to him than it does to any other person. He was certainly the first to let the American public see, at '291,' the work of Picasso, Matisse, Marcel Duchamp, etc., and it is safe to say that the epoch-making Armory show in 1913 was a byproduct of Stieglitz's insight and courage.''

Many of Barnes's students, too, remember the doctor more for his magnanimity than for his well-publicized irascibility. A number of them were recipients of the Foundation's fellowships to Europe. In addition to paying all costs of travel to and within Europe, Barnes provided each participant with a generous weekly or monthly allowance, which more than covered living expenses. The itinerary was determined in advance, but the students, though supervised by a leader, were free to do as they pleased during their five or six months abroad. It was an immeasurably enriching experience for many young men and women who would never have been able to travel to Europe on their own.

Others benefited from the doctor's generosity at home. They remember him not as the "Terrible-Tempered Dr. Barnes," but as a dynamic and enthusiastic teacher, who helped them at the Foundation and away from it. Of these, none has fonder memories of Barnes than has Kenneth Goodman, a musician whose affectionate portrait of the collector is a most uncommon one. Goodman came to Merion in the 1940s and was admitted to the Foundation's beginning classes in art appreciation. He enjoyed the courses of instruction—they opened up a new world to him, for he had known little about art—but he enjoyed and gained even more from his remarkable personal relationship with Barnes. The doctor liked him at once: he was young, personable, "undebauched," eager to learn—and he was black. Goodman was equally enthusiastic about Barnes. He was never afraid of him and never understood those who were; instead he was touched by what he remembers today as the collector's unfailing warmth and sincerity.

In the course of their many long talks, Barnes often spoke to the young man of his profound interest in the heritage of the black people and of his enthusiasm for African sculpture, and Goodman once described to Barnes another, living part of the African tradition: the Maryland singing and praying bands. The doctor's interest in his description was such that the young man invited him to see how this tradition was still carried on, at the Tindley Temple in Philadelphia. Barnes accepted the invitation enthusiastically, and the experience was a memorable one for Goodman and for all those who had a rare opportunity to see Barnes unguarded and at leisure. As soon as he entered the church, the doctor entered into the spirit of the occasion. Taking off his coat and loosening his collar, he joined the circle of celebrants, clapping his hands and bowing and turning rhythmically along with the rest of them. Barnes, too, never forgot the experience—he gave generous donations to the church for the rest of his life.

Goodman left the Foundation in 1945 to study organ at the Juilliard School in New York, but his friendship with Barnes continued. Money for his studies in Juilliard had been provided by another generous patron, but Barnes, too, wanted to contribute his part and did so by sending monthly checks to Goodman's mother (who reciprocated by baking a fruit cake for the doctor each Christmas). These checks continued to arrive after Goodman's graduation, and when the young man protested, his benefactor explained that he knew organists always needed money, and he would do well to accept the checks. Goodman was remembered even after Barnes's death; the doctor had known of his desire to travel to France to study with the world-renowned organist, Marcel Dupré, and stipulated in his will that the young man should be sent there at the Foundation's expense. Barnes himself had already arranged it with Dupré.

Goodman, who today lives near Chicago, can't understand those who continue to characterize Barnes as a cantankerous tyrant. "God be praised that there are such people," he says. "I have revered no other man so much, except my father. If there were more such people, there would be no wars."

There was no sign of Barnes's belligerence either on the night of January 14, 1943, when he gave an extemporaneous talk at Pembroke College in Providence, Rhode Island. It was further evidence that the devil occasionally relinquished possession of his soul. His subject was "Having a Hell of a Good Time Playing with Art,

Education, Science, and Philosophy," and he was playful and good-natured as he delivered the speech. He told his audience of his childhood, of his evolution as a collector, and of the development of the Foundation's educational methods. He told them that firefighters, too, were artists, and reminded them that valid aesthetic experiences could be gained away from art—from watching Joe Louis fight, for example (though he admitted that the quality of that experience was not as high as that provided by art).

He was relaxed during the question period that followed. Asked why most visitors were excluded from the gallery, he explained that he had become tired of people "who went about exclaiming, 'Oh, isn't that nice, isn't that lovely?' and letting their children slide on the floor," and he had reached the conclusion that it was best to reserve the gallery for his serious students. When asked on what basis he selected the paintings for his collection, he replied modestly that some people considered him the anointed of God, while others thought he didn't know a damned thing, and that the truth was probably somewhere between the two.

The audience was stunned by the doctor's performance. A writer from the Providence *Journal* reported: "By reputation, Dr. Barnes is a surly firebrand of the most dangerous sort, but, all in all, he appeared rather benevolent. He is solidly built, gray headed and clean shaven. His untamed black eyebrows push out over unrimmed spectacles. He wore a suit of brown and high laced shoes, also brown. He spoke in a quiet voice. . . ."

22

There were no signs of Barnes's generosity or playfulness (if he was playing, his games were cruel ones which only he enjoyed) as he waged what proved to be his final battles with two long-standing enemies—the Philadelphia Museum and the University of Pennsylvania. Though past his seventy-fifth birthday, he had not lost his well-known skills as a streetfighter; age had not softened but merely lowered his blows.

He had, for years, remained silent about the museum. According to his own statement, following his struggles with the institution in 1937 and 1938, he had negotiated a truce with its president, Stokes. In return for the museum's promise to refrain from the use of his name or that of the Foundation in any of its publications, he had agreed not to "expose" the museum for its deceptions of the public. In 1948, however, the truce came to an end, and according to Barnes, the museum alone was to blame.

The occasion was a large Matisse retrospective, and the battle began with an innocent request. Aware that Barnes had made an exception to the Foundation's policy by lending works by his friends Glackens and Prendergast to two major retrospectives, Henry Clifford, the museum's curator of paintings, wrote the doctor on February 23, 1948, asking for the loan of three Matisses for the Philadelphia exhibition. He added that when he had last seen Matisse in Paris the artist had expressed the hope that the doctor would agree to the request. Barnes was unimpressed. In his answer to Clifford, Barnes informed him that Matisse had "an unerring sense in spotting phonies, a wit and humor that is both subtle and penetrating" and was obviously joking when he said the loan would please him. Probably, he added, the artist was merely interested in finding out how Barnes would react to such a presumptuous suggestion.

Clifford never answered the letter, realizing that any further attempt to obtain the paintings for the exhibition would be futile. Instead he went ahead confidently with his plans to mount the exhibition. He had Matisse's full cooperation. The artist had worked with Clifford during the latter's three trips to Europe, had agreed to lend several of his own paintings as well as seventy-five of his drawings, and had even written the curator a letter of endorsement, which he allowed the museum to use as the preface to the catalogue of the exhibition. "I hope that my exhibition may be worthy of all the work it is making for you, which touched me deeply," he wrote. He was not joking, Clifford knew.

Nor was Barnes joking, Clifford learned. The museum's refusal to join the battle, coupled with proof of Matisse's generous cooperation, infuriated him. Shortly after sending off his first unanswered letter, Barnes found another, more serious pretext for a fight. The March issue of the *Philadelphia Museum Bulletin* was using a reproduction of a Matisse masterpiece, *The Joy of Life*, which belonged to the Foundation, as an illustration for its article on the forthcoming exhibition. This, Barnes claimed, was a violation of a law prohibiting the use of reproductions of works of art without the permission of the owner. Even worse, use of the illustration implied that the painting would be part of the exhibition—another act of deception on the part of the museum.

This time, Barnes directed his protest to his old enemy, Fiske Kimball. In a letter of March 29, hand-delivered, Barnes demanded that the issue of the *Bulletin* be withdrawn. Predictably there was no reply. Undaunted, the doctor repeated his demand a few days later, this time writing to Ingersoll, whom he addressed as "Dear

Sturgeon." Again there was no response. Obviously the museum had reverted to its former policy of ignoring all communications from the doctor.

Barnes, however, refused to be ignored. On April 7 he led a group of his students on a visit to the museum, and, afterward, he had mimeographed copies made of a "stenographic report" of excerpts from a talk he had delivered during the visit. It was a defense of his own refusal to lend the Foundation's paintings—"the owner of the paintings would not be associated with people who prostitute art and education by habitual deception of the public"—and a lengthy, confused attempt to explain why Matisse had cooperated with the museum. "This is consistent," he noted, "with the intelligent, clear-thinking, worldly-wise artist whom everybody respects and admires. . . . That the phonies who run the museum are all set to occupy the center of the stage with their socialite parties, bothers neither Matisse nor serious students of his work."

Copies of this report, together with copies of Barnes's correspondence, past and present, with the museum, were given to members of the press and mailed to any and all he felt would be interested in learning of the museum's immoral practices. They were even distributed throughout the museum—several were found in a telephone booth. Again, however, there was no response. The exhibition was, deservedly, a great success, and nobody was concerned with the doctor's irrational diatribe.

Barnes was frustrated. He wanted to fight, but no one would climb into the ring with him. Finally, a few weeks later, he found an opportunity to humiliate the museum, and he took full advantage of it. Along with its Matisse exhibition, the museum scheduled a series of lectures on various aspects of the artist's work. One of them was to be delivered by David Robb, a professor of art at the University of Pennsylvania, a man Barnes had already placed prominently among those "debauched" by conventional academic training. Since Barnes had learned that Penn was once again eager to collaborate with the Foundation, he felt he was in a position to make a formal protest to the university, claiming that the museum wanted Robb only because of his prestige as a member of its faculty. He warned of the dire consequences and threatened retaliation. Initially Penn's officials pleaded academic freedom—they could not dictate to a faculty member—but in the end they gave in to Barnes's insistent demands. Robb's lecture was canceled, and he was replaced by Fiske Kimball, who agreed to step in at the last moment.

Kimball's gesture was a gracious one; he didn't want to let the museum's public down. It was also an act of courage. He was not, admittedly, a Matisse expert, and he was inadequately prepared for his last-minute assignment. Nonetheless, he could in no way have known that Barnes, having planned the event well in advance, was fully prepared; nor could he have anticipated the debacle that awaited him on the afternoon of April 30.

The doctor had mustered all of his forces. Friends and students of the Foundation packed the lecture hall. Led by Barnes and by Abraham Chanin, a former student and at the time a member of the staff of New York's Museum of Modern Art, their task was to discredit both Kimball and the Philadelphia Museum. They succeeded brilliantly, but in doing so—because of their methods and manners—they brought no credit to the Barnes Foundation. It was a sorry spectacle for all concerned, yet Barnes apparently was proud of his role in it, for the following day he distributed mimeographed excerpts of notes taken during Kimball's lecture. They read, in part:

CHANIN (*to Kimball*): What makes a still-life a masterpiece?
KIMBALL: The *life* with which the artist has impressed it.
CHANIN: Can you give me an idea of what you mean by that?
KIMBALL: Do *you* know the secret of organic life?
CHANIN: There are no specifics that make it a Matisse?
KIMBALL: I think there are, but they are not the ones that give it life.
CHANIN: What does "life" mean?
SOMEONE: That's a mystery.
KIMBALL: Yes, that's a mystery. . . .
CHANIN: You have not made a single statement that would enable a person of average intelligence to learn what makes

a painting a work of art, or what makes a painting by
Matisse different from the work of any other modern painter.

KIMBALL (*to Chanin*): Young man, art can't be explained like
that. The only specific thing about Matisse is his being Matisse. . . .

BARNES: Wouldn't you point out what that "life" in Matisse
consists of?

KIMBALL: Yes! Wouldn't *you* tell us, Doctor Barnes?

BARNES: It is *you* who are here to talk about Matisse; *I* came
here to learn.

KIMBALL (*to Chanin*): We are very happy to welcome guest
artists . . . and . . . uh . . . Doctor Barnes, you know a lot
about Matisse, you began in 1921.

BARNES: Nineteen *twelve* is correct.

KIMBALL: You own sixty-odd Matisses.

BARNES: Sixty-*five* is correct.

KIMBALL: I wish you would interpret them to me.

BARNES: I would if you would come out there and enter as a
student in the first-year class, learn what the first principles
of psychology and education are, and learn something about
paintings by being shown, not by banalities and platitudes.
I have been swamped by questions here this afternoon.

KIMBALL: Won't you answer them?

BARNES: Why should *I* answer them? They refer to *your* talk,
which seems to have confused everybody. For instance, here
is one question: "Do you mean that what you pointed out
is what makes Matisse a great artist?"

KIMBALL: Yes, the *life*!

BARNES: A very vague thing. As I understand it, these people
came to learn something about Matisse and what makes the
difference between Matisse and any other painter.

WOMAN: Couldn't what you said about Matisse be said of any
other artist?

KIMBALL: Yes, it could.

VOICES IN AUDIENCE: What! My God!

BARNES: There is no difference then? That's what we want to

know. That fellow (*pointing to Chanin*) asked you what you mean; you didn't tell him.

KIMBALL: I have no pretense, as I said, of being a master of interpretation. (*To Chanin*) Maybe *you* want to talk to the audience; why don't *you* enlighten these people . . . ?

CHANIN: Well, it's not my job, but I will, if they want me to. If you select a painting, I'll show you what I mean.

SOMEONE: How about *The Blue Window*?

KIMBALL: Yes—

VOICES IN AUDIENCE: Oh! Yes.

CHANIN: All right, if you want me to prove a painting can be analyzed so that it makes sense, I'll talk on *The Blue Window*. . . .

(*Turning to the picture and facing the audience, Chanin began his talk.*)

KIMBALL (*interrupting Chanin's analysis*): My dear boy, I am sure we have all enjoyed—

SOMEONE: Hey! Let him go on! He hasn't finished.

BARNES: You can't interrupt him. He [Chanin] has the floor. That's not very polite, and you know, Mr. Kimball, that *I* am *never* impolite.

KIMBALL: I am *director* of the museum—

BARNES: That doesn't mean you own the museum. It's tax-supported and you are expected to serve the tax-paying public. Besides, you asked the man to speak and he has the right to finish what he wants to say.

AUDIENCE: Yes! Yes!

KIMBALL: Unfortunately, I have to leave myself and I wanted to thank our young friend here [Chanin]. . . .

Barnes was in a triumphant mood in the weeks following what he considered to be Kimball's—and the museum's—overwhelming defeat. He wrote Dewey that he was celebrating with fireworks and guns. At the same time, because of his genuine interest in Matisse's art, he returned to the exhibition several times. These unofficial visits were reported by various employees of the museum, and on May 16, taking note of them, Clifford, who had started the struggle with his innocent request, wrote Barnes, in a light vein: "All joking aside! You have been to the Philadelphia Museum a number of times to see my selection of Matisse. Will you now let me come out to Merion someday to see your selection?"

Barnes's reply was typed on the back of one of the Foundation's printed rejection forms. It read:

> Your "all joking aside" of May 16th fills me with chagrin: that a Museum official should inform me now that the Matisse project was a joke is a fatal blow to my self-esteem. . . .
>
> A proper question to you is—Why the hell did not one of the Museum officials inform me earlier that it was a joking matter?—*Pardon, monsieur; je termine ici afin d'éviter le danger de dévier de ma politesse accoutumée.*

A few days later, Barnes, enjoying himself, made his own joke. "You were right after all," he wrote Clifford. "People far and wide saw the joke. Enclosed, from a famous leader of the legal profession, is a sample of my extensive mail." The enclosure, signed "Bella Donna van Byttsche," read:

> I want you to know that you are too, too, awfully perfectly horrid to say all the nasty things about us aristocratic art lovers who have done so much for the common herd by making the Philadelphia Museum of Art the truly marvelous institution it is today. There is no need whatever for me to apologize for my aristocratic lineage, which naturally has been recognized and is reflected in my acknowledged social leadership.
>
> Of course, recent immigrants like you would hardly understand true quality, but I will have you know that my ancestry is *simply* unassailable. I am a direct descendent of the Blighs, of Dartmoor. Our great-great-grandfather was Lord Costermonger, of Billingsgate Mews, and founded that great British institution, "The Hulks." Another ancestor was the Earl of Droolingtoole, of Houndsditch Manure, Sluppington-

on-Slops, Herts. And besides Herts, many of the great nobles of Harts, Nerts and Farts are my relatives. There the old traditions are still preserved, with tea and strumpets served every afternoon. . . .

With such a background it was only fitting that my consort should be of equal distinction, if that could be possible. He is a direct descendent of that greatest of early Dutch poltroons, Mynheer Ludwig van Gott Damm, of Spuyten Duyvil, Weehawken and Flatbush. Beginning with the Revolution and on through World War II, successive generations of that famed family have done their patriotic duty to their Country. Not behind the breastworks (don't you dare titter at that) or in the trenches, as any fool could do, but by using their brains to supply our armies with clothing, arms and other supplies. After such public service for centuries, the government showed their ingratitude by compelling us to pay nullions in taxes on the modest profits we made.

Pish, and Tush, too, on you for suggesting that persons of *our* position, who have practically created Art by our patronage for hundreds of years, do not know what is best for the illiterate and unwashed masses. Why I just *love* all of that fellow Matice's works. I simply go all over with goose-pimples every time I barely glance at one. Such depth! Such breadth! Such height! Such width! The daring and dash to it all, along with exquisite technique and flashing colors. Of course they are different. I searched my soul to the bottom for fully an hour when I saw my first before I had the answer. Then it came to me, suddenly, like a revelation, what Mattis's genius really meant.

Naturally the peasantry, being without my advantages, could not understand this rapprochement between the great and would need labored explanations. Noblesse oblige rests heavily on us leaders, and that is why I suggested to Director Sinballs he talk to the proletariat on Mattice. I am informed that certain ruffians, including yourself, were most unappreciative of this condescension.

If Hendrynk were not down with the gout, I would send his seconds to call on you, you horrid odious, villian. You have me so overwrought that I have dropped and broken my lorgnette. I shall defend us aristocrats with all my vast resources against your scurrilous attacks. So be warned.

Along with this piece of vintage Barnesiana, the doctor sent a copy of a reply allegedly written by his own secretary, "Phallus Leucorrhea," which read: "The doctor read your letter of May 21st, rose from his chair, and I pushed him out of the third story window. As he hit the stone pavement, he cried—'ah Jan Masaryk, our martyrdom . . .' We incinerated him two hours later—the bastard!"

In spite of having "irrevocably" ended his relationship with the university in 1947, Barnes, reluctantly and with considerable skepticism, was willing to give his alma mater one more "last chance." The occasion was Penn's appointment of a new president, Harold E. Stassen. Stassen was the wonder boy of American politics. Elected governor of Minnesota in 1938, at the age of thirty-one, he had been twice reelected when, in 1943, he resigned to join the Navy. In 1945 he had been a delegate to the San Francisco Conference called to create the United Nations. Though defeated in his attempt to become the Republican candidate for president of the United States in 1948, he remained a major political force to be reckoned with in the future.

Barnes didn't think much of Stassen. He realized that Stassen's appointment, which took effect in July 1948, was politically motivated and that his new job was only a stepping stone to the White House. However, he accepted what he was told was a purely social invitation from Horace Stern to meet the new president at a dinner party on June 23, 1949. Once there, he understood that it was not, after all, a purely social occasion. Both Stern and Fogg (who was present at the dinner) assured him that with Stassen's arrival on the scene there would be a new deal at Penn. They also made it clear that they hoped Barnes himself would somehow participate in this regeneration of the university. After both Stassen and Fogg had left, Barnes politely informed Stern that he was indeed sympathetic to the idea of sweeping change at the university, and that he was willing to share his ideas with its officials when asked to do so. He insisted, however—and he confirmed this in a letter sent the following day—that the resources of the Foundation were not, and would never be, available to Penn.

Both Stassen and Fogg were disappointed. Barnes's offer fell far short of their expectations. Nonetheless, he had not closed the door, and in the fall, when the doctor returned from his annual trip to Europe, they resumed their efforts to convince him to work with the university. In the beginning it was Fogg who did his best to involve the doctor, tactfully urging him to give Stassen his candid opinion of just what he believed Penn's problems to be, without pulling any punches. Finally on October 27, 1949, Stassen himself wrote to Barnes. It was a curious letter. After taking note of "the general observation of Professor John Dewey's ninetieth birthday," he asked Barnes if the philosopher had expressed any written or spoken opinions about Nehru's approach to the world situation. More to the point, he then invited the doctor to lunch to discuss recommendations concerning the School of Fine Arts.

Barnes replied within a few days. Ignoring Stassen's question and brushing off his invitation to lunch, Barnes wrote that he had spent four hours with Dewey, during which he had shown him all of his correspondence with university officials. The way the philosopher "sized up the situation," he noted, "expresses my attitude so well that I quote what he wrote me: 'It would be wonderful if Stassen had the insight and foresight to break away and do something sound in educational policy on his own.' "

Personally, however, Barnes remained skeptical, and he made no effort to hide his feelings from the new president. "To expect you, a man not trained in educational science and not having around him anybody who has evidenced such knowledge, to bring about the desired results, is practically a confession of a belief in miracles," he wrote. "And your suggestion to discuss with me 'the reported recommendations as to the School of Fine Arts' would be like a

Frenchman and a Chinese trying to convey to each other, each in his own language, the essentials of a problem in which both are interested. Your problem, I think, is the very old one of how to eat your cake and have it too, and is, it seems to me, not unlike that of Hercules when he had to clean out the Augean stables."

If Stassen was interested in working with Barnes, he made no effort to show it. It took him several months to answer the doctor. In the meantime Barnes continued sending countless letters to both Fogg and Stern, giving them his candid opinions concerning university affairs. He admitted that he had initially been sympathetic to Stassen's problems, but bitterly expressed his subsequent disillusionment with the president, whose sole function at the university was to raise money. "The attempts to get me into the game were really to further that end," he wrote Stern in a letter of November 25.

Apparently Barnes was genuinely distressed and hurt. This latest attempt to cooperate with Penn would be no more successful than his earlier efforts had been, he realized. He felt he had been used and that even his friend, Fogg, whom he trusted, had, willingly or not, deceived him into believing that something concrete might come of a dialogue with Stassen. On February 8, 1950, weary of the struggle, Fogg gave up his role as intermediary. Having been repeatedly bombarded by the doctor's frequently abusive letters, he lost patience: he wrote that in the future it would be best if Barnes would direct his correspondence to Stassen himself. The collector answered at once, authorizing Fogg to inform the president that he saw no reason to write to him in the future. Nonetheless, he continued to write to Fogg—angry, often irrational letters, justifying his behavior by attempting to prove that he had done his best to help Penn and had failed only because of the university's ignorance and insensitivity.

With Fogg out of the picture, the battle degenerated. Though he must have seen copies of the patient intermediary's correspondence with Barnes, Stassen chose to write to the doctor on March 29, 1950, responding directly to the letter Barnes had written him—five months earlier. "I appreciated the bluntness of your letter," he began. "Even though the task may be 'not unlike that of Hercules'; and even though I lay no claim to being a twentieth century Hercules, I am determined to make progress on the task." Repeating his invitation to lunch or to an afternoon conference, he added, inexplicably, that he thought the State Department had made a mistake in refusing to issue a visa to Picasso.

Barnes needed only a few days to answer, and he did so on April 3, concluding with a tasteless joke:

> How to avoid "bluntness" is always the problem of the person whose painful duty it is to pronounce a death. In the present instance, the cause of death is meticulously set forth in documents in Penn's official records. . . .
>
> In view of the finality of death, your numerous invitations to me to luncheon and to discuss with you the situation at Penn stimulate the imagination. When I received the third such invitation last week, it recalled a story, ascribed to Abe Lincoln, about a Negro woman in Georgia who supported her no-good husband and their children by taking in washing. She was young, beautiful, buxom and flirtatious—in short, a potent aphrodisiac. On one occasion, as she was scrubbing clothes outdoors, a slick looking black man lingered at her side. Her husband called out the window—'Mandy, what you doin' there?' She replied—'Dis man wants me to go over to his house to do some washin'.' The husband said—'Come on in heah; dat man don't want no washin' done—I see the front of his pants move.'

This time it took Stassen little more than a month to reply. In a letter written on June 12, he challenged Barnes's manhood, pleading that he himself was doing his best at his Herculean task and regretting that the doctor lacked the courage to help him. "If you are afraid to tackle it, because of its many difficulties, that, of course, is your privilege," he taunted his adversary. "I did have the impression, however, that you were a man of courage and determination."

The real issue, of course—the Foundation's cooperation with Penn—was a dead one. Barnes had no intention of working with Stassen, and the president must have known it. Nonetheless, the two men exchanged senseless letters—and insults—for several weeks. Stassen, according to Barnes, still wore "the dunce cap that Tom Dewey placed on him in the 1948 presidential campaign." He was a dull politician, tied to a corrupt political machine, the perennial candidate who should be sent back to the sticks. In replying, Stassen again accused the doctor of cowardice, claiming that it took no courage to throw insults at men in public life, but that it did take courage to work toward the improvement of the university.

They wrote to each other about communism and quarreled over Great Britain's National Health Service and other irrelevant issues. Finally, in answer to Stassen's repeated charges of cowardice, Barnes dared him to give copies of their correspondence to the press, and let its readers decide just who was afraid of whom. The doctor had reached his own irrefutable conclusion: the president of the University of Pennsylvania was "what psychologists term a 'mental delinquent,' variously known to laymen as 'dumb bunny, false alarm, phony.'"

With this correspondence, any hopes that Barnes might have had for a collaboration with Penn, any hopes that the university might someday be entrusted with his collection, came to an end. On October 20, 1950, he took the legal measure he had avoided for many years. The bylaws of the Foundation were amended so that Penn would no longer be responsible, after his death, for nominating any of the Foundation's trustees and would play no role in the Foundation's future. He further stipulated that no member of the faculty or board of trustees or directors of the University of Pennsylvania could ever serve as a trustee of the Barnes Foundation.

Following what was really his final break with Penn, Barnes continued his efforts to find an institution qualified to assume responsibility for his collection after his death. But he did so with little enthusiasm and, because of the impossible conditions he set, with little hope of success. He was almost eighty years old, and it was time to reach a decision—even the doctor must have been aware of his mortality—but it seemed that he really didn't care what happened to his paintings when he himself could no longer look after them.

For practical reasons—proximity to Merion—it would have been best to entrust supervision of the Foundation to a neighboring institution, but in the same amendment to the bylaws that ruled out the possibility of Penn's participation in the Foundation, Barnes had specifically denied any role in its future to Temple, Bryn Mawr, Haverford, Swarthmore, or the Pennsylvania Academy of the Fine Arts. Though all were logical choices and all were distinguished schools, they were, according to Barnes, too closely associated with the Philadelphia Museum. Instead, in the summer of 1950 his search took him farther afield—to Sarah Lawrence College in Bronxville, New York.

Sarah Lawrence had been Dewey's idea. Largely because of the great esteem in which he held its young, dynamic president, Harold

Taylor, the philosopher believed that the small women's college might be ideally suited to take charge of the Foundation's collection and continue its educational program. Barnes, having been favorably impressed by a few of Taylor's published articles, agreed to pursue the matter.

Taylor, too, was interested, and a weekend meeting at Merion was arranged. Dewey and Taylor were to come to the Foundation to hold serious discussions with Barnes. At the last minute, Dewey canceled—he was ill—but Taylor, who had been sent a copy of the *House & Garden* article so that he might be prepared, kept the appointment. The talks were not successful. After a day and a half, Barnes informed his guest that he found him somewhat lacking in his knowledge of art. This, he felt, could be remedied—and Sarah Lawrence subsequently offered the collection—but only if Taylor agreed to travel to Merion each week to attend de Mazia's classes. Without hesitation, Taylor turned down the suggestion. Running a college, he told Barnes, was a full-time job.

When he returned home, Taylor wrote Barnes a formal note rejecting the idea of any cooperation between his college and the Foundation. He told Dewey that on the basis of their discussions, he was certain that Barnes wasn't interested in turning over his paintings to any institution and that he probably wanted no one to see them after his death. Informally, he confided to a colleague that he thought the doctor was "off his rocker."

Only a few weeks after having been rebuffed by Sarah Lawrence, Barnes turned to his final hope. It was a surprising choice: Lincoln University, at the time one of the most distinguished black schools in the country. Located conveniently near Oxford, Pennsylvania, thirty miles from the Foundation, Lincoln had been established in 1854. Its distinguished graduates included Thurgood Marshall, Langston Hughes, and Kwame Nkrumah, and among its trustees, several of whom were white, was Owen J. Roberts, Barnes's friend and former attorney. Lincoln's art program was practically nonexistent, and it was small—its student body numbered fewer than 350 students—but these seemed advantages to Barnes, since he could more easily manage and dictate to it.

Barnes had, for some time, been interested in Lincoln's activities, and on August 18 Dr. Horace Mann Bond, the university's first black president, had written inviting him to join Lincoln's faculty as a lecturer in art for the year 1950–51. The job, Bond explained good-naturedly, involved little work—four to six lectures a year—and small monetary compensation—the usual fee paid to faculty members was $9.25 an hour. But as an inducement he noted that a lecturer was "endowed with complete prerogatives of giving the President and his fellow-faculty members Hell with no restrictions." More seriously, he concluded, "The African people, from whom I have the honor of claiming descent, are people generally blessed with a loving, affectionate and grateful soul. I believe that you could help increase that fund of love and affection and arm it with greater intelligence and appreciation. Certainly we should repay your gift of yourself to us with loving affection and gratitude, if with little else."

Barnes was charmed by the tone of Bond's letter—"so overwhelmed with joy and admiration at the ease with which you disposed of the work and worry that face me in the future, that I danced the cancan," he wrote him. Nonetheless, he was unable to consider any teaching offer, but he did have a counterproposal of his own: that Lincoln hire, at the Foundation's expense, a Barnes-trained professor of art to teach twelve to fifteen of the university's best students one afternoon a week at the Foundation's gallery. He had the right person for the job, too, Jon Longaker, another talented young man whom he had briefly envisioned as Chisholm's successor while the experiment with Penn was reaching its conclusion.

It was the same offer he had made to Sarah Lawrence, but Bond, unlike Taylor, responded positively. Barnes was delighted. He wrote Bond that the arrangement with Lincoln would give him a chance to show the world that "when given the proper opportunity, the Negro demonstrates that his intellectual capacity is at least equal to that of the white man" and "his endowment for aesthetic appreciation is even greater than that of the average white man." It would also, though he failed to mention it, give him a chance to show his contempt for the white, Main Line establishment.

Barnes had little chance to prove his point about the natural endowment of Lincoln's students. Classes began in September 1950, and by October it was already obvious that they would be no more successful than those held in conjunction with Penn. The students were enthusiastic and alert, but they were totally unprepared for their studies. In spite of this, Barnes took his final revenge on his enemies: he amended the Foundation's bylaws, giving Lincoln the power to nominate its trustees following his death and that of his wife.

The doctor seemed to have lost interest—in the future of his Foundation and in its classes. He rarely attended Longaker's lectures (the teacher would leave the Foundation after the end of the academic year) and spoke to the Lincoln students on only a few occasions. Once he played some records of Paul Robeson and Marian Anderson, comparing their singing to the work of the great painters. "Barnes tended to ramble on as he spoke in a low, gruff voice and a belligerent manner," Longaker remembers today. "He had piercing eyes under bushy black brows. He got red in the face as he spoke and white gobs of spittle appeared at the corner of his mouth if he spoke long. On one occasion, he worked up to a climax. 'Don't ever forget you're Negroes,' he thundered. I was flabbergasted because it sounded like the most virulent racist remark. Then, of course, I realized what he meant, that they should be proud of their heritage."

Barnes's own feelings about the Foundation's relationship with Lincoln were summarized in a letter to a Lincoln official, Joseph Newton Hill. "The only possible way to make our resources really serviceable to Lincoln is by the method of 'trial and error' and to fulfill conditions which experience shows are indispensable," he wrote. "These are: 1) a rational philosophic foundation; 2) a trained teacher; 3) selected students; 4) a first-year class in fundamental principles of orderly thinking, scientific method, authentic experience. This year the experiment with Lincoln failed in practically all of these requisites, in spite of your zeal and intelligent cooperation, and my efforts to start it right . . ." The language was familiar to anyone who had followed Barnes's efforts to work with Penn, and the outcome of the Lincoln experiment could have been predicted. Lincoln, however, was never officially fired. There was no time for Barnes to take this step.

During the 1940s, Dr. and Mrs. Barnes paid frequent and regular visits to their country house, Ker-Feal—Breton dialect for "Fidèle's House"—named after the black and white mongrel dog the doctor had brought from Port-Manech, Brittany, where he spent many summers. Set in the midst of 165 acres of farmland in the rolling hill country of Chester County, not far from Merion, it had been purchased to house Barnes's large collection of antique American furnishings and to give the collection meaning within the scope of the Foundation's educational program. An eighteenth-century stone farmhouse, it had been restored and expanded with skill and taste by three young architects—H. Martyn Kneedler, Henry D. Mirick, and C. Clark Zantzinger. Its rooms furnished with examples of the most important styles of American eighteenth-century craftsmanship, it admirably served its purpose. "Indeed, not a room, not a piece of furniture, a door hinge, a pewter mug, a potter's crock or plate, fails to elicit in the alive, informed observer the impulse to journey into the past and share the joy of the artist's new insight and knowledge," Barnes wrote in *House & Garden*.

Ker-Feal became a badly needed retreat for the doctor and his wife. They came there regularly each weekend, arriving at ten-thirty on Saturday mornings and leaving at two o'clock, after lunch, on Sundays. They did little entertaining; most of the time, they were alone with their cook and three gardeners, all of whom lived in the house. Among the few weekend guests was Charles Laughton, who spent so much time there that one room became his own, identified by a cookie-cutter, shaped like the actor, which hung over its doorway. It was, Barnes liked to say, Fidèle's house. The mongrel shared his master's room. Above the dog's bed was an eighteenth-century map of Brittany, in case he felt lost; above the doctor's bed was a drawing of Fidèle's hometown.

During their time at Ker-Feal, Laura Barnes gardened. She had managed to convert what was once barren land into a monument to her considerable skills as a gardener and horticulturist—she was as much a stubborn perfectionist as was her husband—and Ker-Feal's botanical garden came to be used as an adjunct to the Foundation's arboretum in Merion, where formal classes in horticulture, botany, and landscape were held. On the side she raised turkeys and chickens, selling eggs to the Foundation's students through an intermediary so that they might never learn where they came from. She also sold her chickens—she was spied by a neighbor carefully wrapping the breast meat at the kitchen table in front of her husband.

While his wife worked in her garden, Barnes spent his time rearranging furniture, just as he rearranged paintings in the gallery. Shifting pieces from place to place, forming new designs and compositions of iron, glass, china, and fabric, he saw to it that each corner of each room became an artistic unit in itself, each his own creation, a reflection of his personal taste, and concern.

In spite of the tranquility of the setting, Barnes's behavior at his country retreat was essentially unchanged from his behavior at the Foundation. At Ker-Feal he could be as childish and deliberately offensive as he was at Merion. His need to scandalize, to call attention to himself, extended even to a formal ladies' party given by his wife, when he burst on the scene naked following his afternoon swim. Laura Barnes had asked him to wear a robe when going down to the pool but failed to ask him to wear one when returning to the house. His days at Ker-Feal, too, were marked by his need to control and his unreasonable anger. His repeated attempts to buy adjoining property in order to protect his own home so antagonized one neighbor that the latter left a deed restriction in his will forbidding the sale of his home to either Barnes or the Foundation, at any time. In the early days of the war, the doctor asked for a postponement of Russell's suit on the grounds that he had no time to prepare his defense because he was too busy running his farm in order to grow food for the war effort; yet when the county agent wrote him that he was not doing enough for the war effort with all his land and suggested that he grow tomato plants, Barnes angrily replied that he would buy the plants and feed the county agent with them every day. He was ready and eager to do battle until the end of his life. When he learned that a pipeline was to be built through his property, he responded by urging all farmers and gardeners in the area to patrol the grounds and arm themselves against any invaders.

He never had a chance to fight this battle; officials, knowing their adversary, feared that his protests would delay any action on their part for years and diverted the pipeline. Nor did he have a chance to change the bylaws concerning the fate of his collection. On the afternoon of July 24, 1951, the disposition of his collection not yet satisfactorily provided for, Dr. Barnes's life came to a sudden and violent end. He had gone to Ker-Feal in the morning, leaving after lunch to return to Merion. Driving alone in his Packard, with only Fidèle at his side, he failed to observe a stop sign at what he knew to be a dangerous intersection; he had often warned visitors of it. Apparently he was distracted this time, and his car was struck by a ten-ton trailer truck. He was killed instantly, his body hurled forty feet into a nearby field. (Fidèle survived but was put out of his misery by a state trooper.) It was, Fiske Kimball commented upon learning the news, a fitting end for a man who had spent his life figuratively ignoring stop signs.

According to his wishes, Barnes's body was cremated, and there was no funeral service. His death was officially commemorated only by the Narberth Fire Company, its headquarters draped in black and its flag flown at half-mast. His lasting memorial is the extraordinary collection of paintings which remain in Merion, but he and his collection remain the subject of controversy even today.

Immediately following the death of Dr. Barnes, Nelle E. Mullen, the Foundation's secretary and treasurer, announced that the collection would remain, intact, in Merion and that the educational program would continue to function as it had in the past. In other words, nothing would change.

Nonetheless, six months later, in February 1952, the status quo was challenged by the Philadelphia *Inquirer*, which filed a suit in the Court of Common Pleas of Montgomery County in the name of Harold J. Wiegand, both as an individual taxpayer and as an editorial writer for the *Inquirer*. The suit sought to require the Barnes Foundation to adopt "reasonable rules and regulations" for admitting the public to the gallery, during specified hours on a reasonable number of specific days throughout the year. It contended that the Foundation had not been operated according to its charter as a tax-exempt corporation "to promote the advancement of education in the appreciation of the fine arts."

One month later, attorneys for the Foundation filed an answer claiming that the court had no right to change the bylaws of the Foundation, that the Foundation enjoyed no special tax privileges, and that Wiegand had no legal right to bring suit, because he was not a member of the Barnes Foundation Corporation. The following December, the Foundation was vindicated when the court dismissed the suit on the grounds that neither the plaintiff nor the court "may set themselves up as judges of the proper method of conducting a course in the fine arts."

The *Inquirer* and its publisher, Walter Annenberg, however, refused to let the matter rest. Joined in the battle by *Art News* and its editor, Alfred M. Frankfurter, who solicited and received letters from eminent art historians and scholars attesting to the Foundation's unwillingness to admit recognized experts to study the collection, it appealed the lower court's decision before the Supreme Court of the State of Pennsylvania. That appeal, too, however, was unsuccessful, the court ruling in June 1952 that it could not interfere with the bylaws of the Foundation unless the trustees were guilty of bad faith. Furthermore, holding that only a state government had the right to investigate the conduct of a tax-exempt foundation, it questioned the right of Wiegand to institute the action.

It took the state several years—until April 1958—to exercise that right. At that time, largely through the efforts of a stubbornly determined deputy attorney general, Lois G. Forer, who had been assigned to the supervision and regulation of charities, the matter was again brought before the Montgomery court. This time it was the state which petitioned the Foundation to show cause why it should not be compelled to open its gallery to the public, as stipulated by the original charter. According to the state, the Foundation's educational facilities and art gallery were separate, and the latter should be opened to the public.

A year later, the court again ruled in favor of the Foundation. According to the judge, Alfred Taxis, the gallery was an integral part of the educational institution, and the trustees were not obliged to open its doors to the public. Nonetheless, Mrs. Forer persevered, and in January 1960 this latest decision was appealed before the Supreme Court of Pennsylvania. This time, the state won its case: the court agreed that it did have the right to investigate the operation of a tax-exempt foundation. In his opinion, Judge Michael A. Musmanno, speaking for the unanimous court, noted that if the gallery was open to only a selected, restricted few, it was not a public institution; and that if it was not a public institution, it was not entitled to tax exemption. Consequently, the lower court was ordered to review its decision.

Several months later, in December 1960, Judge Taxis issued an order to the Foundation. It directed its trustees to compile and make available a list of its assets, income, and expenditures; an inventory of its collection; a list of persons who had applied for admission to the gallery and a list of those who had been admitted; a list of its employees; and a floor plan of the gallery. He also directed that three art experts be permitted to visit the gallery to evaluate the collection and to ascertain the optimum number of people who could be admitted at any one time.

A few days later, the Foundation complied with part of that order. It allowed the experts to view the collection, and it submitted to the court a floor plan of the gallery, as well as what Forer described as a "heterogeneous jumble of unfiled papers," which included a visitors' register for the years 1956 and 1957. It did not provide any information concerning the Foundation's finances, which the trustees maintained were none of the state's business, or an inventory of the collection, which they claimed did not exist.

It was hardly an adequate response, but it signaled the Foundation's capitulation. On December 10, two days before the case was to come to trial, an out-of-court settlement was reached. According to its terms, the Foundation agreed that the public would be allowed to visit the gallery on each of two days a week, one of them a Saturday, except during the months of July and August. The number of persons would be limited to two hundred—half of them by previous appointment and half on a first-come, first-served basis. No cards of admission would be required, and special arrangements would be made for art students and art instructors, under "reasonable regulations." A listed telephone would be installed at the Foundation—for the first time—to facilitate requests for admission and information. In addition, it stipulated that, following the death of Laura Barnes, who then lived in a building adjoining the gallery, the gallery would be open on one additional afternoon each week.

Though the Foundation's trustees protested and did their best to delay compliance with the agreement, the gallery of the Barnes Foundation was finally opened to the public on March 18, 1961. The staff of the Foundation braced itself for the invasion of outsiders, but there was no stampede to gain admission. At six-thirty in the morning, a dozen or so visitors formed a line in front of the Foundation's gate, but by nine-thirty, when the gallery was formally opened, no more than fifty art lovers were on hand. The quota of one hundred was not reached until noon, and at three-thirty, an hour before closing time, the last of the one hundred persons with reservations arrived.

Inside the gallery, white-haired Laura Barnes, then eighty-six years old, was seated on a bench in the main gallery. As she observed the visitors, she admitted to a reporter that they were nice-looking people and not the vandals she had expected; but she insisted that the gallery had always been open to the public and saw no reason why it had to be done this way. Nonetheless, she did comment that it was annoying to have so many people there at one time.

Outside the Foundation's gate, a dozen or so men and women, identifying themselves as "Friends of the Barnes Foundation," handed out broadsides expressing their strong opposition to the opening of the gallery. The four-page statement was headed: NOTICE TO THE PUBLIC: DESTROYING OUR EDUCATIONAL FACILITIES IS NOT BUILDING OUR CULTURE. It could have been written by Barnes himself; he would have been proud of them.

While the *Inquirer*, scholars, and art lovers all over the world congratulated themselves on their victory—the incomparable collection could finally be viewed by the public—the attorney general's office, and above all Mrs. Forer, were not satisfied. The out-of-court settlement had deprived the state of an opportunity to launch a full-scale investigation into the Foundation's operations. Before long, however, such an opportunity arose. In August 1961, claiming that additional expenses had been incurred since the opening of the gallery, the trustees of the Barnes Foundation announced that an admission fee of two dollars would be charged beginning in September. The state acted quickly. Charging that this was contrary to the earlier decree, which stated that there would be no admission fee—and contrary to Barnes's own wishes that his collection be seen by the "people"—and that such a fee was just another way of harassing the public, it obtained a temporary court injunction barring the fee until the matter could be settled in court.

Finally, after ten years of litigation, the stage was set for a thorough inquiry into the policies and practices of the Barnes Foundation. The case was brought to court on April 5, 1962. Lois Forer, representing the state, was determined to wage an all-out battle to protect the public's interest in the matter, and she was well prepared for her task.

Among those appearing in court—for the first time—were the Foundation's five trustees. Under questioning, three of them—Joe W. Langran, a landscape architect, Sidney W. Frick, an attorney, and Nelle E. Mullen—admitted to no training in art or in the management of a museum. The testimony of the fourth trustee, Violette de Mazia, whose only training had been at the Foundation, was confusing and contradictory. The testimony of the fifth trustee, Barnes's widow, who testified voluntarily, was more satisfactory. Emphasizing her role in the administration of the Foundation's arboretum, she noted that the arboretum welcomed visitors and cooperated willingly with botanists all over the world. (It was pointed out that no complaint had ever been made to the state that the arboretum, unlike the gallery, had ever denied information or admission to scholars.)

Others who appeared in court included art historians and museum curators, all of whom gave convincing evidence that the gallery was not being properly managed. Paintings were being moved about recklessly—a dangerous practice—to illustrate points made during the Foundation's classes; misattributed works or forgeries, which would have been removed by a competent director, were retained; professional museum directors were not consulted concerning management and security problems; groups of qualified scholars were still denied admission to the gallery; and the Foundation's funds were improperly administered—adequate steps had not been taken to increase income and reduce expenses.

At the end of the hearings, the state moved to have four of the trustees (Laura Barnes was the exception) removed from their positions for incompetence, but in March 1963, while agreeing that some of the charges of mismanagement were valid to some extent, the motion was denied by the court, which merely ordered that the admission fee be reduced to one dollar. The Foundation's trustees had again been vindicated.

Laura Barnes, who, following the doctor's death, continued to devote most of her energies to the Foundation's arboretum, died in 1966 at the age of ninety-two. The bulk of her estate was left to a number of hospitals and charitable institutions, and her personal art collection was bequeathed to the Brooklyn Museum. Nelle E. Mullen, who replaced her as president of the Foundation, died in 1967 at the age of eighty-three. Her own collection of seventy-eight paintings (including some which had been left to her by her sister Mary, who had died several years earlier) was sold at auction for more than a million dollars.

Following the death of Mrs. Barnes, the Foundation's gallery was opened on one additional afternoon—Sunday—per week, but nothing has come of further halfhearted efforts to change the Foundation's basic policies. It has been art and education—both under the direction of Violette de Mazia—as usual in Merion. Many of Barnes's critics have forgiven the doctor himself—after all, he created the magnificent collection and, in doing so, earned the right to exercise his eccentricities. Yet these same critics and many others find it impossible to forgive those who followed him and over-zealously perpetuate the Foundation's high-handed regulations.

Visitors to the Foundation have voiced many complaints. In spite of the marvelous paintings that adorn its walls, the atmosphere in the gallery is decidedly unfriendly. Before entering, visitors are required to check coats, cameras, packages, umbrellas, and even handbags—lockers are provided for the latter. Children under twelve are not admitted, and those between the ages of twelve and fifteen must be accompanied by and remain with an adult. (In all fairness, it must be noted that New York's Frick Collection also bars children—under the age of ten—and demands that those under the age of sixteen be accompanied by an adult.) The gallery itself is inadequately lighted. There are no titles or dates under the paintings—merely the names of the artists, some of which, because of their position on the walls, can barely be read. There are no reproductions for sale, and no catalogue of the collection is available. Guards are, for the most part, unwilling or unable to answer questions.

Scholars, too, continue to complain of the Foundation's erratic policies. At times, their requests for information and permission to visit the gallery by special arrangement have been granted, but at other times, equally legitimate requests for cooperation have been refused—for no apparent reason. The Foundation's regulations concerning the reproduction of its paintings in books and periodicals are inflexible. No color reproductions are ever allowed, and black-and-white photos are supplied, according to Miss de Mazia, only when intended for use "in educational publications dealing with paintings from the aesthetic standpoint." Presumably, Miss de Mazia is the sole judge of whether or not these standards have been met.

The Foundation's educational program remains essentially unchanged. Candidates for admission to its first-year classes are interviewed either at the Foundation or at Miss de Mazia's home. They are asked why they want to study at the Foundation and whether there might be any reason they could not attend classes regularly—each Tuesday. The majority, it seems, are accepted. Most of these are housewives or retired persons, since the workers Barnes wanted to educate are unable to devote each Tuesday to the study of art appreciation.

At this writing, Miss de Mazia still presides over these beginning classes, as she has for several decades. (Lesser members of the faculty teach the advanced classes.) She remains a remarkably dynamic teacher, able to hold the attention of more than one hundred students for several hours without interruption—and she still remembers the name of each student after only one meeting. Her lectures never deviate from the fundamental Barnesian doctrine, and she continues to enforce the Foundation's rigid rules concerning class attendance. Recently, when a student missed several lectures because of the death of her husband, she received a letter of condolence from Miss de Mazia—together with word that, since she had missed more than three consecutive classes, she was dismissed from the school and could not resume her studies there until the following academic year.

Clearly, time has stood still behind the Foundation's walls. Yet change seems inevitable. Since the state seems unwilling to act again in the matter—though it might be convinced to do so through pressure from the press or the public—that change would most likely come from within the Foundation itself. Of the five trustees who govern it today, three—Frick, Langran, and de Mazia—are veterans, still determined to carry out the doctor's policies. The other two include a representative of the Mellon Bank and Benjamin F. Amos, who was appointed to his post by Lincoln University. According to Barnes's written wishes, the bank representative, upon expiration of his term, is to be replaced by another representative of the same bank; and when each of the other four trustees resigns, becomes incapacitated, or dies, he or she is to be replaced by persons nominated by Lincoln University. The Foundation's future is in their hands. Officials of Lincoln are proud and aware of their responsibility in the administration of one of the world's great art collections; when the time comes for them to exercise this responsibility, it can only be hoped that they will act in the best interests of art, education, and the public.

A NOTE ON SOURCES

Neither footnotes nor a detailed bibliography of sources seems to be appropriate in a book of this nature. When possible, I have cited these sources in the main text and see no reason to repeat them here. By the same token, I have, elsewhere in this book, acknowledged those who granted me interviews and will not repeat these acknowledgments here.

I have gathered a great deal of information from a number of libraries and archives. Among these are the Archives of American Art and the Library of Congress in Washington; Yale University's Beinecke Rare Book and Manuscript Library; the Manuscript Division of the New York Public Library; Philadelphia's Free Library; the Center for Dewey Studies and the Morris Library of the University of Southern Illinois at Carbondale; the archives of M. Knoedler & Company, New York; the library of the Pennsylvania Academy of the Fine Arts, the Rosenbach Museum and Library, the Temple University libraries, the archives of the Philadelphia Museum of Art, and the files of the Philadelphia *Inquirer* in Philadelphia; the archives and library of New York's Museum of Modern Art; the Harry Ransom Humanities Research Center of the University of Texas, Austin; and the Rutgers University Art Library in New Brunswick.

In addition, I would like to mention a few books that have

been especially useful in providing background material for this portrait of Dr. Barnes. These include William Schack's *Art and Argyrol* (New York, 1963), the first biography of Barnes, which served as a starting point for my own researches; Ira Glackens's *William Glackens and the Eight* (New York, 1957); *The Perennial Philadelphians*, by Nathaniel Burt (Boston, 1963); *Philadelphia: Patricians and Philistines, 1900–1950*, by John Lukacs (New York, 1981); Leo Stein's *Journey into the Self* (New York, 1950); Pierre Schneider's *Matisse* (New York, 1984); *The Life and Mind of John Dewey*, by George Dykhuizen (Carbondale, 1973); *Triumph on Fairmount: Fiske Kimball and the Philadelphia Museum of Art*, by George and Mary Roberts (Philadelphia, 1959); *Bertrand Russell's America* (Volume I), by Barry Feinberg and Roland Kasrils (New York, 1974); Milton W. Brown's *American Painting: From the Armory Show to the Depression* (Princeton, 1955); and Abraham A. Davidson's *Early American Modernist Painting: 1910–1935* (New York, 1981).

Finally, a most important source has been the published writings of Dr. Barnes himself—not only his books, pamphlets, and articles (in the *Journal of the Barnes Foundation*, *Les Arts à Paris*, *The New Republic*, *Arts and Decoration*, and elsewhere), but his many letters, which he generously distributed to the Philadelphia press, which frequently printed them.

INDEX

FOR THE BEST IN PAPERBACKS, LOOK FOR THE

In every corner of the world, on every subject under the sun, Penguin represents quality and variety—the very best in publishing today.

For complete information about books available from Penguin—including Pelicans, Puffins, Peregrines, and Penguin Classics—and how to order them, write to us at the appropriate address below. Please note that for copyright reasons the selection of books varies from country to country.

In the United Kingdom: For a complete list of books available from Penguin in the U.K., please write to *Dept E.P., Penguin Books Ltd, Harmondsworth, Middlesex, UB7 0DA*.

In the United States: For a complete list of books available from Penguin in the U.S., please write to *Consumer Sales, Penguin USA, P.O. Box 999— Dept. 17109, Bergenfield, New Jersey 07621-0120*. VISA and MasterCard holders call 1-800-253-6476 to order all Penguin titles.

In Canada: For a complete list of books available from Penguin in Canada, please write to *Penguin Books Canada Ltd, 10 Alcorn Avenue, Suite 300, Toronto, Ontario, Canada M4V 3B2*.

In Australia: For a complete list of books available from Penguin in Australia, please write to the *Marketing Department, Penguin Books Ltd, P.O. Box 257, Ringwood, Victoria 3134*.

In New Zealand: For a complete list of books available from Penguin in New Zealand, please write to the *Marketing Department, Penguin Books (NZ) Ltd, Private Bag, Takapuna, Auckland 9*.

In India: For a complete list of books available from Penguin, please write to *Penguin Overseas Ltd, 706 Eros Apartments, 56 Nehru Place, New Delhi, 110019*.

In Holland: For a complete list of books available from Penguin in Holland, please write to *Penguin Books Nederland B.V., Postbus 195, NL-1380AD Weesp, Netherlands*.

In Germany: For a complete list of books available from Penguin, please write to *Penguin Books Ltd, Friedrichstrasse 10-12, D-6000 Frankfurt Main I, Federal Republic of Germany*.

In Spain: For a complete list of books available from Penguin in Spain, please write to *Longman, Penguin España, Calle San Nicolas 15, E-28013 Madrid, Spain*.

In Japan: For a complete list of books available from Penguin in Japan, please write to *Longman Penguin Japan Co Ltd, Yamaguchi Building, 2-12-9 Kanda Jimbocho, Chiyoda-Ku, Tokyo 101, Japan*.